IMAGES
of America

WESTFIELD

VOLUME II

I0792675

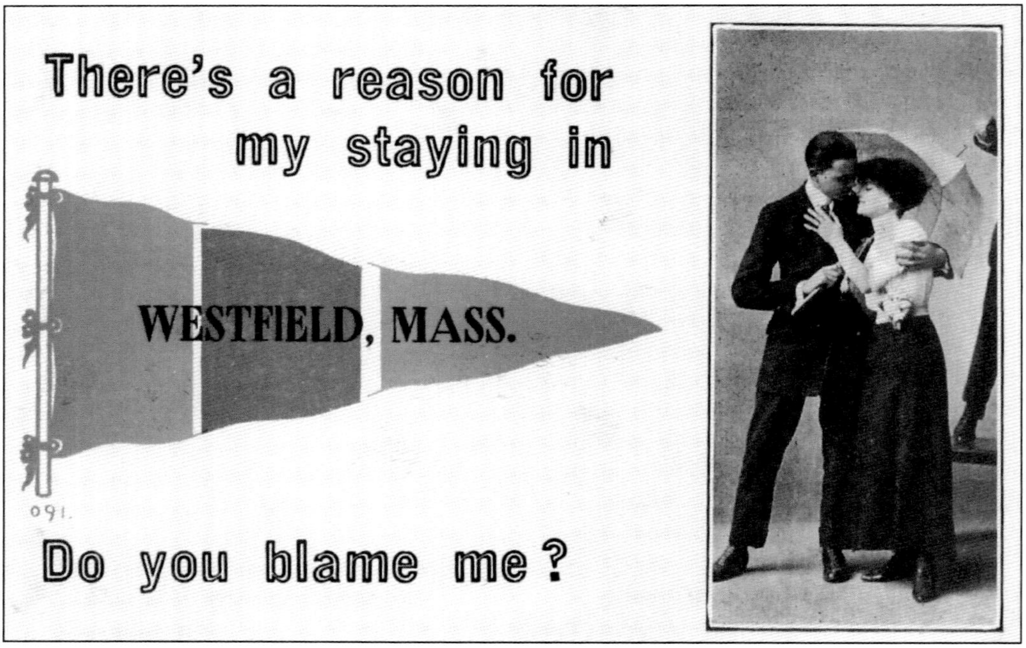

"Penny Postcard," dated 8 pm, April 16, 1913.

IMAGES
of America

WESTFIELD
VOLUME II

The Westfield Athenaeum

ARCADIA
PUBLISHING

Copyright © 1997 by The Westfield Athenaeum
ISBN 978-0-7385-6484-5

Published by Arcadia Publishing
Charleston, South Carolina

Printed in the United States of America

For all general information contact Arcadia Publishing at:
Telephone 843-853-2070
Fax 843-853-0044
E-mail sales@arcadiapublishing.com
For customer service and orders:
Toll-Free 1-888-313-2665

Visit us on the Internet at www.arcadiapublishing.com

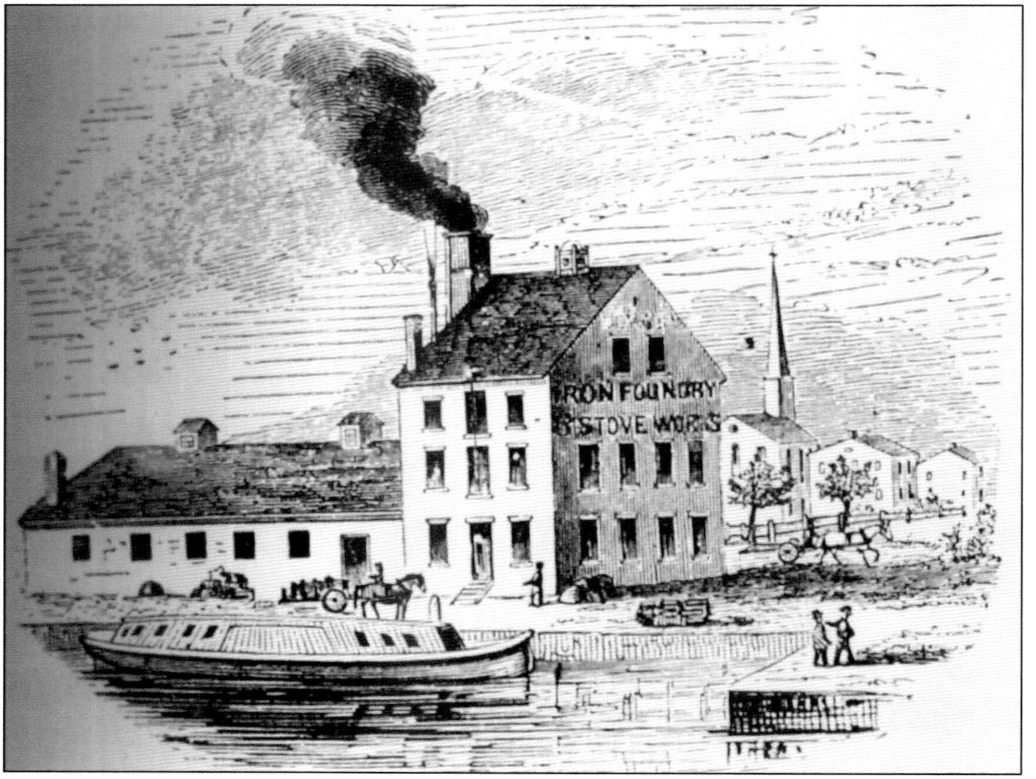

Canal Basin of the New Haven and Northampton Canal and the Iron Foundry and Stove Works, c. 1840. Basins were located at intervals the whole length of the canal to allow boats going in opposite directions to pass each other. This basin was also used occasionally for baptismal purposes and as a swimming pool by local children. In the background is the Iron Foundry and Stove Works, the property of Lyman and Thomas A. Lewis. This was purchased by Henry B. and Edwin Smith in 1853, and it became the H.B. Smith Company.

Contents

Introduction 7

Acknowledgments 8

1. Places We Remember 9

2. Faces We Remember 23

3. Historic Homes 37

4. Business and Industry 49

5. Fires and Floods 63

6. A Variety of Vehicles 77

7. Roads and Bridges 89

8. The Younger Set 103

9. Schools and Sports 115

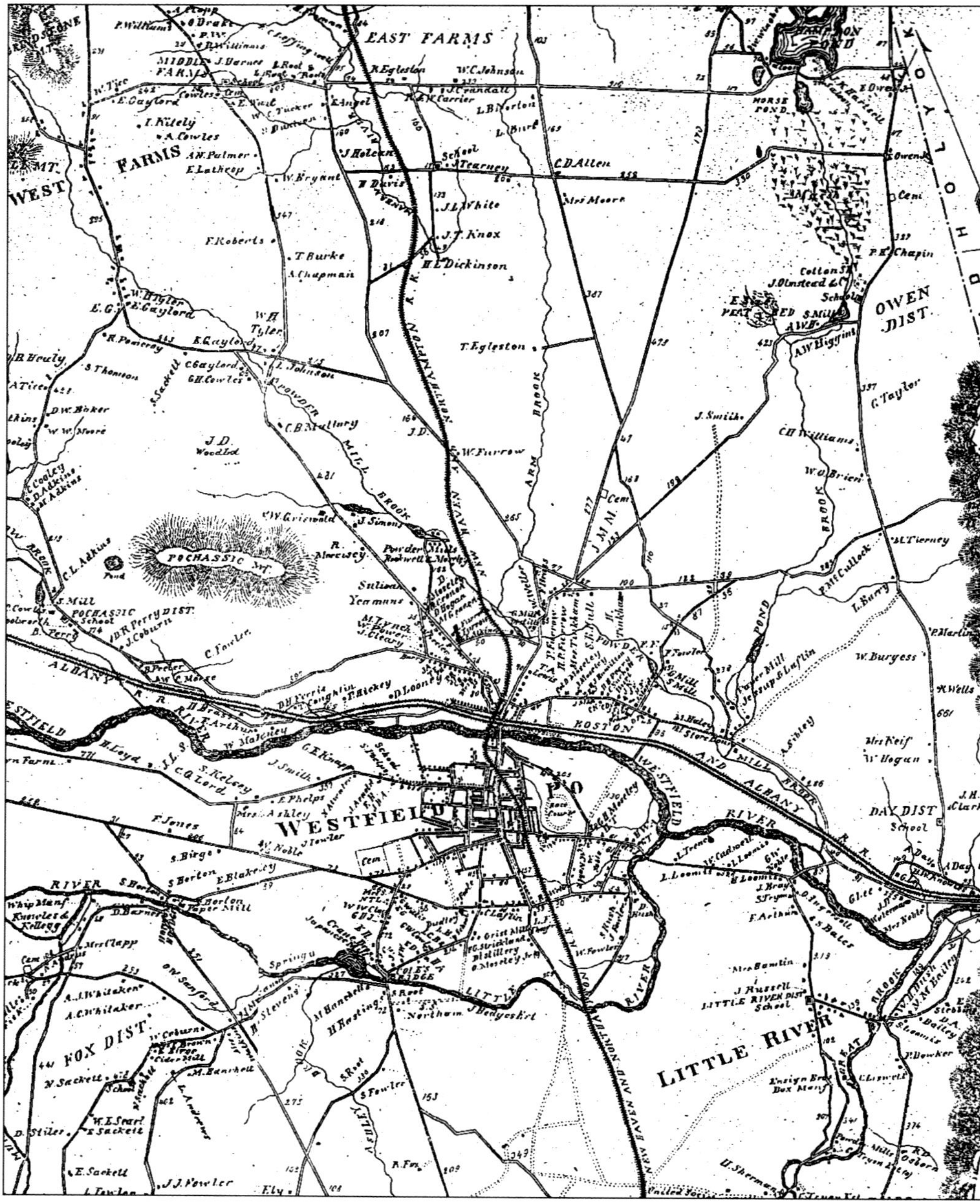

Westfield, c. 1870.

Introduction

In the early 1600s, the Native American name for what we now call Westfield was *Wau-wau-nock-oo*, meaning "it is fat hunting." Game of all kinds was plentiful here in the rich meadows and primeval forests. White men came to this place as early as 1641 to trade with the Native Americans who had settled where Little River joins the Westfield River. When Westfield was incorporated in 1669, it was suggested that it be named Streamfield because of its location on those two "streams." The name Westfield was preferred, however, because the town was then the most westerly settlement in New England.

Many years have passed since those early times and Westfield has a heritage and a history of which to be proud. Authors Joan Ackerman and Patricia Cramer of the Westfield Athenaeum have compiled this photographic collection so that you may share some of its history and see how Westfield has changed throughout the years.

On an editorial note, we have tried to make the pictures more meaningful by providing some explanatory text with each one. In most cases, the facts presented here have been well-researched, checked, and rechecked, but it is impossible to be one hundred percent accurate in a work of this kind. Sometimes we have had to rely on a person's "best memory" of an event or just a brief note on the back of a photograph. Also, we have tried to spell names correctly, but sometimes the available documentation has been faded or illegible and, once again, we could only do our best.

Compiling this book has been a wonderful experience for us and we have certainly expanded our knowledge of Westfield history. We very much enjoyed hearing from those of you who liked our first book. We hope this one is even better!

Acknowledgments

Collecting the photographs for this, our second book of Westfield images, has truly been a joy. For our first book we used photographs that were readily available here at the Athenaeum. Now we have had to dig deeper. We sent out an SOS to the people of Westfield asking if they had any pictures they could make available for our new endeavor. The response has been heartwarming, as so many have shared not only their photographs but also information and personal stories from the past. Our thanks go out to Shirley Pomeroy, Elizabeth Forrish, Marlene Hills, Lydia Malone, Bill Oleksak, Quentin Sizer, Arthur Bush, Florence Cennamo, Jan Steele-Perkins, Carol Fowler, Robert Weinberg, Audrey Sherman, Edward Zorek, Alfred Rios, Bill Ensign, James and Mary Condron, Florence Rogers, Ray Bush, Jim Curran, Peter Boguszewski, Mary Parody, Patrick and Peggy Dowd, Helen Coleman, Ralph Cortis, James Johnson, Don Weinle, Charles L, Darling, Mary O'Connor, Philip Pitoniak, Arlene Bole, Anthony Parisi, Frances Dupuis, Ruth Sperry, Joan Corell, Joan Miller, Doris Snyder, Rita Dupont, and Robert Agan.

Postcards from the Barbara Bush collection and photographs from the Western Hampden Historical Society were also a valuable resource. The following reference books supplied information and some of the pictures: Alfred Minot Copeland, ed., *A History of Hampden County*, MA; Interstate Press, ed., *A Photographic Record of the New England Flood;* Edward C. Janes, and Roscoe S. Scott, eds., *Westfield, Massachusetts, 1669–1969*; Edgar Holmes Plummer, ed., *Westfield's Quarter Millennial Anniversary Official Souvenir*; Eloise Fowler Salmond, *The Spirit of the Old House*; *Westfield Historical Calendar, 1669–1920*; *Westfield, MA, Tri-Centennial Industrial & Business Directory*; the 1930 and 1950 editions of the Westfield High School *Gammadion*; and the 1962 and 1970 editions of the Westfield Trade School *Tradesman*.

Our personal thanks go to Jan Gryszkiewicz and Ann Tumavicus, whose help with the research and writing has been invaluable. Thanks also to Candy Pennington, who patiently typed and retyped our text, and to Chris Morrill, who attended to the many details that were so important.

A project like this is rewarding in so many ways. The willingness of everyone to help has shown the true community spirit that exists in Westfield today. Once again, thanks to all.

Joan B. Ackerman
Patricia Thompson Cramer

One

Places We Remember

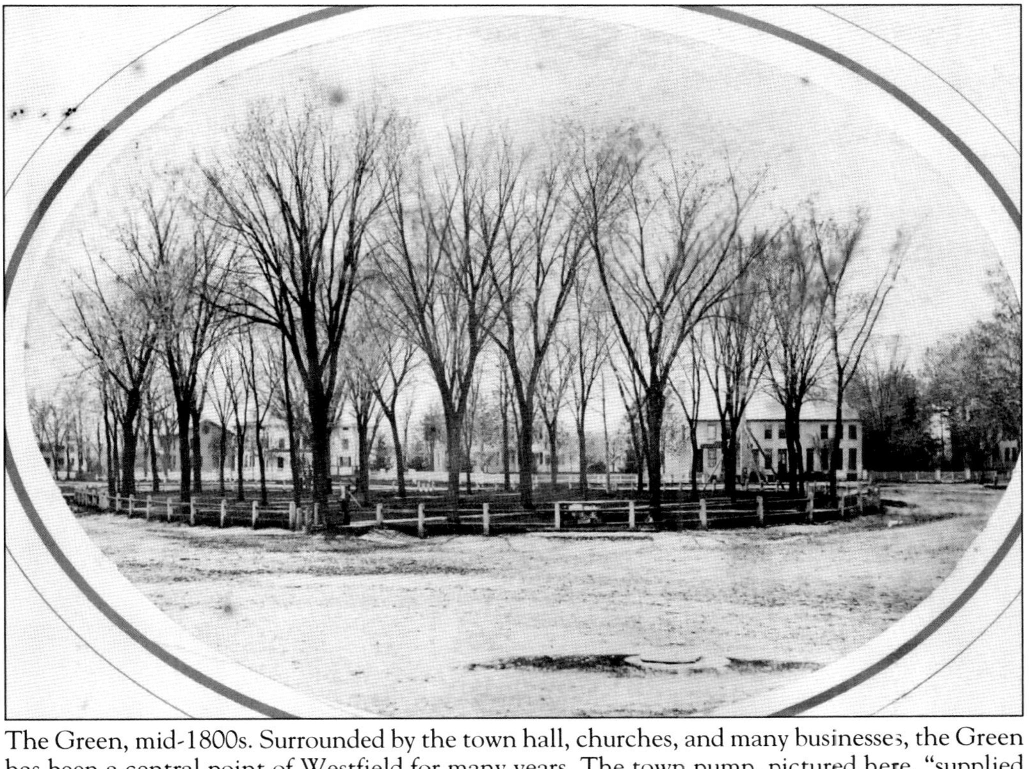

The Green, mid-1800s. Surrounded by the town hall, churches, and many businesses, the Green has been a central point of Westfield for many years. The town pump, pictured here, "supplied the entire neighborhood with water as well as drink for the horses." The picket fence was put in about 1835 and remained around the Green until the posts started rotting and a party of "mischievous boys took the fence up bodily."

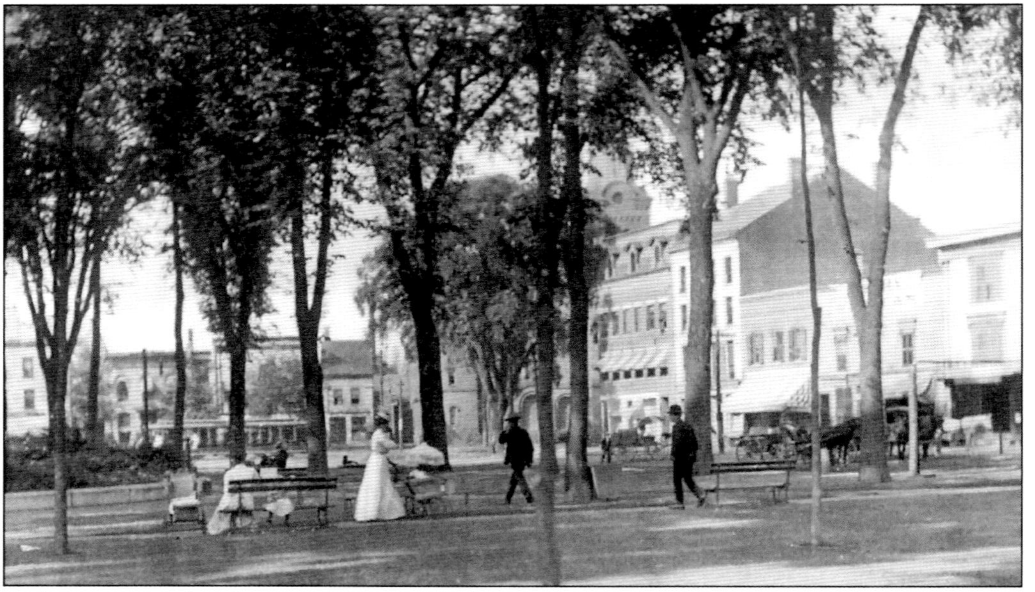

Park Square, mid-to-late 1800s. In the mid-1800s the area around the Green became known as Park Square. A fountain surrounded by granite was constructed on the Green in 1898. The northern section of the Green, now a parking lot, was a favorite place for people to congregate for "music and campaign oratory."

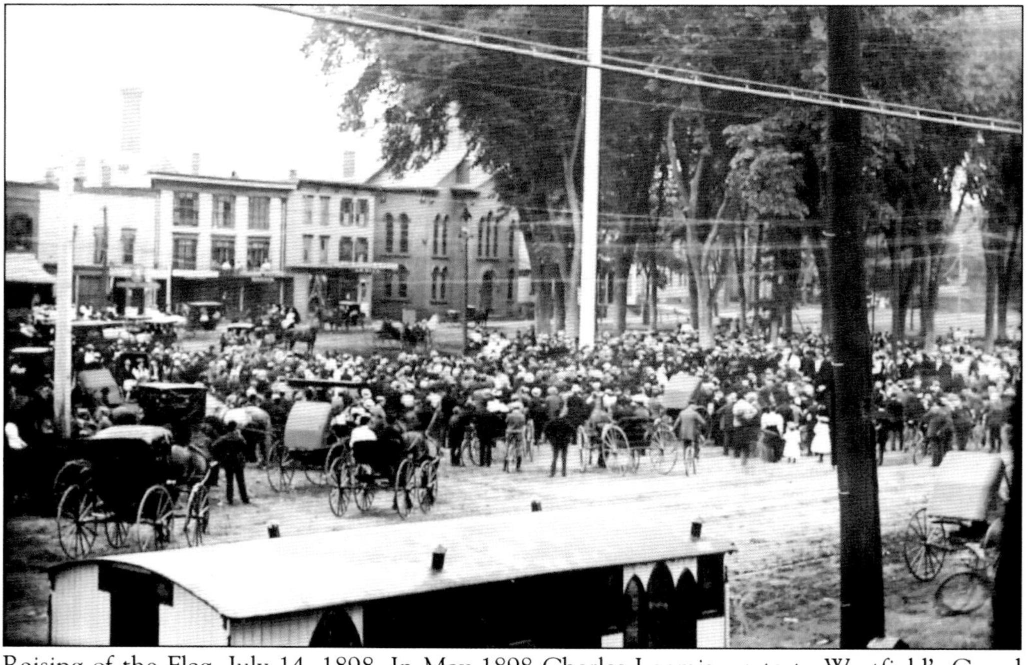

Raising of the Flag, July 14, 1898. In May 1898 Charles Loomis wrote to Westfield's Grand Army of the Republic offering to "provide a flag if the pole can be secured." The GAR decided to receive "popular subscriptions" to purchase the pole. By June the money was collected and the liberty pole bought "of a Connecticut firm." The heated discussions on choosing its location delayed the July 4th raising to July 14th.

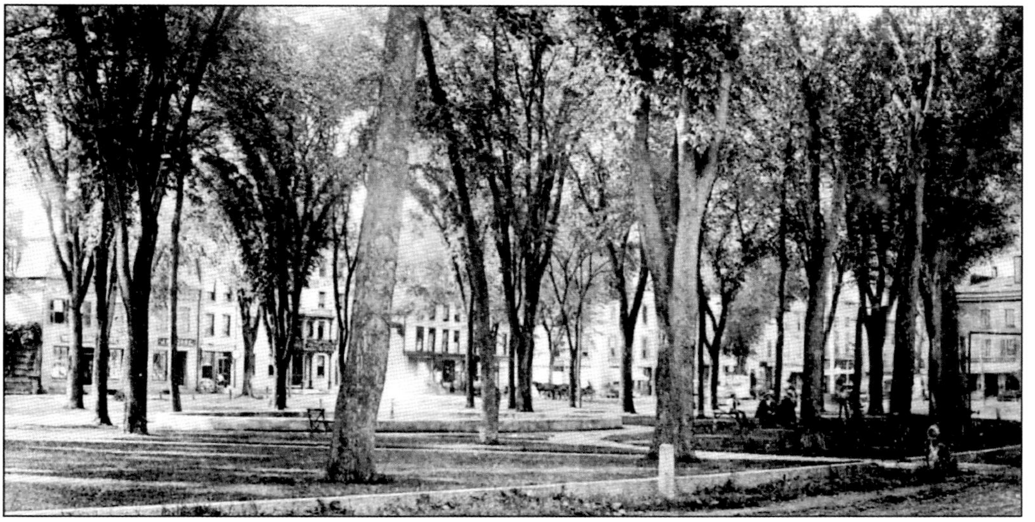

Park Square, late 1800s. Around the turn of the century, Westfield used to celebrate the Fourth of July with a large bonfire at Park Square. Old wooden packing cartons from local merchants would be collected and placed in the center of the square. It is said that the pile could reach as high as 75 feet. The fire would burn from midnight until morning, Thousands of people would gather downtown to celebrate.

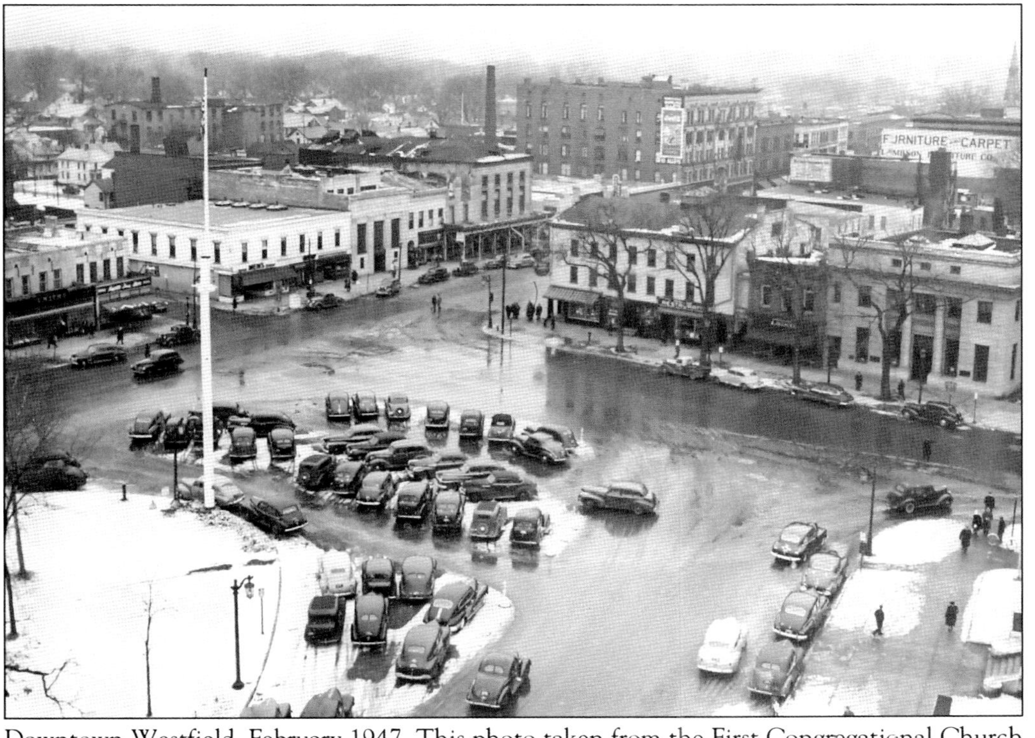

Downtown Westfield, February 1947. This photo taken from the First Congregational Church steeple shows the many changes that had taken place around Park Square over the years. With the increasing use of automobiles the north end of the park became a parking lot. Many of the elm trees had already succumbed to Dutch Elm disease.

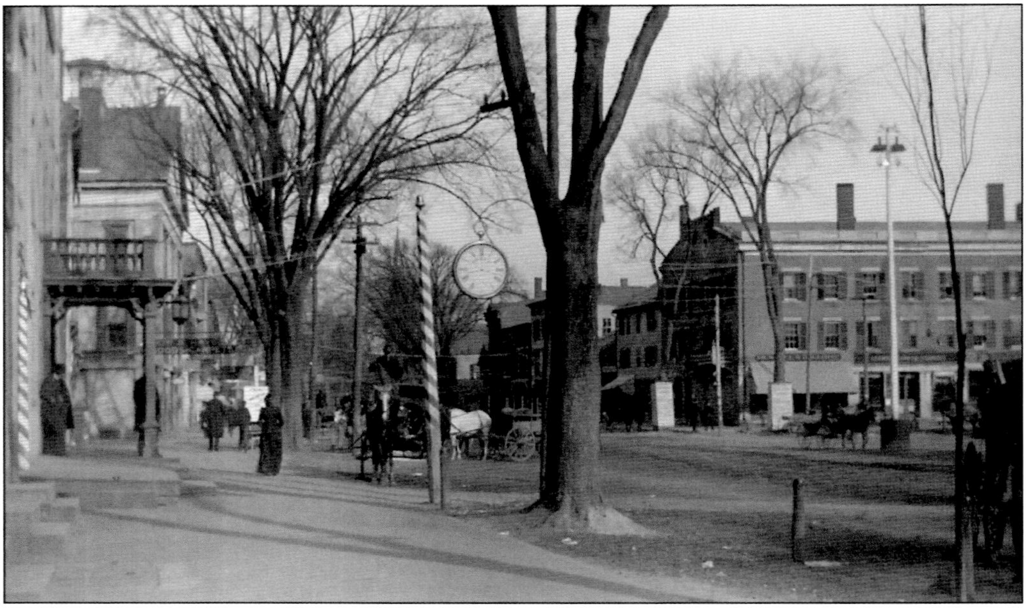

Downtown Westfield, *c*. 1885. The large pocket watch shown here advertised James H. Morse's jewelry and watch store on Elm Street next to Willmarth House Hotel. Snow and Hays, dry and fancy goods, is on the other side of Willmarth. Russell and Holliday, "choice family groceries and provisions," is pictured here on the corner of Main and Elm Streets. Note the gas lamp and hitching post.

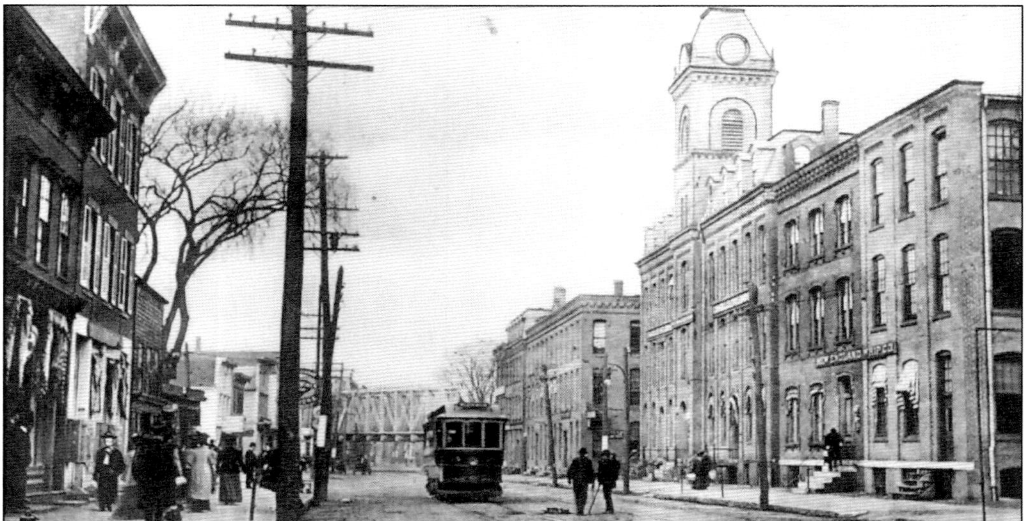

Elm Street. This is a view of Elm Street, looking north, taken around the turn of the century. The streetcar service began in 1890. At first, horse-drawn cars were used, then compressed air cars in 1894, and followed by electric cars in 1895. Lines ran from the Green to the railroad center at Depot Square. Other lines ran along Court, Main, and Union Streets. By 1905 interurban trolley routes extended to Hampton Ponds, Holyoke, Huntington, and Springfield. The streetcar service was abolished around 1920, as more automobiles took to the roads.

Westfield Schools, 1914. *Pochassic:* The original building was destroyed by fire in 1874. A new school was erected and served the area until it closed in 1900. It was reopened in 1914 and finally abandoned in 1932. *Fox:* In 1793 Munn's Brook District was divided into Munn's Brook West and Munn's Brook East. The school in the east became known as Fox District School and was located on the east side of Sackett Road. *Wyben:* Built about 1864, this schoolhouse was later used as a community center. *Mundale:* The old Mundale School was built in 1867 at a cost of $2,690.16. Miss Maria H. Loomis was schoolmistress there for twenty-five years.

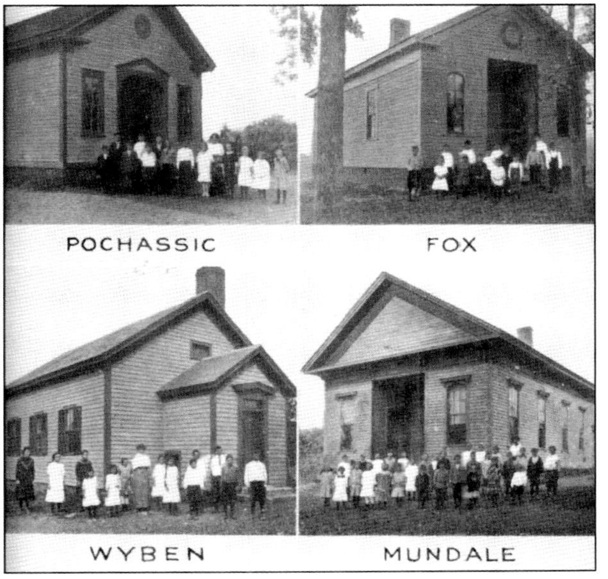

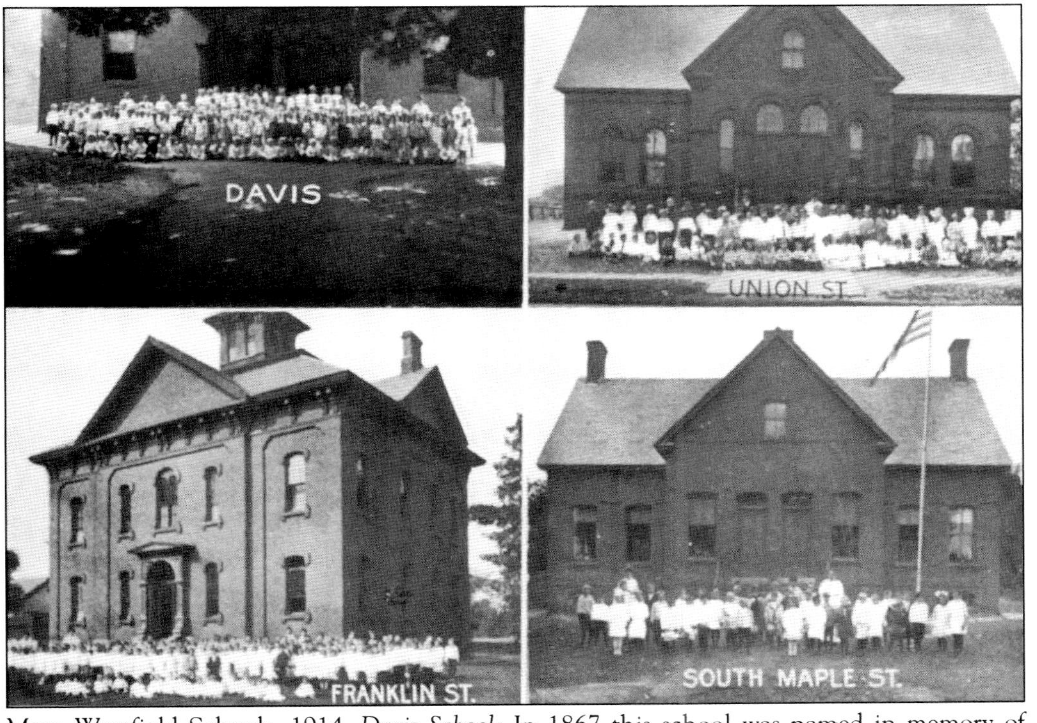

More Westfield Schools, 1914. *Davis School:* In 1867 this school was named in memory of Rev. Emerson Davis. It was formerly the Bartlett Street School. *Union Street:* The Great River District was divided in 1835 and the East Building was located on Union Street. In 1865 it was renamed the Union Street School. *Franklin Street:* In 1866 a lot on Franklin Street was purchased from Solomon Phelps. This two-story, four-room school was erected and continued in use until 1953. *South Maple Street:* This brick building served as a two-room schoolhouse from 1888 until 1918. It later became the Grange Hall in 1931.

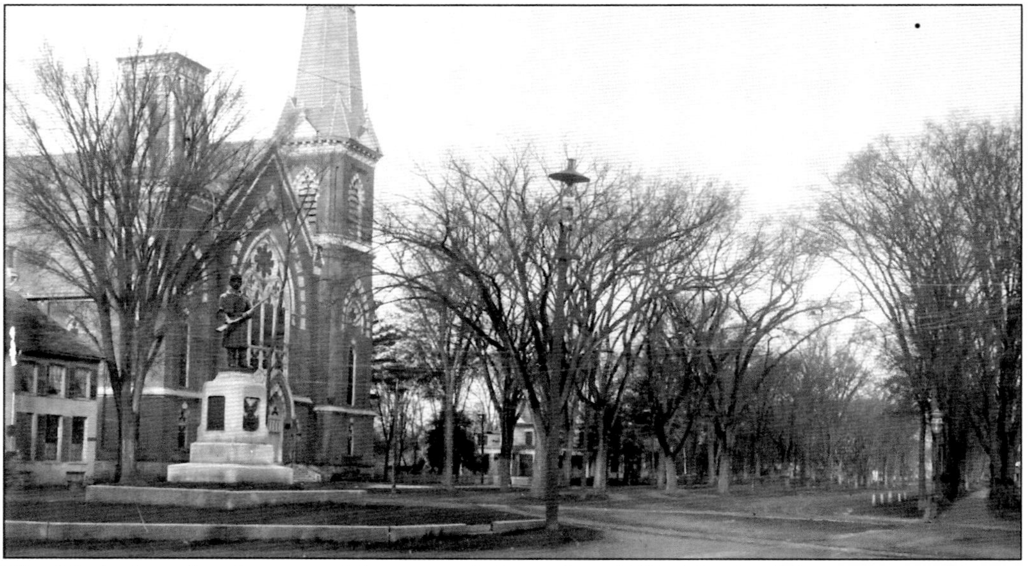

The Methodist church pictured here was dedicated in 1876. The land for it was a gift from Dr. James Holland. The house that once stood there was the home of Lt. Richard Falley, and there was a little shop behind it where he forged gun barrels and polished muskets. This church building has since been torn down and a new one stands in the same location today.

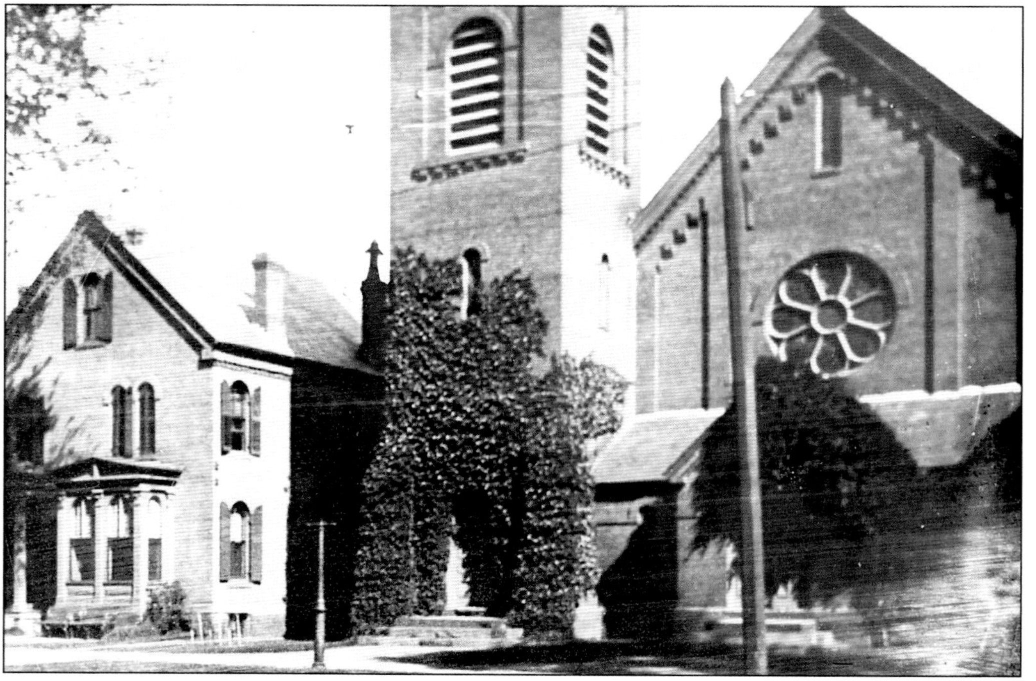

Baptist Church and Rectory, *c.* 1899. This church was built in 1867. The rectory next to it originally was a "gentleman's club" and its bar was closer to the church than the liquor laws allowed. To solve this problem Mrs. Florence Allen Hays bought the property and gave it to the church in memory of her father, Allen Hays. It was used as a parish house until it was razed in 1959 to make room for a new educational building.

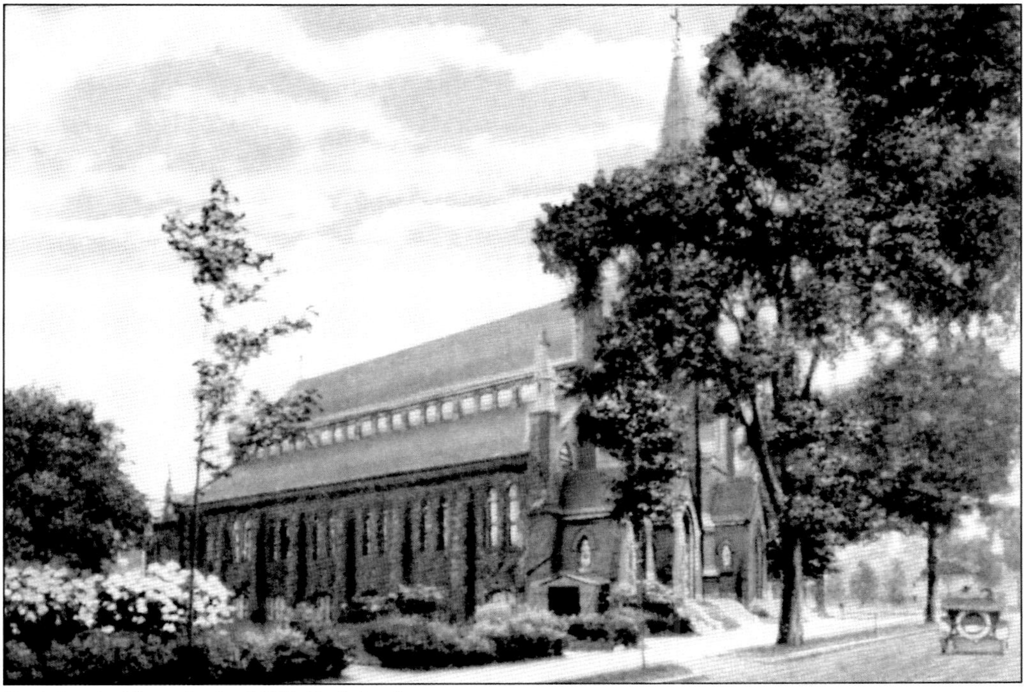

St. Mary's Church. In 1885 St. Mary's completed this new church. The old one had been damaged by flood in 1879 and by a fire three years later. As time passed, more land was purchased, and the convent, the rectory, and the school were built. From about 1908 on, some of the parishioners referred to the priests as "Brick and Mortar Priests," because of their vigorous building program.

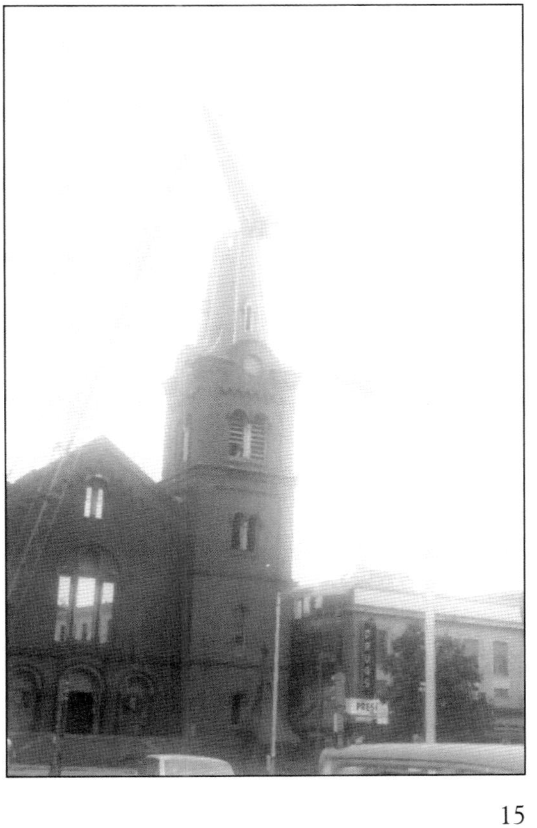

Second Congregational Church, Main Street. The removal of the church's steeple attracted a lot of attention in August of 1962. The more-than-one-hundred-year-old church was being demolished to make way for a parking lot for the Third National Bank of Hampden County. A new Second Congregational Church was built on Western Avenue.

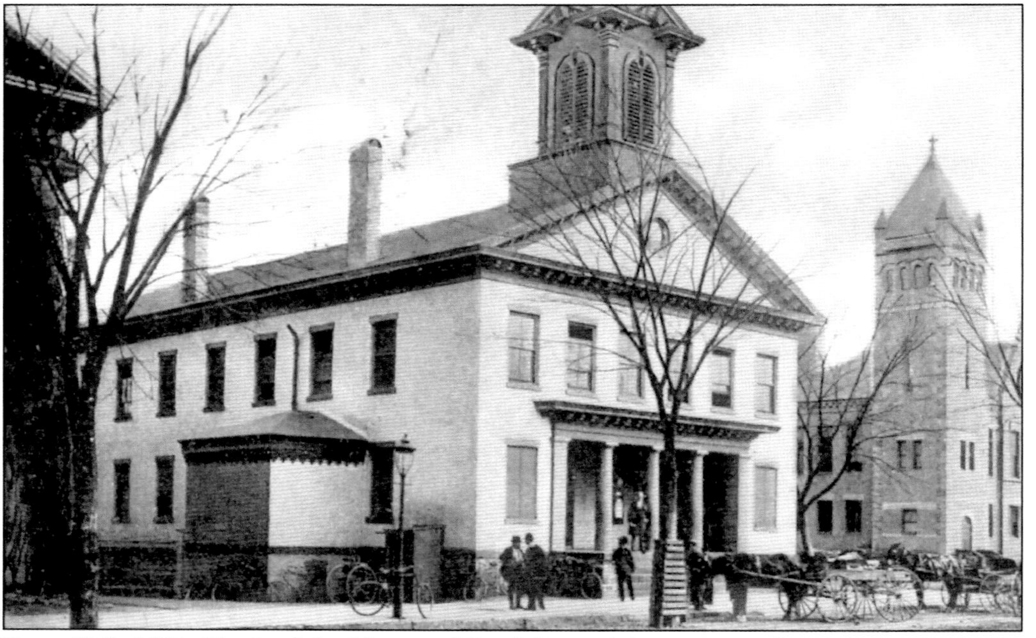

Town Hall, 1906. This brick building is of Greek Revival design, a significant feature being the three round columns in front. The cupola on the roof was removed about 1912, and then the space was covered with slate to match the original roof. Built in 1837/38, it originally served as the town hall and subsequently the city hall. Throughout the years it has also served as the police department and district court, a high school, an elementary school, a child guidance center, and a mental health clinic.

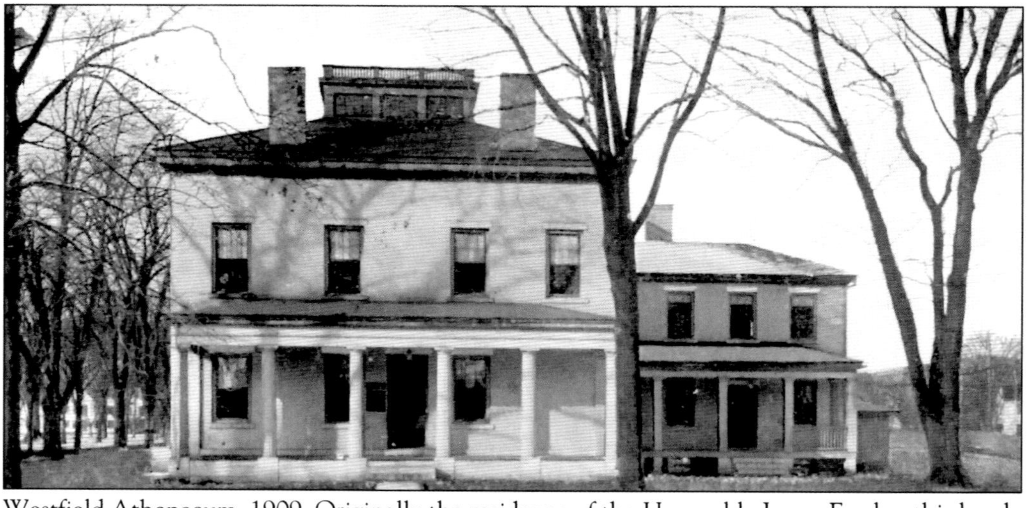

Westfield Athenaeum, 1909. Originally the residence of the Honorable James Fowler, this lovely Georgian building came into the possession of the Westfield Academy upon his death. The exterior was of mellowed buff brick, and there were black marble mantels and mahogany windows, sashes, and banister rails inside. It was said to be the finest house in western Massachusetts in 1838 when the Fowlers moved into it. Realizing that a larger library was needed in Westfield (the old one had one room), the Academy presented this building as a gift to the Athenaeum. After being reconstructed for library use, it was dedicated on March 6, 1899.

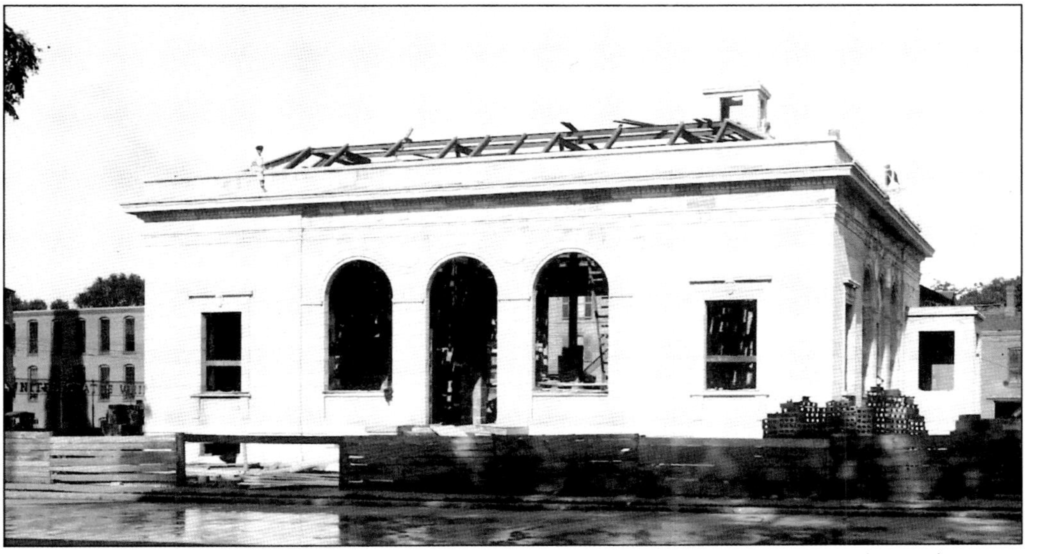

Westfield Post Office under construction, 1913. Land at the corner of Main and Broad Streets was purchased for the post office by the U.S. Treasury Department in 1912. It was constructed with a granite base, a limestone superstructure, and a marble lobby. It has several arched doors and windows, a slanted metal roof, and ventilated cupola. The window sills and baseboards are made of serpentine marble quarried in Westfield. In 1975 a new post office was built on the corner of West Silver and Broad Streets, and this building is now vacant.

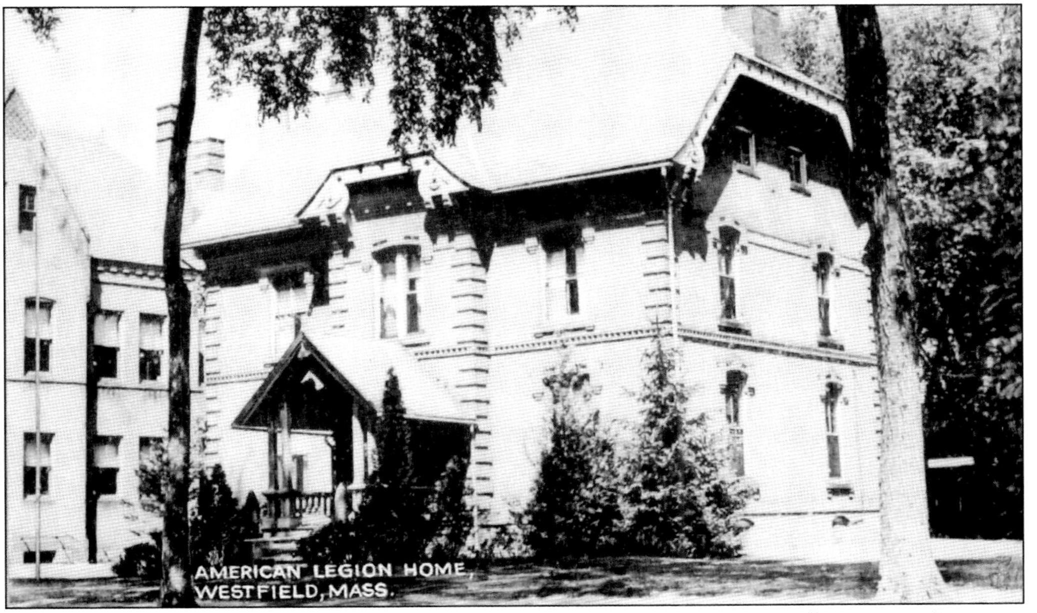

American Legion Home. Noah Strong built this brick home in 1873. It reflects a combination of styles ranging from Italianate, with its corbelled hood molds, paired brackets, and ornamental quoining; to the Stick style porch; and a unique jerkinhead roof. H.B. Smith owned it for a time, and then in 1909 the City of Westfield purchased it for use as a vocational school. Later, the American Legion leased the building for their headquarters for many years and eventually bought it from the City in 1962.

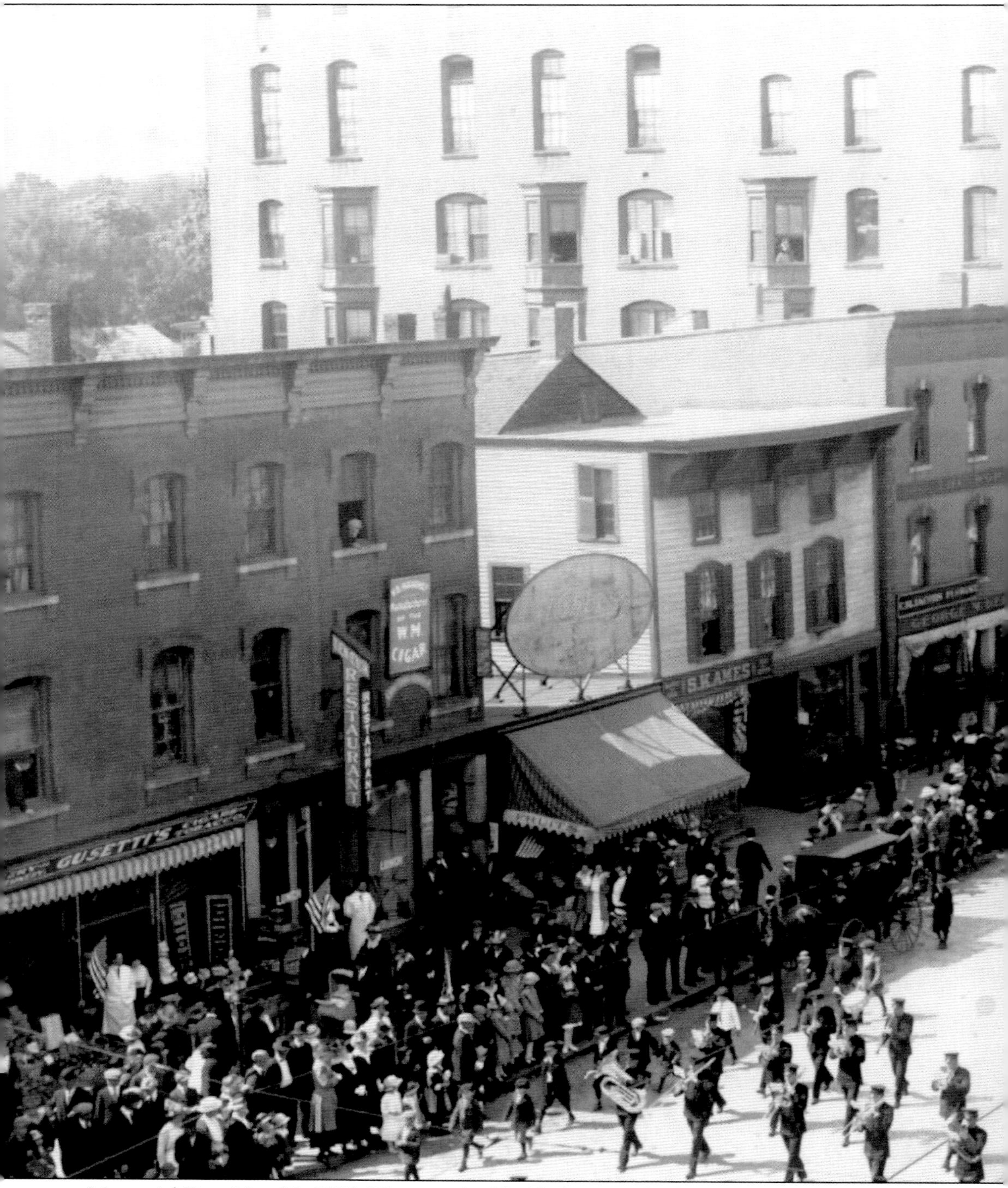

Memorial Day, May 30, 1917. This wonderful old photograph of a parade on Elm Street shows many signs of the times. There were wires overhead and tracks below for the trolleys, a horse and wagon parked by the curb, a boy on a bike, men on horseback, and of course, all those fine automobiles. There were about a thousand marchers who followed a route to Broad Street, Pine

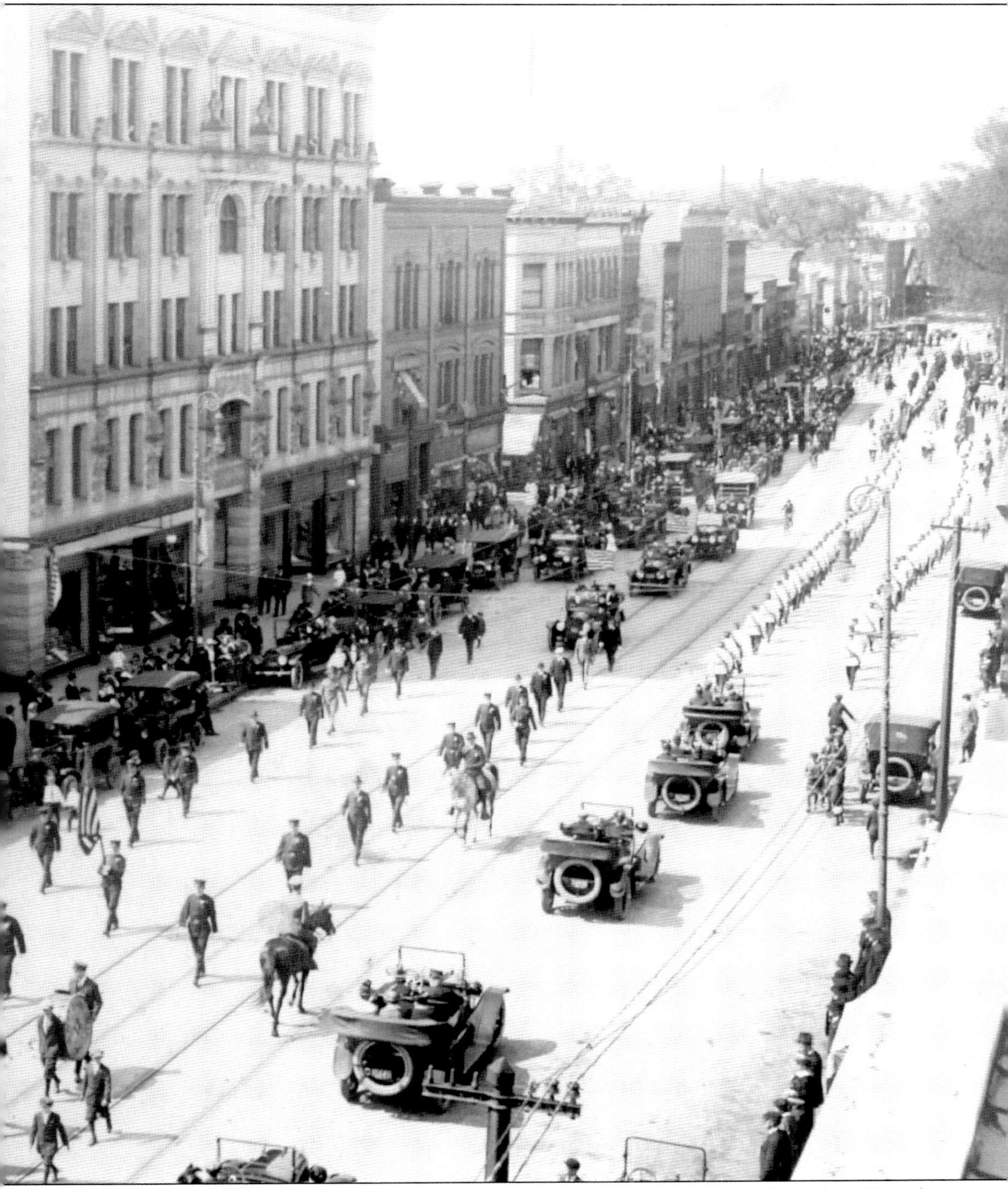

Hill Cemetery, Elm Street, Franklin Street, and then made a counter-march back to Broad where they disbanded. The counter-march explains why the parade seems to be going in both directions at once.

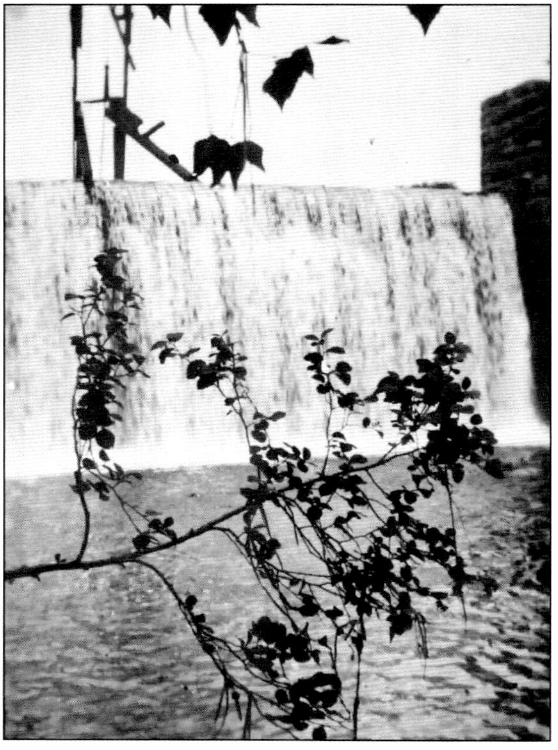

Spillway at Still Pond, 1928. This damsite was spanned by a footbridge between abutment tops. To the left are vestiges of gate-controlling mechanisms. Beyond the visible abutment stood a horse-operated capstan used to lift ice to a runway which led to an icehouse below. About 100 feet to the left of the unseen abutment lay another housed gate for the discharge of water. Supposedly, water was released here by a Buschman employee (Edward Kirby) to provide power for the Buschman-owned Bismark Hotel.

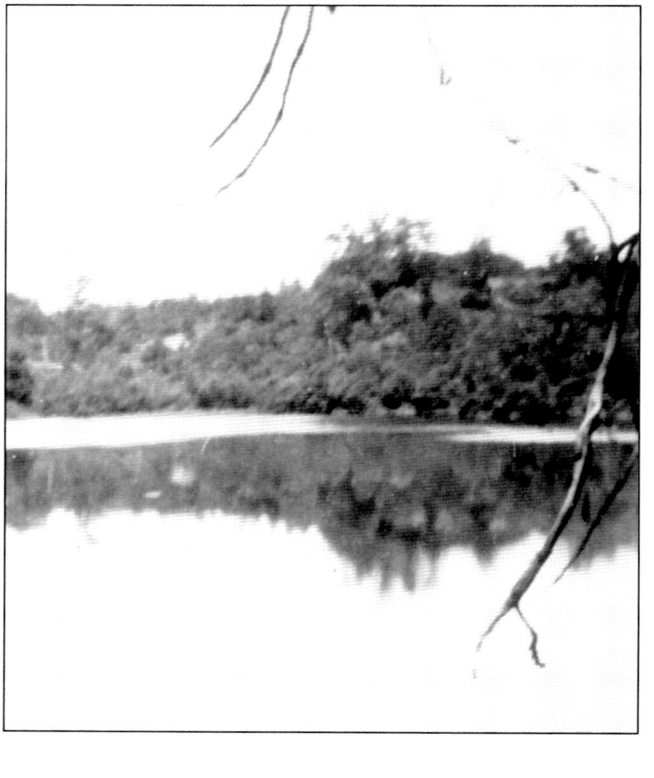

Still Pond, 1928 (near railroad tracks north of Notre Dame Street). There is a stone culvert in the distance at the left. The semaphore and the spur track to Holyoke lie above the culvert. The pond extended past this culvert to the roundhouse and coaling station, almost to a second stone culvert beneath the Northampton spur of the New York, New Haven & Hartford Railroad. Powder Mill and Arm Brooks were the sources of the water. The ponds were later drained to make way for oil storage tanks. In 1955 floodwaters breached both embankments, destroying the culverts and most of the damsite.

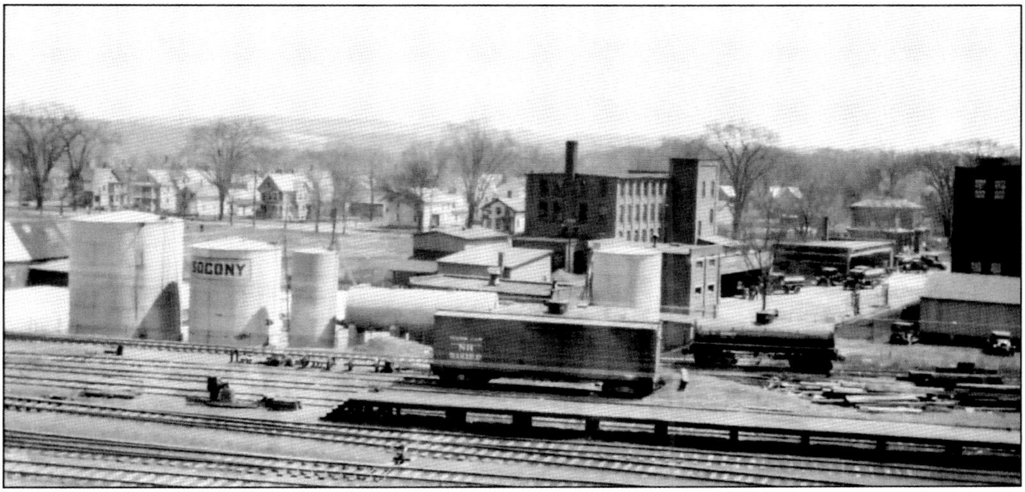

Railroad Tracks behind North Elm Street, 1929. In 1929 Westfield's transportation facilities for freight were considered unsurpassed. With the Boston and Albany Railroad and the New York, New Haven & Hartford Railroad, the city provided direct service to and from the north, south, east, and west. The Standard Oil Company of New York's storage tanks are shown here by the tracks. The Bryant Box Company, a cigar box manufacturer located at 98 North Elm Street, is shown in the center.

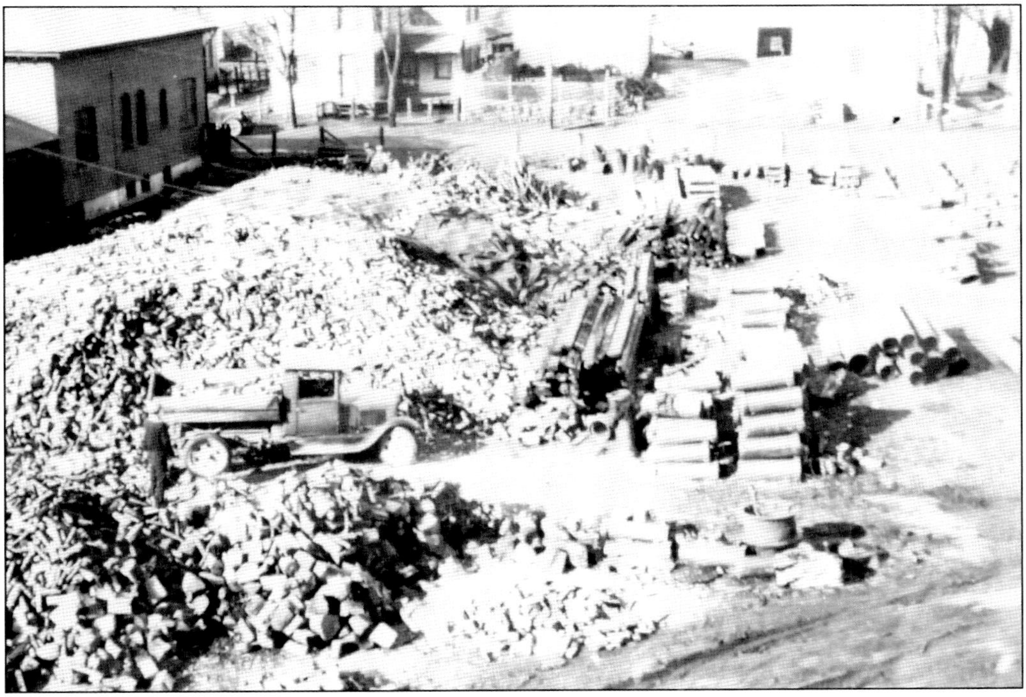

Wood Pile in the City Yard on Sackett Street, February 1933. "Men furnished by the city's unemployment agencies" cleared many dead trees and "undesirable growth" on Westfield Water Department's lands. The wood was hauled to the city yard and cut into firewood. Loads of more than a half cord were sold to the Welfare and Soldier Relief Departments for $2.75 per load. This wood provided fuel for many "needy families."

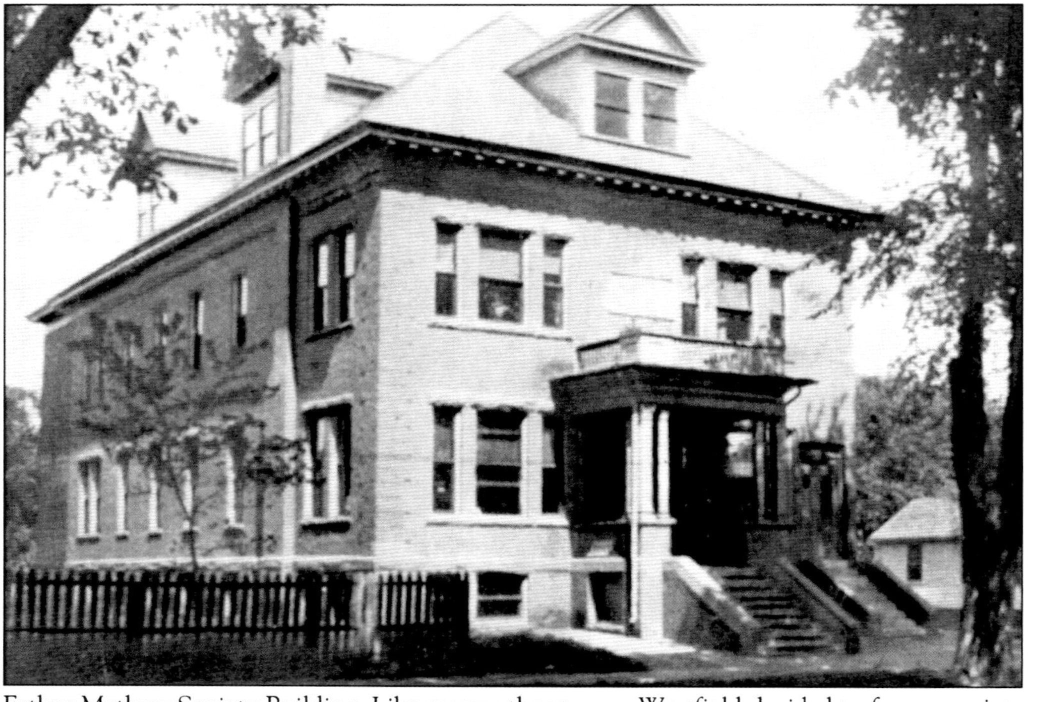

Father Mathew Society Building. Like many other towns, Westfield decided to form a society for total abstinence. The Catholic young men formed the Father Mathew Society in 1871 to reform individuals who were alcoholic. Starting with only thirty members, it grew to over two hundred and fifty members by 1906. This building was erected on Bartlett Street in 1892. It served as a home for those who had been "rescued" and as a social center as well. The facility included a dance hall on the second floor, a gymnasium in the basement, reading rooms, games, and bathrooms. The building is currently occupied by the Fraternal Order of Eagles.

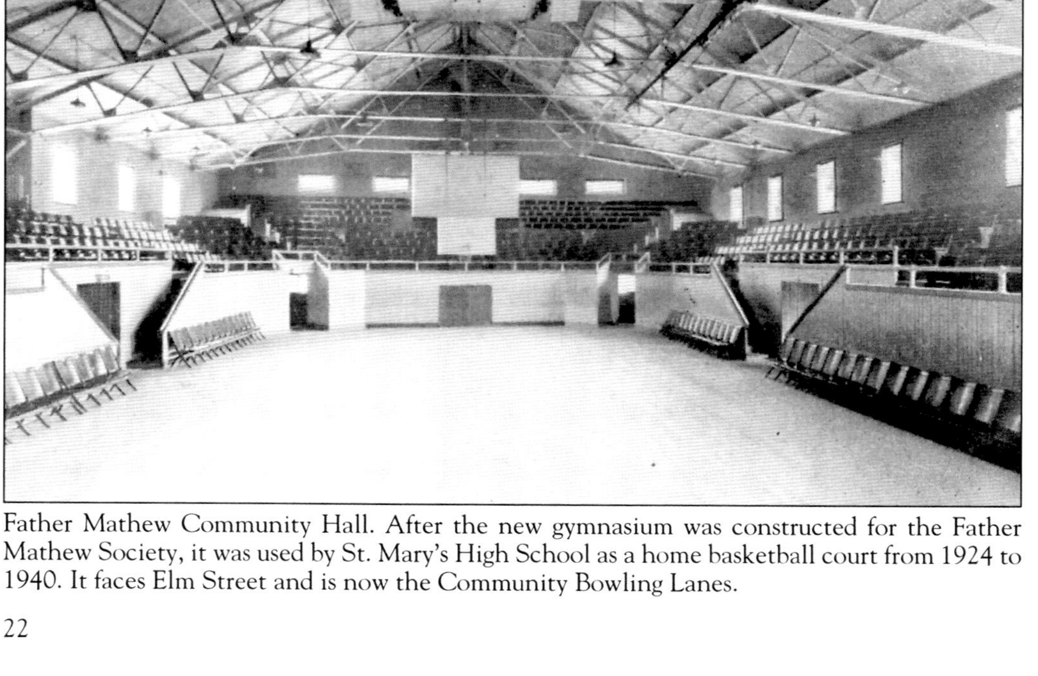

Father Mathew Community Hall. After the new gymnasium was constructed for the Father Mathew Society, it was used by St. Mary's High School as a home basketball court from 1924 to 1940. It faces Elm Street and is now the Community Bowling Lanes.

Two

Faces We Remember

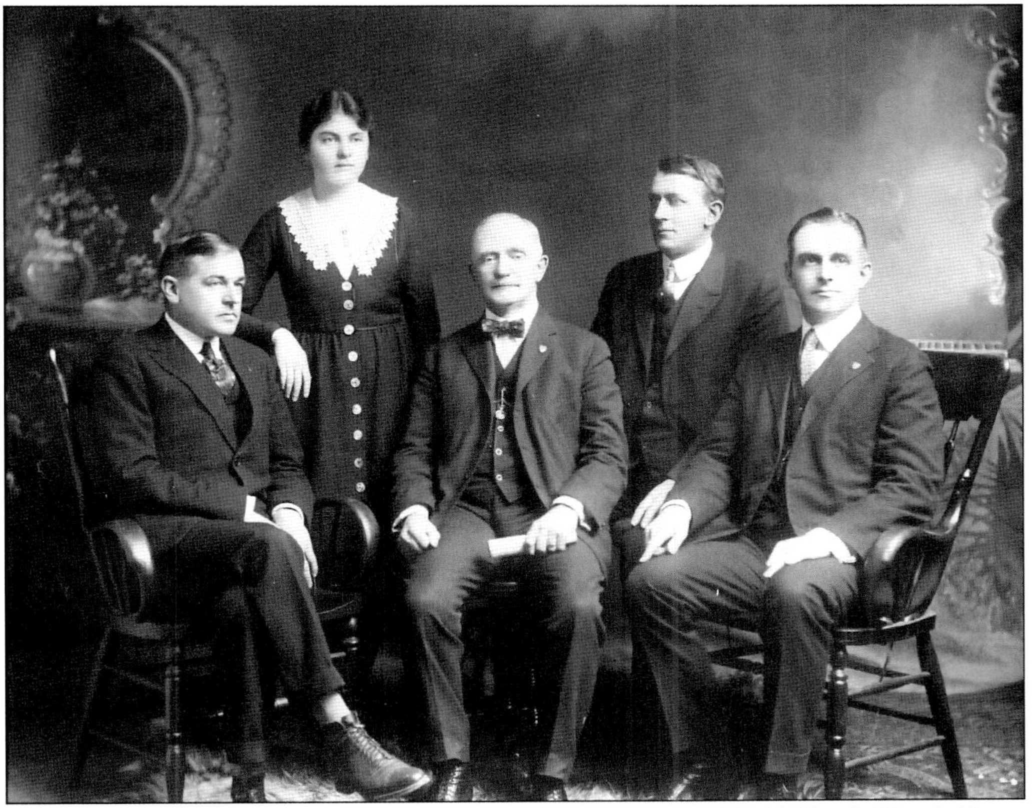

Local Exemption Board, Division No. 6, Massachusetts. During World War I, Westfield was headquarters for the local Exemption (Draft) Board which served Westfield, West Springfield, and Southwick. Arthur J. Descoe of West Springfield (center) was chairman and his associates were Dr. Edward S. Smith (far left) and Florence W. Burke (far right), both from Westfield. Miss Margaret Sullivan (standing) was the stenographer, and Henry W. Hallbourg (back row right) was the chief clerk. Registration took place at the town hall on June 5, 1917; June 5, 1918; August 24, 1918; and September 12, 1918.

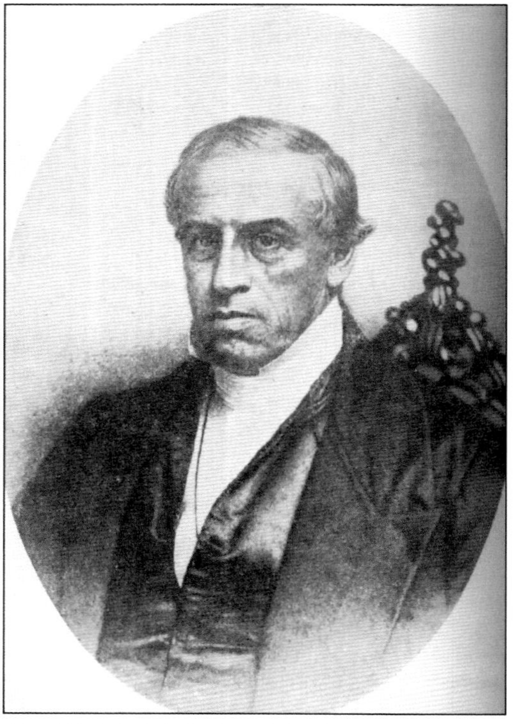

Emerson Davis, D.D. Mr. Emerson Davis, a graduate of Williams College, served for fourteen years as preceptor of the Westfield Academy. In 1836 he became pastor of the Congregational church and served there until his death. He was highly esteemed and well loved by the residents of Westfield.

Hiram Hull and his wife, Drusilla Clark. This couple lived in a big house on School Street, and it was believed they were part of the Underground Railroad. Hiram Hull was the first man to start a whip factory. In 1855 his company merged with another and became the American Whip Company, which through later mergers became the United States Whip Company, the largest in the world.

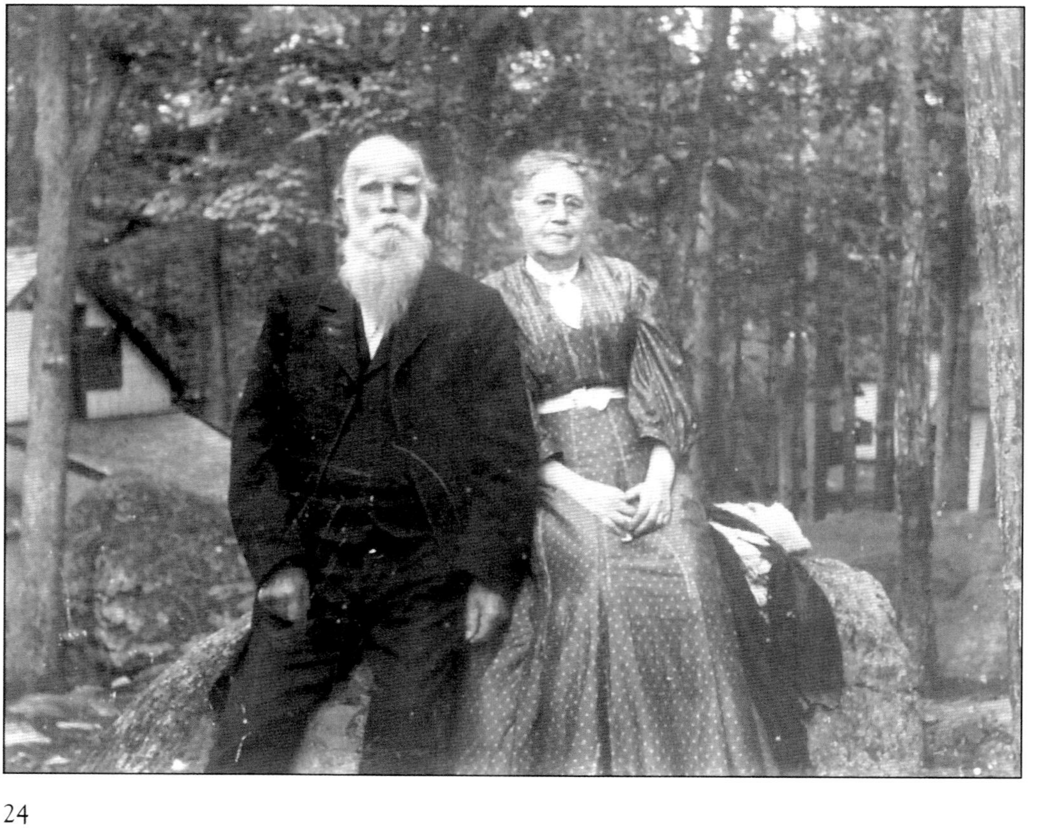

William Nash. The owner of Nash's Bakery and Ice Cream Rooms, Mr. Nash located here in 1871 on Main Street. In 1877 he moved to Broad Street. In 1909 he sold the property to the government for the new post office and built a new bakery on Dudley Avenue. Ice cream sold for 5¢ a plate, 15¢ a pint, 30¢ a quart, and $1 a gallon.

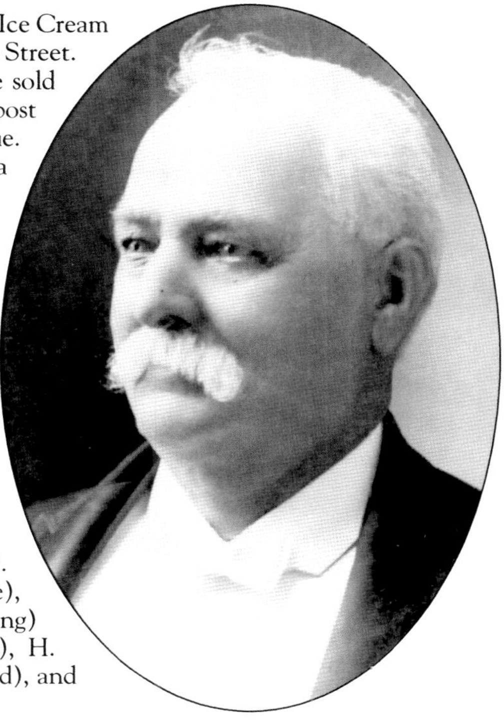

Westfield Firemen's Baseball Team, 1880s. From left to right, the players have been identified as follows: (front row) A. Williams (pitcher), and J. Corcoran (catcher); (second row) H.T. Snow (captain and third base), G. Walkley (shortstop), G.L. Minor (second base), and E. Deihl (first base); (back row, standing) John Sauter (manager), A.L. Reed (left field), H. Nordstrom (center field), G. Cushing (right field), and J. Roach (manager).

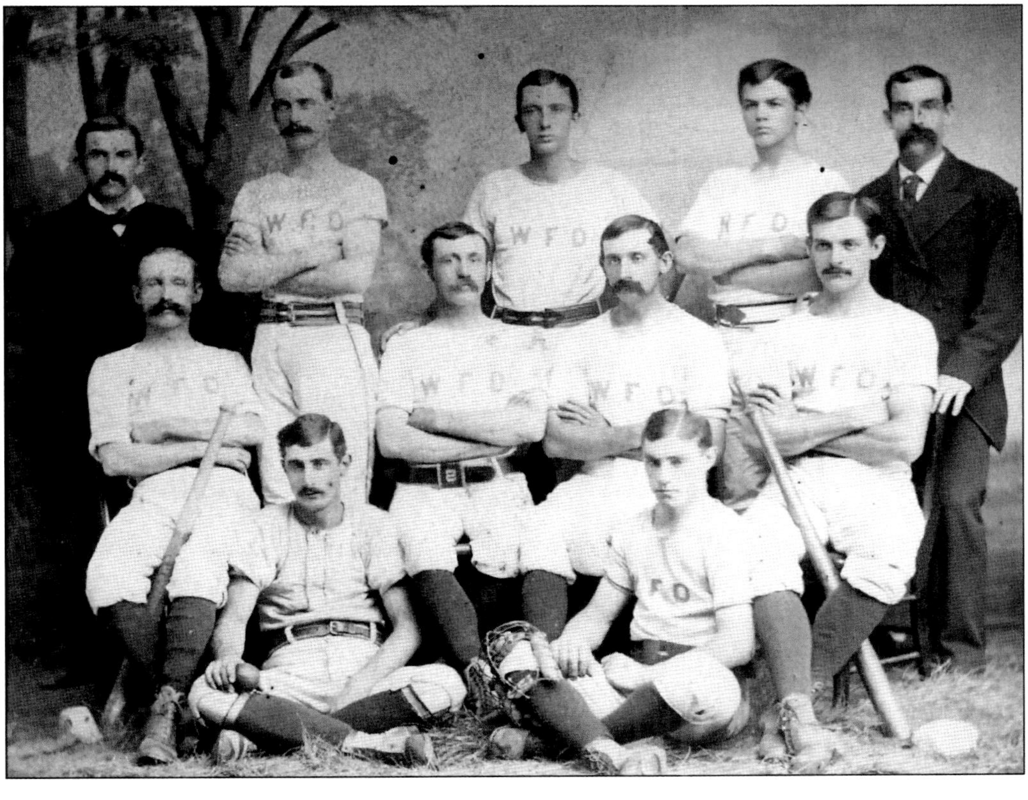

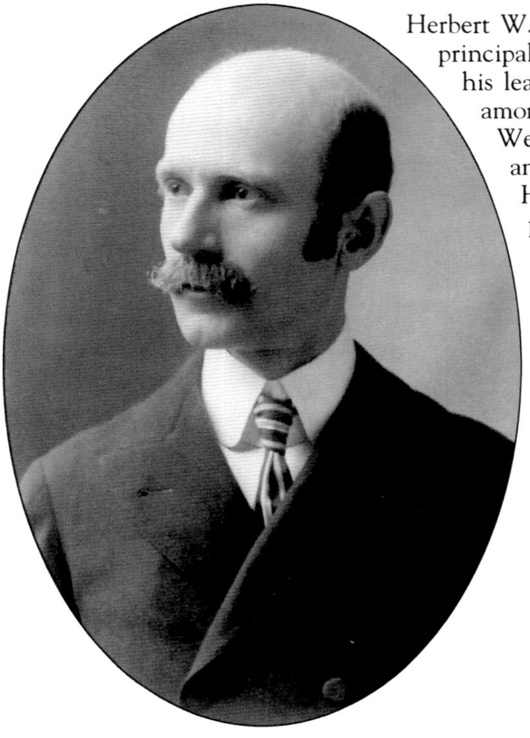

Herbert W. Kittredge. Herbert Kittredge was appointed principal of Westfield High School in 1890, and under his leadership, the school rose to the highest rank among high schools in the state. He came to Westfield when he was only thirty-two, and he and his family bought the well-known Bingham House on Broad Street. He continued as principal for thirty-nine years. During that time he held many honored positions in civic, social, and fraternal organizations. He was deeply mourned by the whole city when he died in 1928.

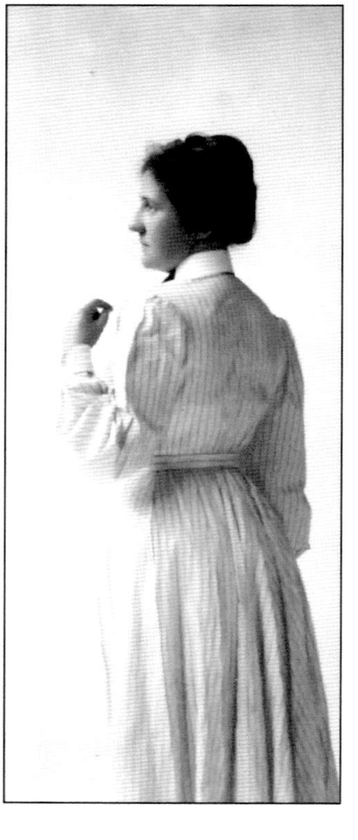

Lucy Jane Dow. Miss Dow was a Latin teacher at Westfield High School in the 1890s. She later married George H. Cushing, the general superintendent at H.B. Smith. They lived at 37 Broad Street.

Rev. David Shurtleff. Educated at the Hartford Theological Seminary, David Shurtleff was ordained a Congregational minister at the age of fifty-one. He lived on Hampden Street and was known as a very warm and sympathetic man. He loved children, and in the late 1800s he established a mission that provided foster homes for them for over sixty years. Funds remaining from the original Shurtleff grant, together with other bequests, were incorporated into the Shurtleff Children's Services, which continues in existence to this day.

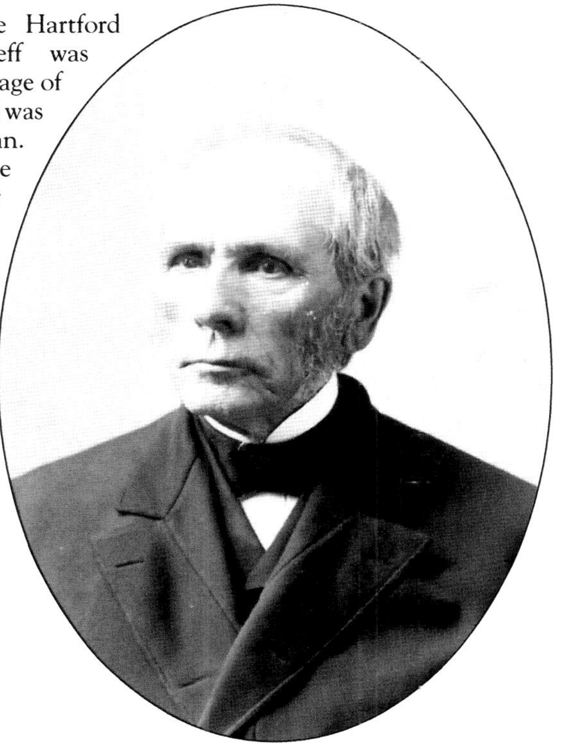

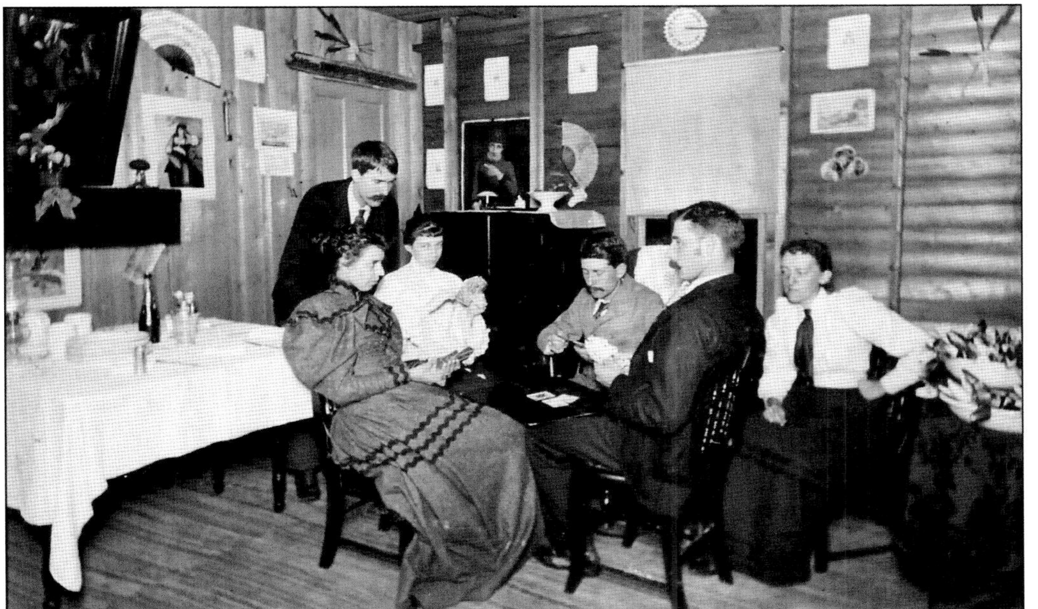

The Card Party, c. 1900. The game is in progress and the table is ready for refreshments. The card players are identified, from left to right, as follows: Mattie Shepard Rees, Belle Shepard Ronan, Ward Rees, and William Ronan. Looking on are Frank Alderman (left) and Mabel Alderman (right).

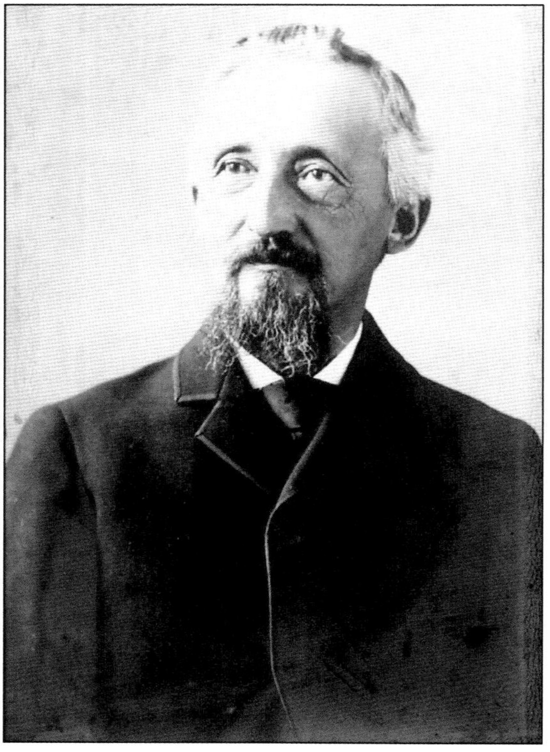

John Schmidt. John Schmidt was an importer and exporter in the early 1900s. His advertising claimed that he was the "sole agent for the Hamburg Enamelled Chair and Basket Cane." His son John, also well known, became the proprietor of the Park Square Hotel Stables at 24 and 30 School Street.

Young men with hats. Included in this picture are Ned and Ian Towle, Oren Parks, Chester Stiles, Ned Fowler, and one unidentified person. Some are wearing the round, hard-felt hats with rolling brims, which were sometimes called Bowler hats after the original hatter in England, William Bowler. In this country, these hats were more commonly called "derbies," and they were very fashionable at the turn of the century.

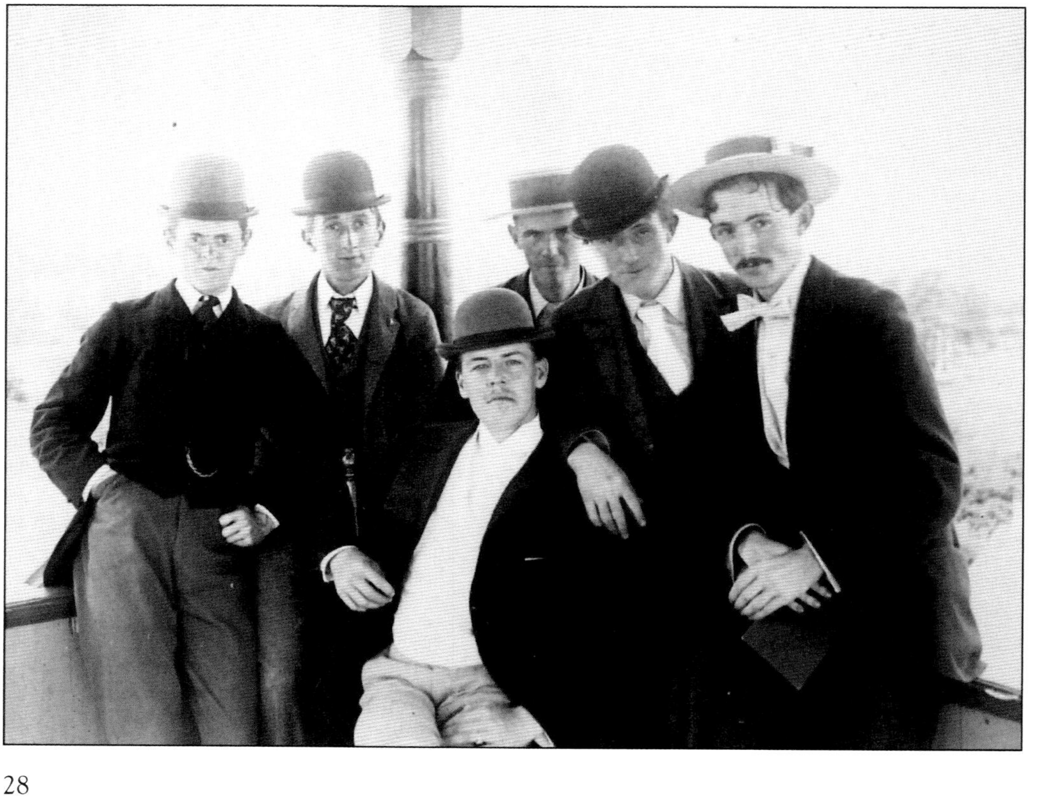

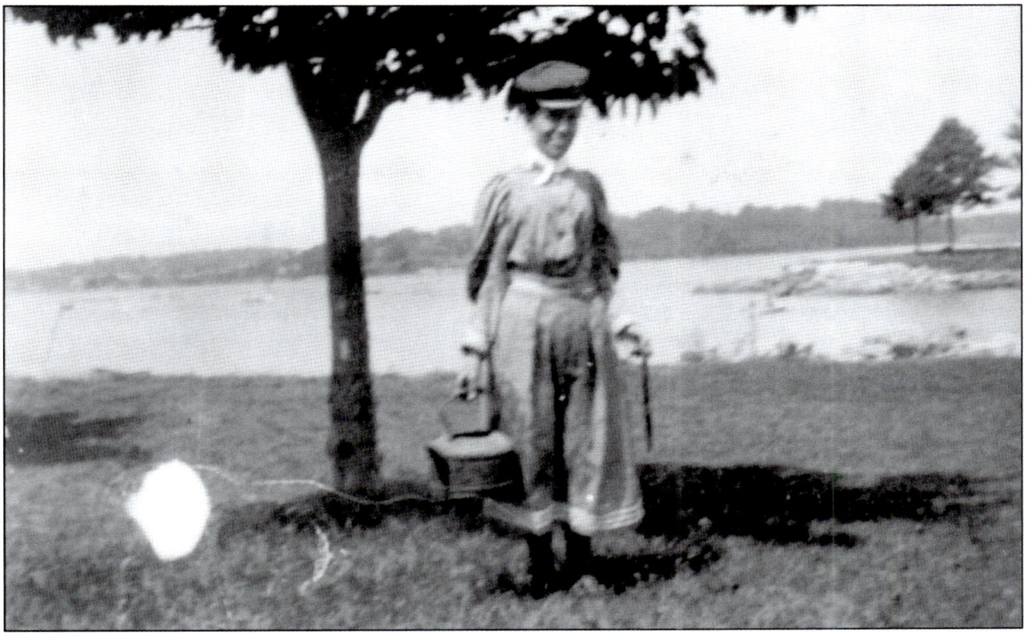

Eloise (Nellie) Ives Fowler on vacation at Linden Point, Stony Creek, Connecticut. Her daughter, Eloise, took this picture with a new Eastman Kodak camera brought to her from Saratoga by her father. On this occasion, Nellie had arisen very early to go fishing. She holds an eel in one hand and an old teakettle for fiddler crabs (bait) in the other.

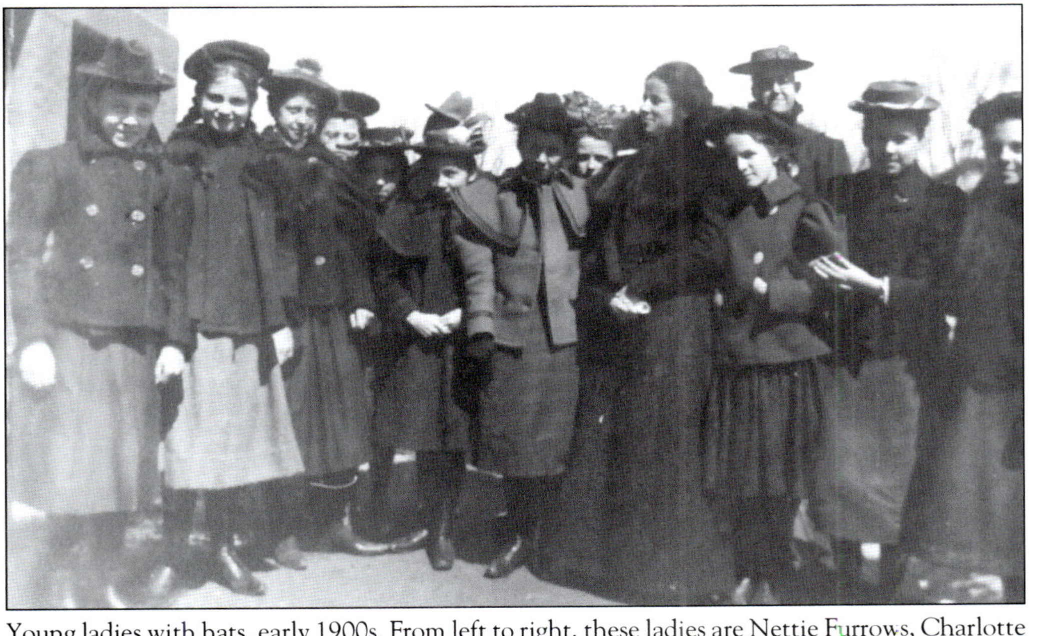

Young ladies with hats, early 1900s. From left to right, these ladies are Nettie Furrows, Charlotte Richardson, Lucia Skiff, Gladys Perkins, Helen Noble, Florence Hosmer (hat in back), Almyra Gaylord, Fay Brown, Vera Simpson, Miss Jennie Austin, Florence Ely, Minna Foster, Clara Gibbs, and Eloise Fowler. Where could they be going, all dressed up in their suits and hats?

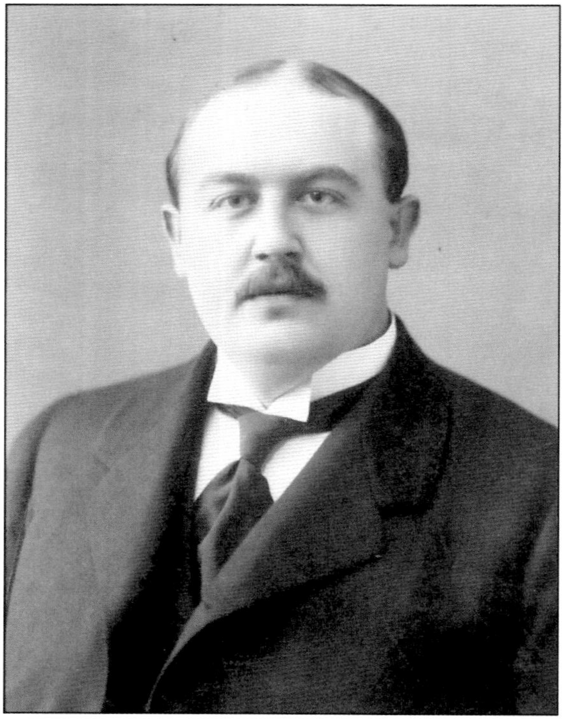

Harold P. Moseley. After graduating from Westfield High School in 1895, Harold Moseley decided to study for a legal profession, He took his B.A. at Williams College and then graduated from Boston University with a law degree in 1897. He began the practice of law in Westfield and became interested in politics. He was elected representative of this district in the legislature for four years, from 1901 to 1904. In 1905 he was elected to the senate. He was married and lived at 12 Chestnut Street.

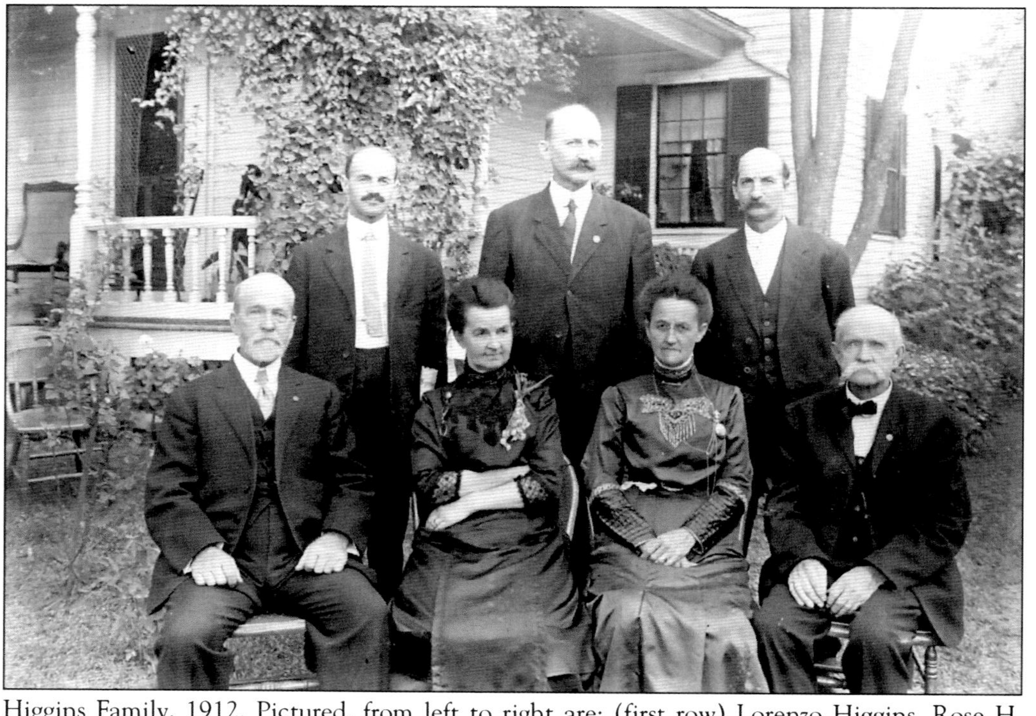

Higgins Family, 1912. Pictured, from left to right are: (first row) Lorenzo Higgins, Rose H. Ormsby, Ermina H. Jones, and Orlando Higgins; (top row) Arthur S. Higgins, W. Higgins, and Herbert Higgins. They lived on East Mountain Road where the country club is now.

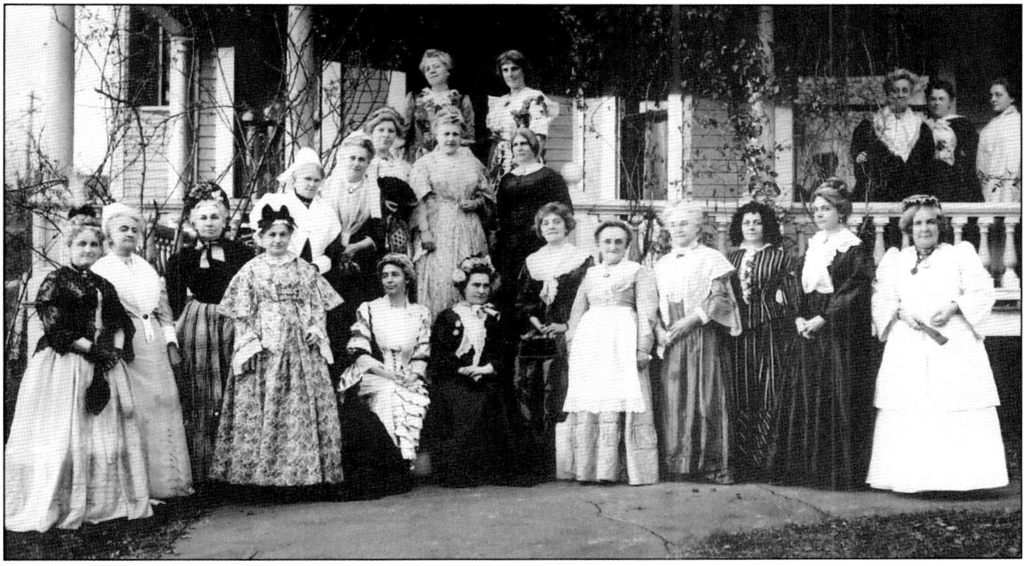

Group of ladies in costume. These ladies were gathered at Mrs. Lyman's house at 81 Court Street on November 18, 1913. Mss. Tooke, Kingsbury, Cooley, Robinson, and Nelson are on the piazza. Others pictured, by last name only, are: Moseley, Whipple, Scott, Mills, Beebe, Jarold, Gladwin, Sanford, Cary, Reed, Ayers, Fowler, Lyman, Grant, Hollister, Kellogg, and Gowdy.

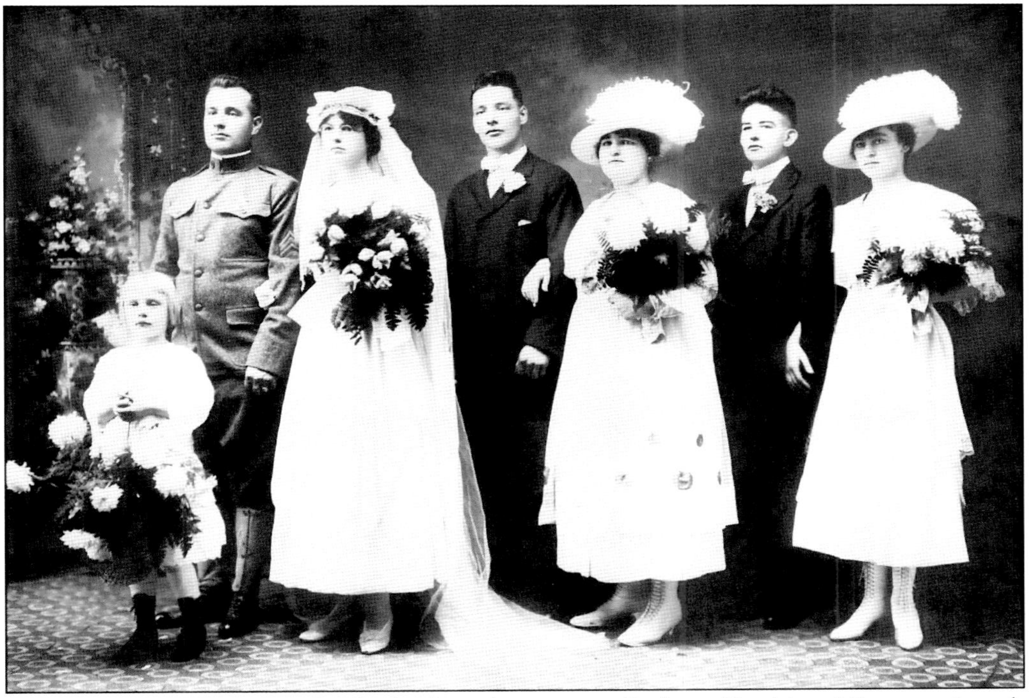

Wedding, November 7, 1917. The bride and groom are Stefania Gorski and Sergeant Joseph Forrish. In the wedding party, from left to right, are: George Forish, Mary Gorski, Peter Gorski, and Josephine Eglinski. The flower girl is Tillie Forish.

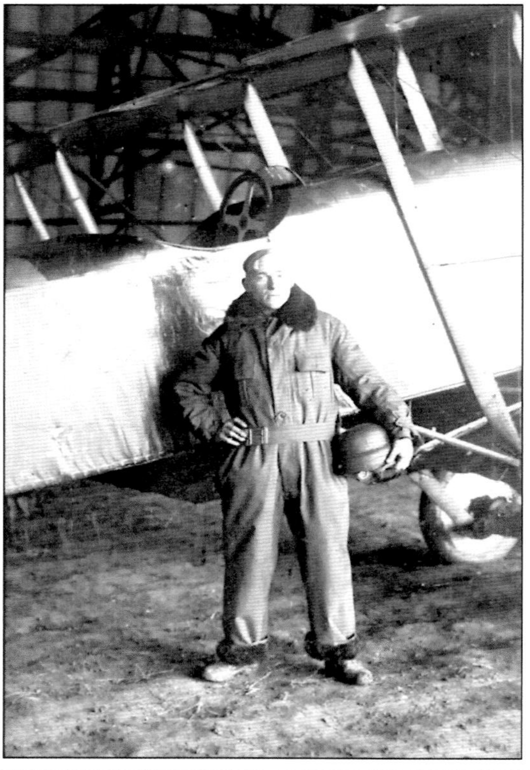

Walter L. Range, 1918. This picture was taken in France where Corporal Walter Range served in the army during World War I. He was a motor mechanic in the Air Service of Company Six, First Regiment. He was born on July 18, 1896, and died on May 3, 1982, at the age of eighty-six. He lived at 20 Southgate Road in a house that was torn down on January 20, 1997.

Mrs. Lewis B. Allyn in "Puritan House." In 1919 Westfield celebrated its 250th anniversary. The Westfield Women's Club, of which Mrs. Allyn was president, selected the former Strong residence to serve as a "hostess house." Townspeople found antiques of every sort with which to furnish it, and tea was served by hostesses in quaint old costumes. Mrs. Allyn was the wife of Lewis B. Allyn, who made Westfield famous as the "Pure Food City."

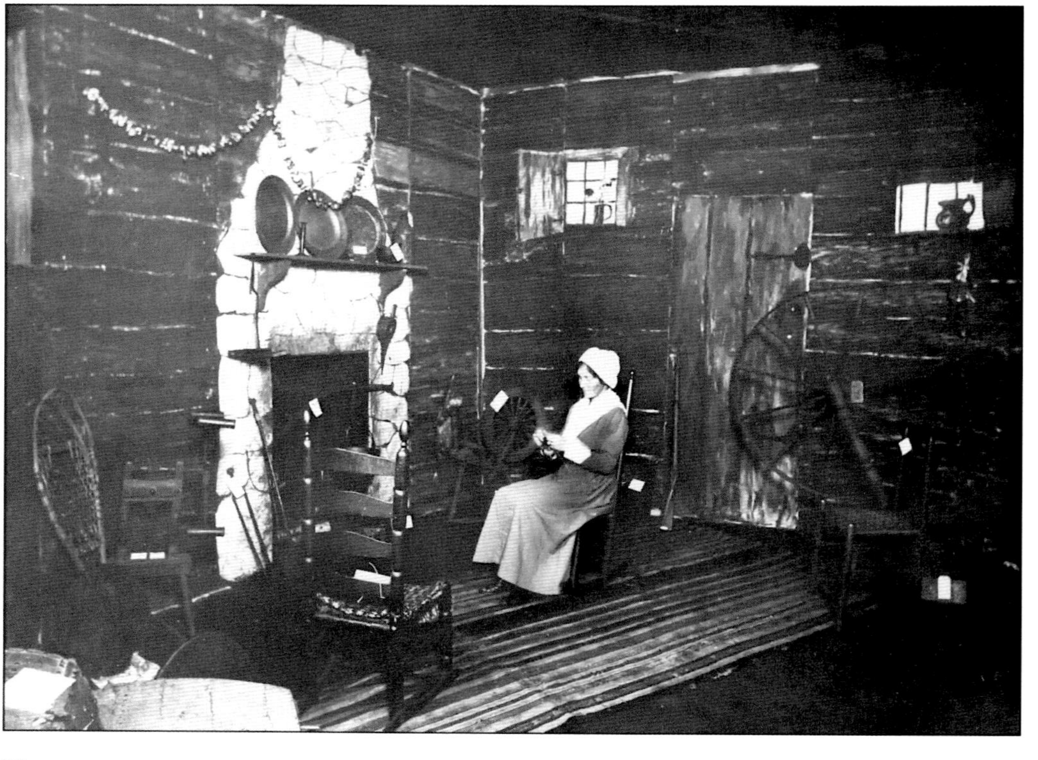

Lt. Richard Jesse King. Lt. King was killed on August 18, 1943, during World War II at the age of twenty-one. He attended Westfield schools, graduated from Williston Academy, and was attending Springfield College when Pearl Harbor was bombed. He left college to enter the service and became a pilot in the Army Air Forces. He and two other pilots were killed in a training accident.

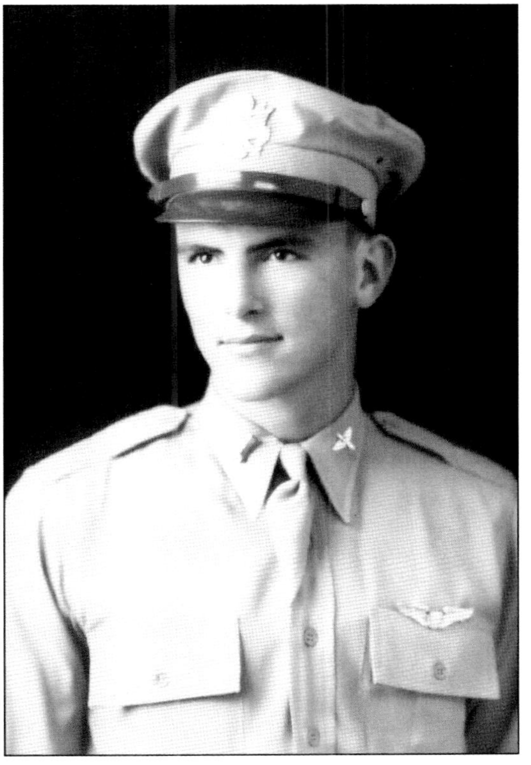

The Pomeroy family, about 1941. These smiling folks lived on Russellville Road. From left to right, they are: Leon Ralph Pomeroy Jr., L. Ralph Pomeroy (with Seth on his lap), Rachel Pomeroy (with Alma in her lap), Gaye Pomeroy, and Lewis Harlow Pomeroy Jr.

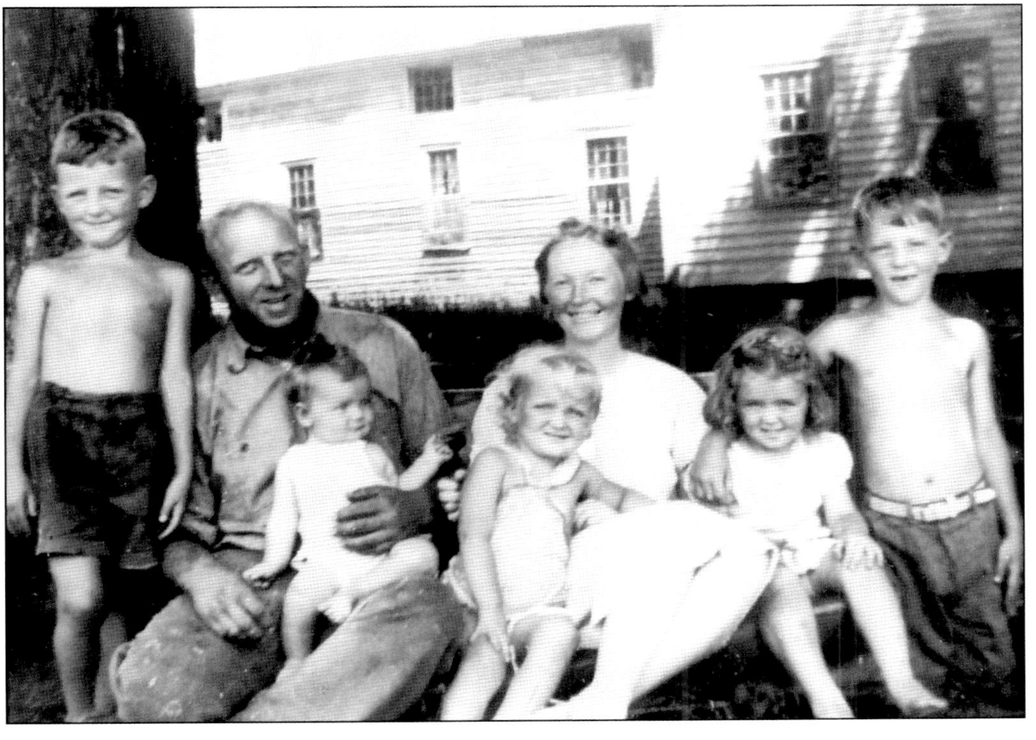

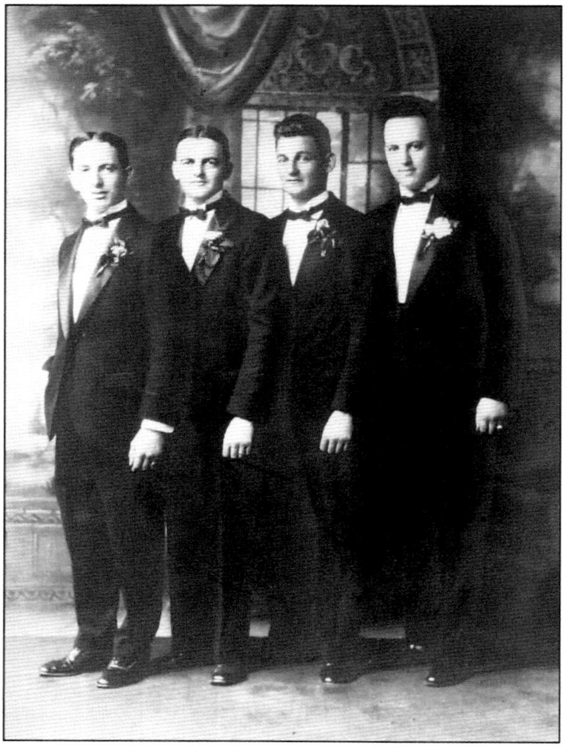

Portrait at a wedding, 1925. The groom was Larry Oleksak (second from the left). Others in the party, from left to right, were: Binky Romani, John Oleksak, and Peter Romani. The two Romanis owned a confectionary and fruit store at 56 Elm Street.

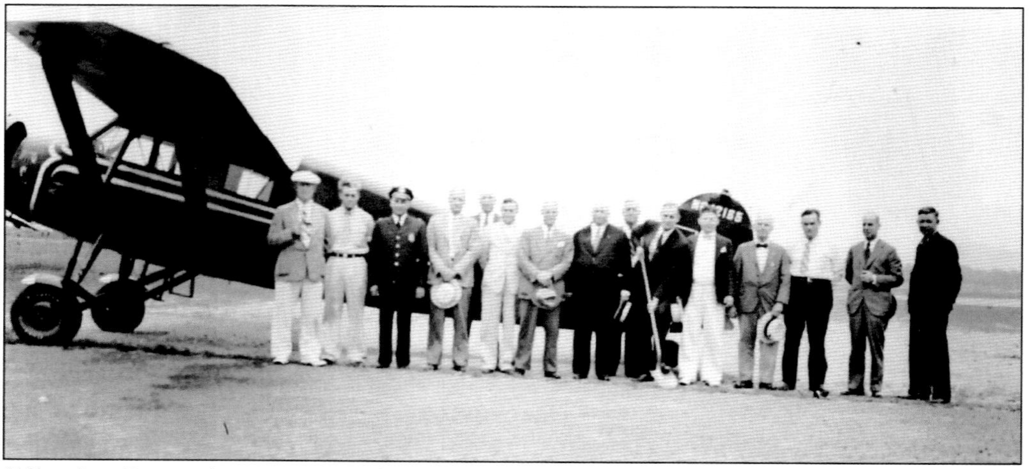

Officials at Barnes Airport, 1936. These men were present at the official start of the development and enlargement of Barnes Airport under an $89,200 WPA project grant. From left to right, they are: Percy N. Hall (secretary of the Westfield Chamber of Commerce), Assistant City Engineer William T. Burke, Police Captain Allen H. Smith, City Building Inspector Ralph M. Sizer, Oren E. Parks (superintendent of the Department of Public Works), Harvey Law (of Newton), Captain W.L. Rockwell (aviation advisor for the WPA), State Senator Harry B. Putnam, License Commissioner Alfred P. Pfeiffer, Major Raymond H. Cowing (with shovel), Attorney Hugh G. Flynn, City Almoner Morrell H. Moore, City Engineer Richard P. Boyle, Glen B. Cowles (from the Board of Public Works), and Charles J. O'Connor (chief pilot of Barnes Airport).

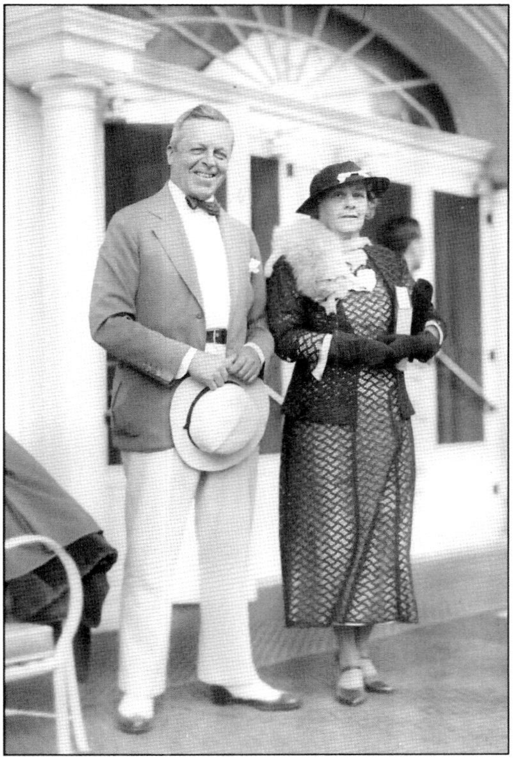

Joseph B. and Harriet D. Ely. Twice-governor of Massachusetts and former district attorney for Hampden and Berkshire Counties, Joseph Buell Ely was one of our most outstanding and respected citizens. He was born in Westfield on February 22, 1888, the son of two native Westfielders. He attended the local schools and then went on to graduate from Williams College and Harvard Law School. In 1905 he began to practice law in his father's firm known as Ely & Ely. He became a power in the Democratic party, and by 1930 he was elected governor.

Homer E. Bush and sons, late 1930s. Former mayor Homer E. Bush is pictured with his sons (from left to right) Everett, Harold, David, and Stanley. They are haying in a field that is now occupied by Eastwood Self Storage on Union Street. People who grew up in the Union Street area may also remember the team of horses, Doll and Belle. They would often pull a wagon or a sleigh when Homer picked up neighborhood children to given them a ride.

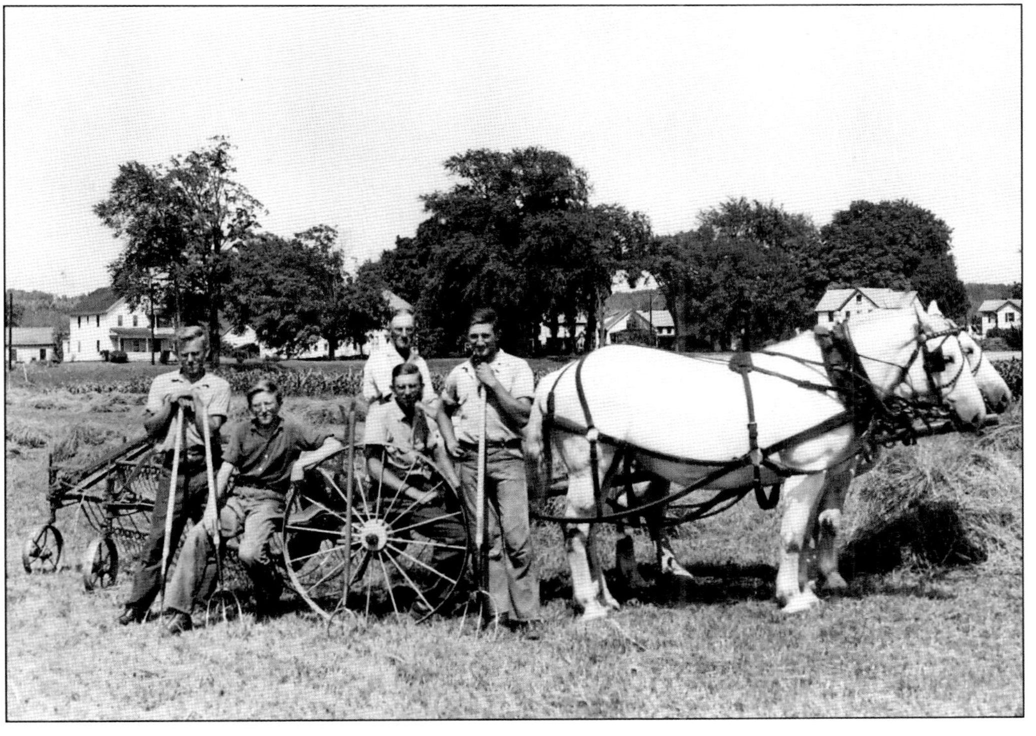

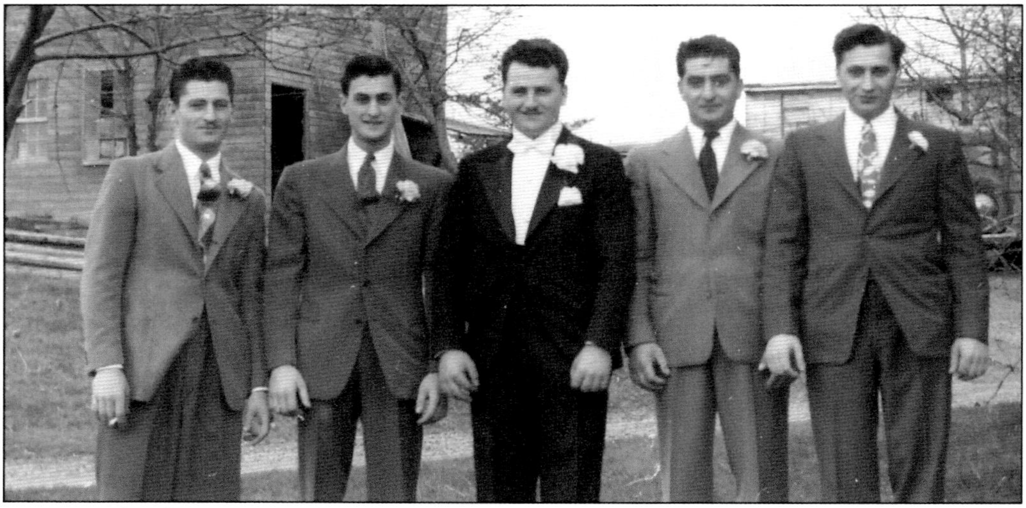

Cennamo brothers, 1947. The five brothers, from left to right, are: Michael, John, Nunzio, Jerry, and Louis. They are pictured at a wedding on the Cennamo property on East Mountain Road. Their father had some of this property taken by eminent domain for the building of Western Massachusetts Hospital.

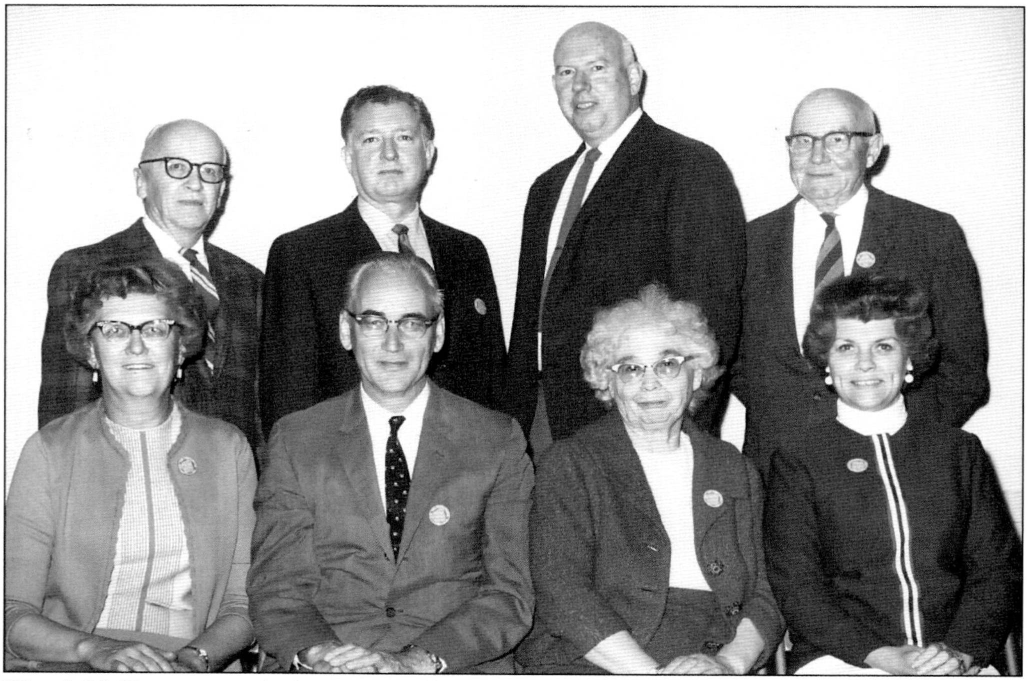

Westfield Tricentennial Association Incorporators. In 1969 Westfield marked the 300th anniversary of its incorporation. A great celebration was planned by the Westfield Tricentennial Association. The incorporators pictured here, from left to right, are: (front row) Barbara Bush, Harold F. Maschin, Mary A. Noble, and F. Evelyn O'Connor; (top row, standing) Roscoe Scott, Leslie A. Chapin, Andrew Anderson, and Edwin Smith. Those not present were: Patricia Martel, Harold N. Jones, Walter J. Zarichak, Edward C. Janes, Edward M. Lee, Ethel F. Oleksak, and John J. Palczynski.

Three

Historic Homes

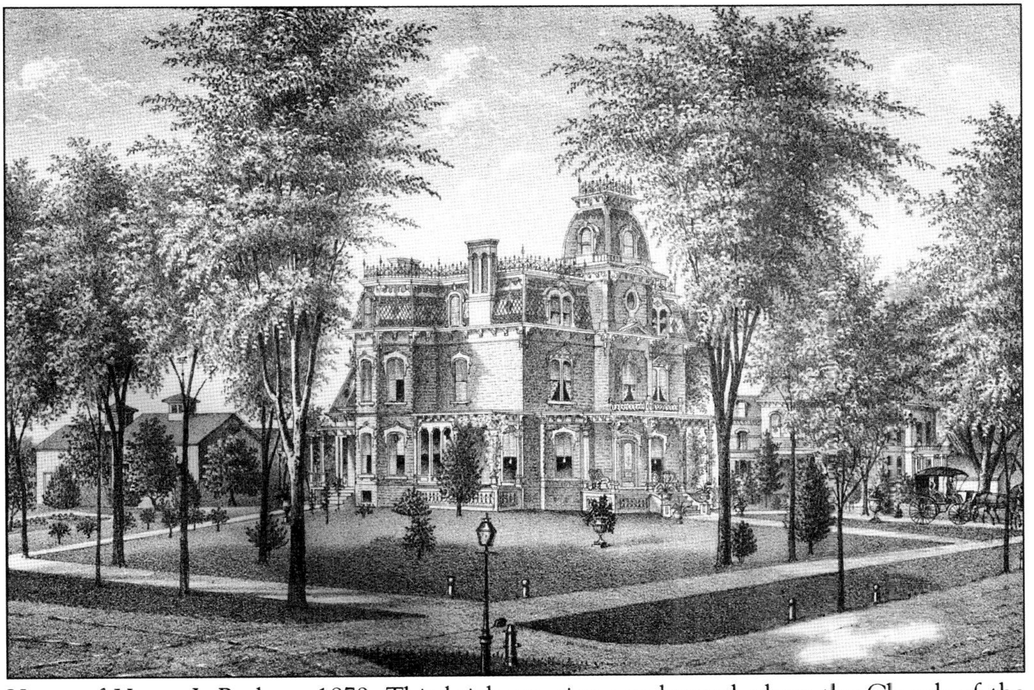

Home of Henry J. Bush, c. 1879. This brick mansion was located where the Church of the Atonement now stands. The house that previously stood on this lot was moved to Holland Avenue in 1876 so that the Bush house could be built. The Bush house later became the home of Ira Miller and subsequently became the property of the Episcopal church, when it began to be known as "The Church in the Home." It was razed in 1952 to allow the present Episcopal church to be built.

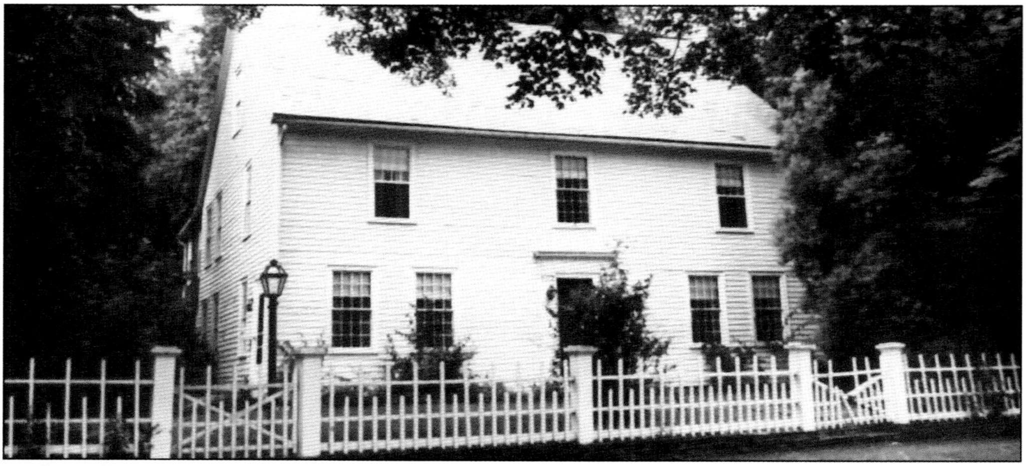

Bush-Collins Homestead at 81 East Silver Street, *c.* 1685. One of the oldest landmarks of Westfield, this is one of the last surviving examples in which the window arrangement of the second floor does not match that of the first floor. Usually houses had five windows on the second floor and four on the first. The house was built by Jonathan Alvard, who deeded it to his adopted son, Ebenezer Bush, in 1709. Until the 1920s the family operated a prosperous farm there and retained ownership until the 1980s. It is now a private residence. In 1983 a rear section was converted to a doctor's office.

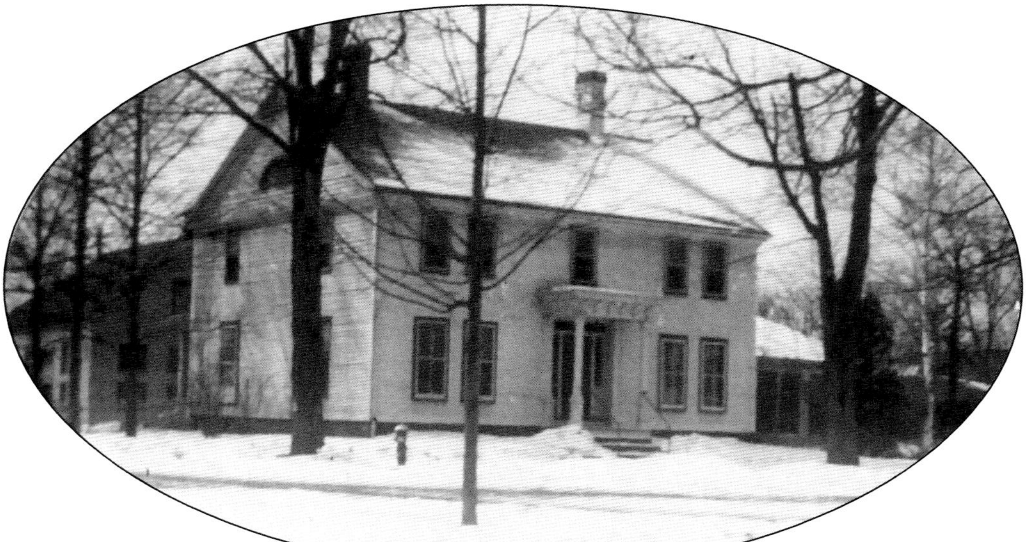

Richard Loomis Fowler Homestead, 87 East Silver Street, 1671. The Fowler's (Ambrose and Joan Alvord Fowler) were one of the first families to settle in Westfield. They settled on the "cellar side" (Union Street). Ambrose moved, after his home was burned by Indians warriors while he was at church, to the west side of South Meadow Road (south of the Richard Fowler house), outside the fortified area. He was allowed to live there on the condition that "he fortify himself well and have 5 or 6 men with him of his family." Ambrose's land was passed down in his family for one hundred years. In 1790 Blackleach Fowler (Ambrose was his great-great grandfather) purchased the house at 87 West Silver Street from Moses Hanchett. This house has been in the Fowler family for another two hundred years, and it remains so to this day.

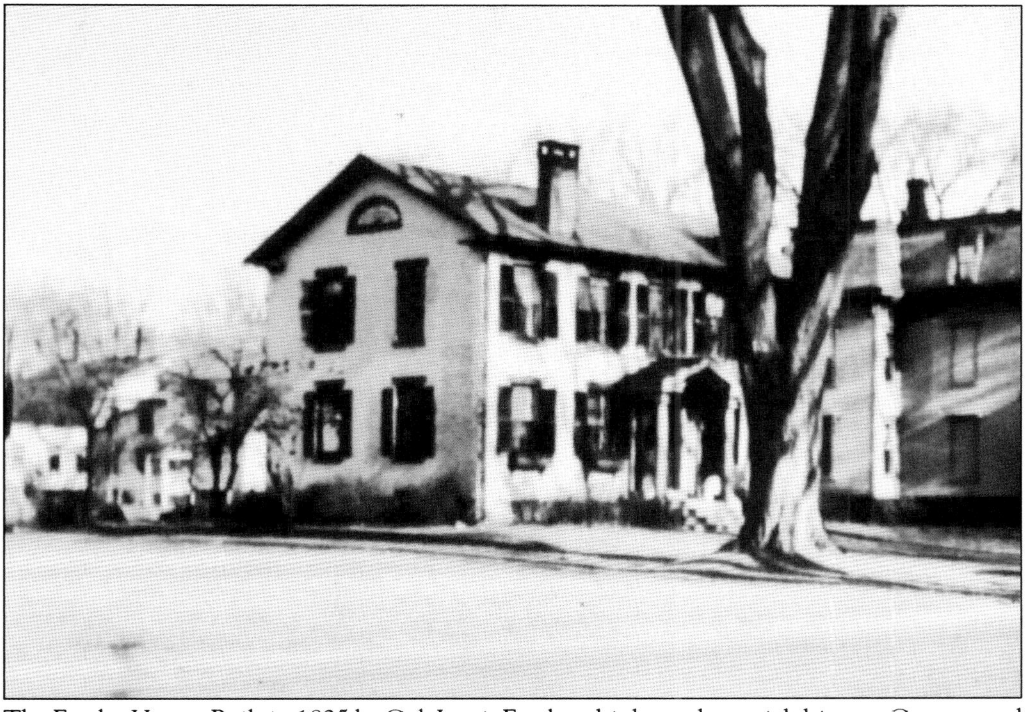

The Fowler House. Built in 1825 by Col. Lewis Fowler, this home has a rich history. Constructed from bricks used as ballast from a Dutch trading ship, the house probably played an active role in the Underground Railroad. It was moved to its current location in 1870 and is considered one of the finer examples of Federal architecture in the city of Westfield.

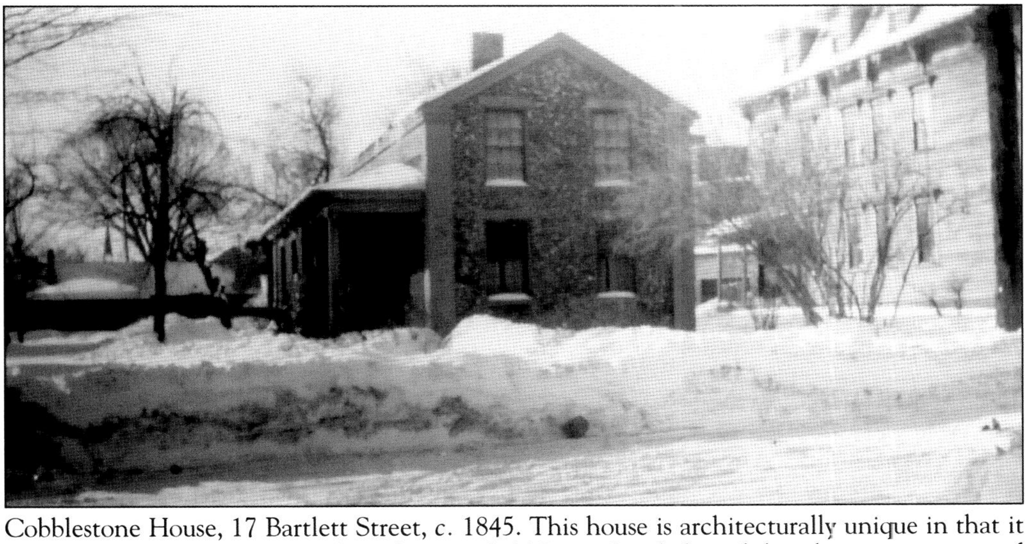

Cobblestone House, 17 Bartlett Street, *c.* 1845. This house is architecturally unique in that it is constructed of cobblestones from the Westfield River. It is believed that the stones were used as ballast in a boat that travelled the old canal. The house was built by Ralph Dewey in the Greek Revival style. Mattie (Boyden) Sizer was the last descendant of Ralph Dewey to live in the house, having died in 1960. During the blizzard of 1888, the snow was up to the second story window. The house is still a private residence.

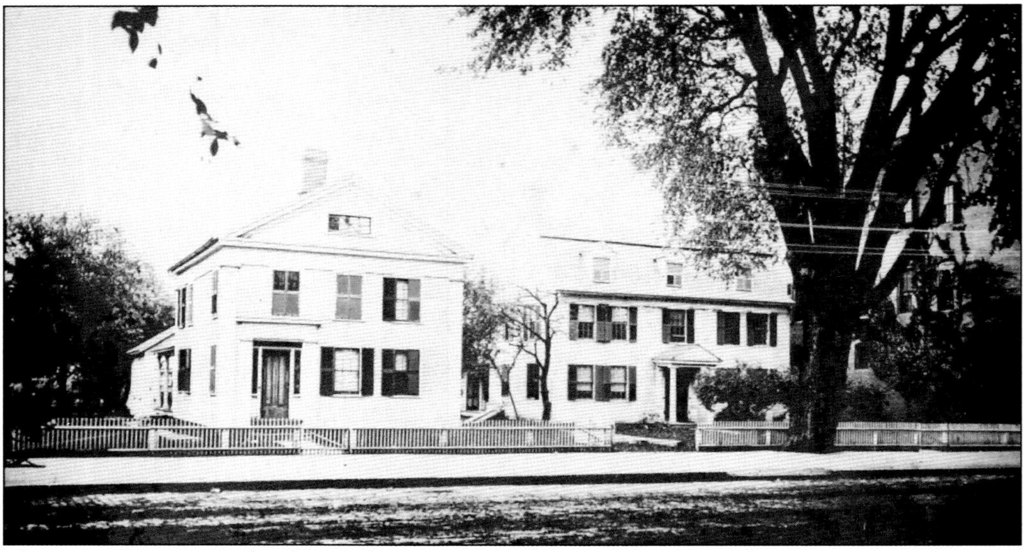

The Loomis House. This house (on the left) was originally located on Elm Street between Church and Arnold Streets. In order to make room for the Parks Block, it was relocated to its present site at 8 Woronoco Avenue. Members of the Loomis family probably occupied the house from the time of its construction (*c.* 1840) until it was moved. Charles Austin, proprietor of Austin Brothers Dry Goods Store, was responsible for having the house moved.

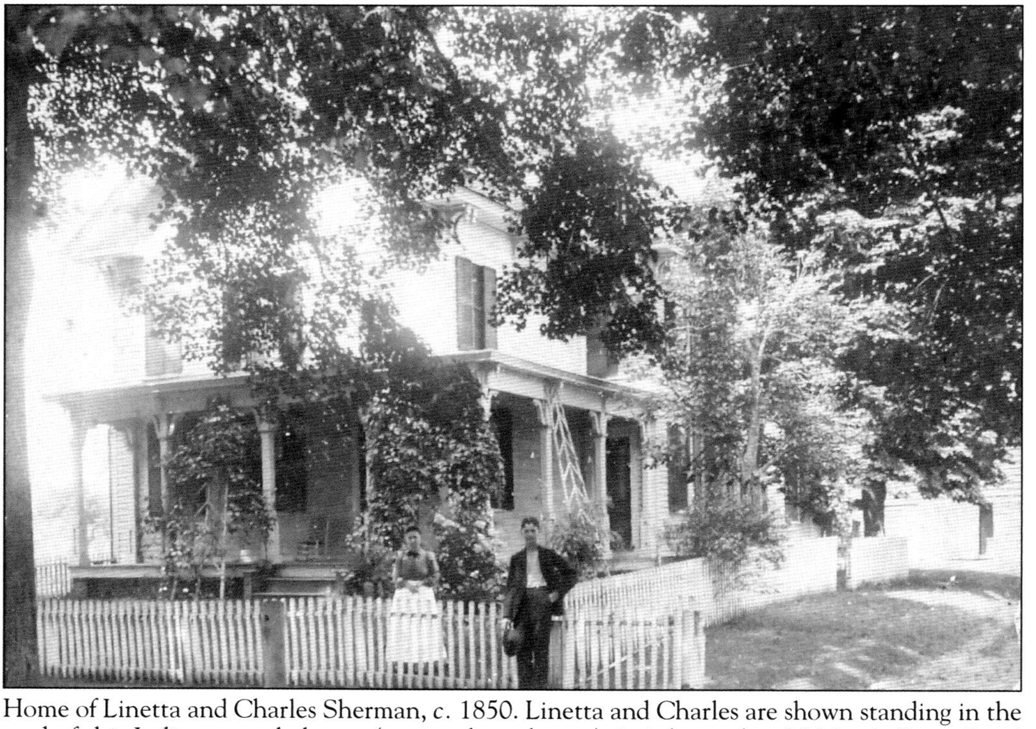

Home of Linetta and Charles Sherman, *c.* 1850. Linetta and Charles are shown standing in the yard of this Italianate-style house (notice the columns). It is located at 356 Little River Road (next to the fire station).

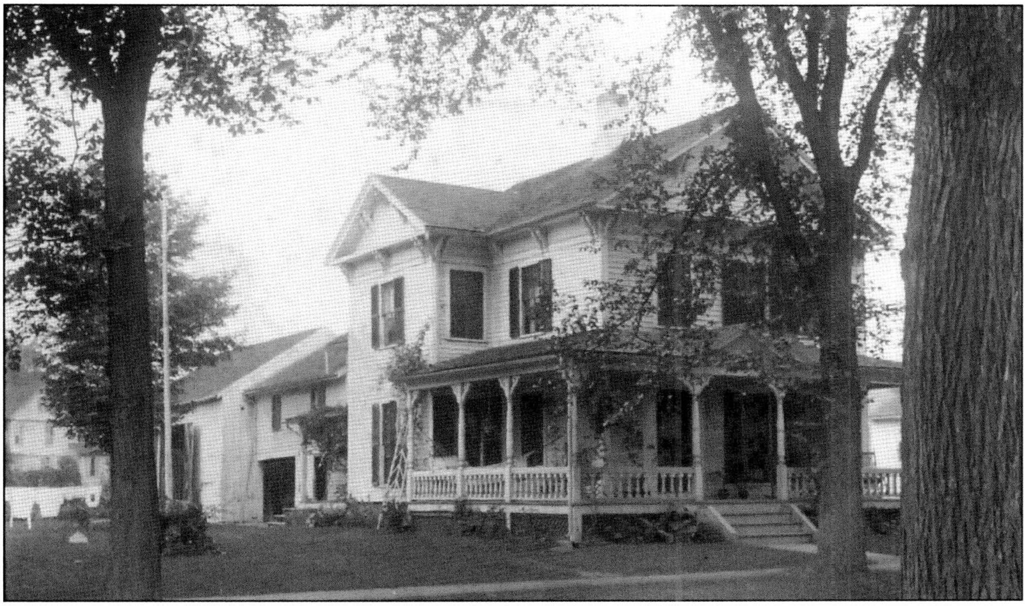

11 East Silver Street, corner of Coleman Avenue and East Silver. This is a good example of a "continuous" style house with the woodshed, carriage house, and other outbuildings attached.

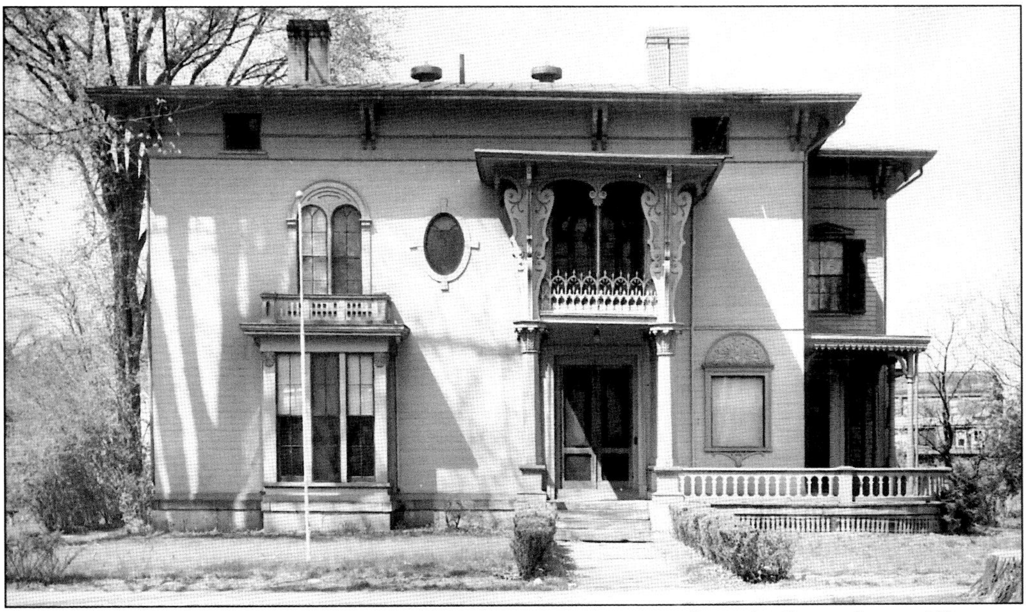

The Gillett House, presently the site of Woronoco Savings Bank, at 31 Court Street. This was the home of Mr. Edward Bates Gillett and his wife, Lucy Douglas Fowler Gillett. They were the parents of Lucy Douglas Gillett (b. 1856), one of Westfield's beloved ladies and beneficiary of the Westfield Athenaeum, the YMCA, and the 4-H. She served as the first president of the Hopefully Well-Affected Club, helped organize the Westfield Women's Club, and was a charter member of the Western Hampden Historical Society. She was a familiar figure in Westfield, driving in her 1916 Model T Ford, with its 27 registration plate—the lowest number in the town.

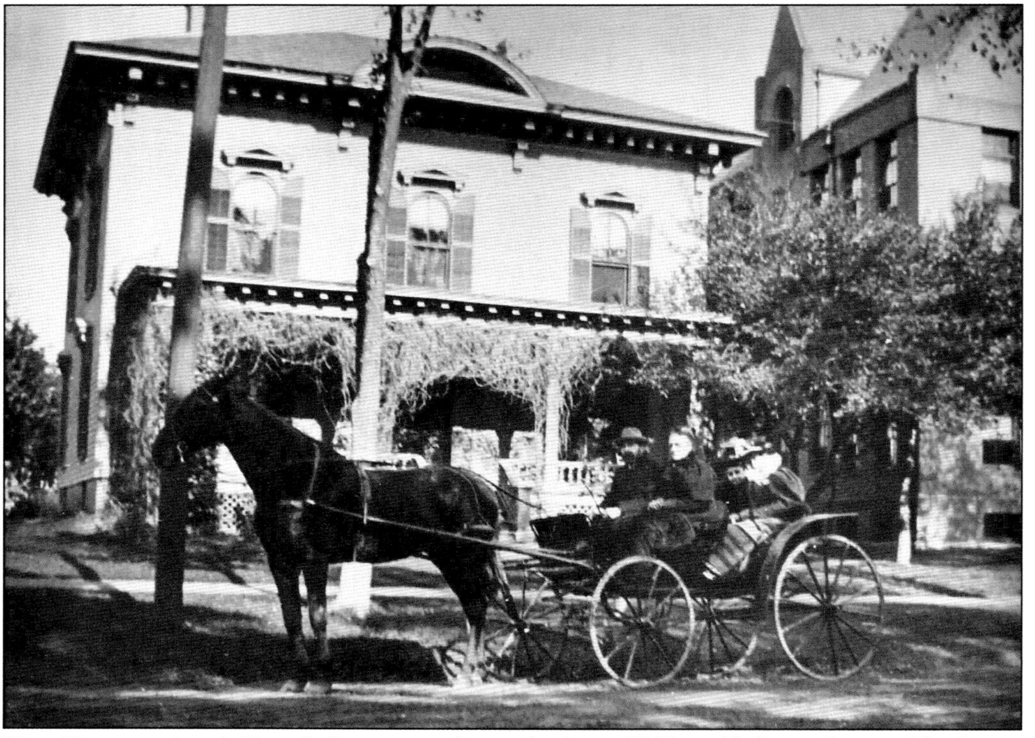

First Congregational Church Parsonage. It was built in 1868 at 65 Court Street. The house was purchased by Miss Lucy D. Gillett and presented to the YMCA in 1944. It was then razed to square out their property. The State Normal School is located to the right (now city hall). Seated in the carriage are Reverend and Mrs. John H. Lockwood with daughters Lucy and Ann in the back.

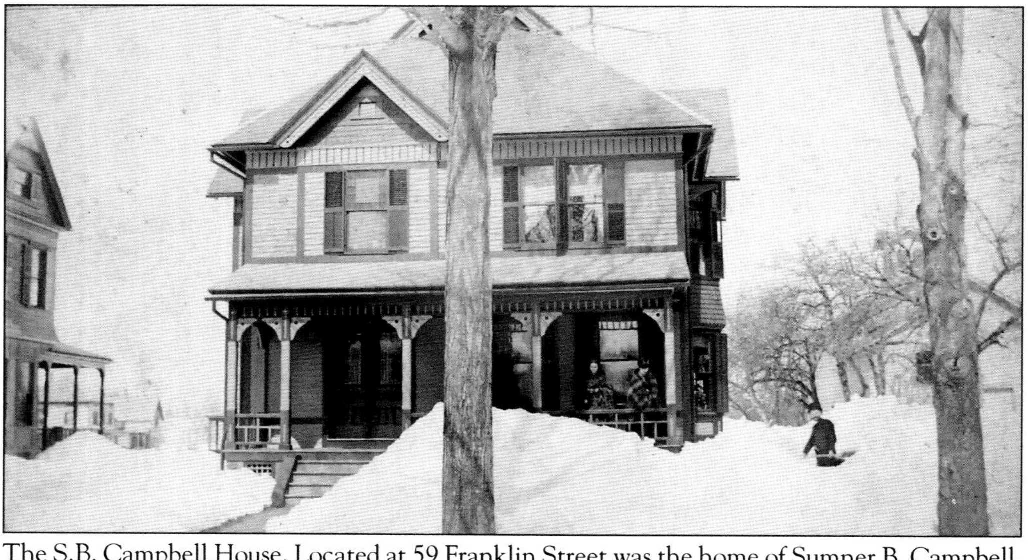

The S.B. Campbell House. Located at 59 Franklin Street was the home of Sumner B. Campbell, who was the treasurer of the Textile Manufacturing Company. The snow was from the blizzard of 1888, and the man in the photograph is Mr. Campbell himself.

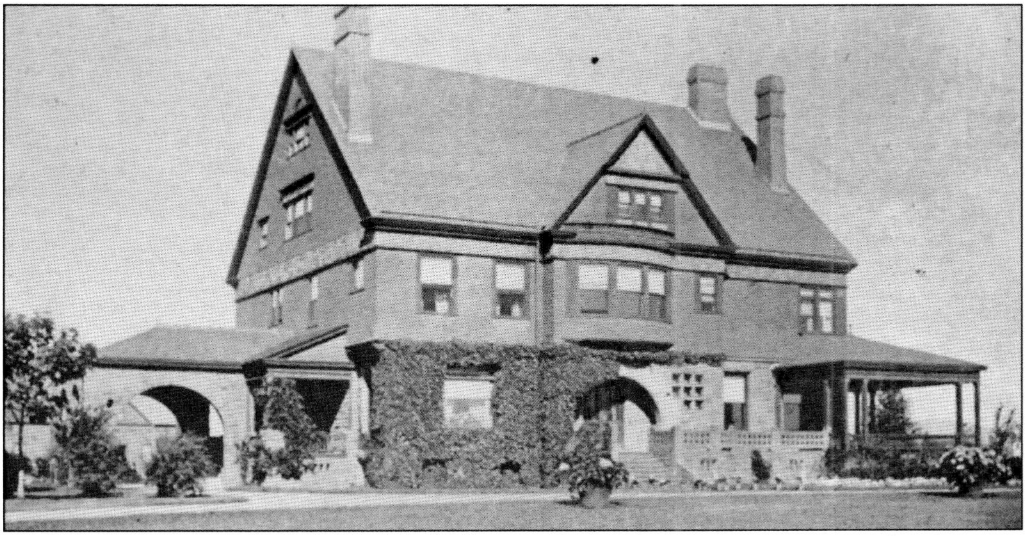

Broadlawn. The residence of James A. Crane, of Crane Brothers paper, on Mill Street was located in the meadow across from the lower mill. He and his brother, Robert, who also lived on Mill Street, developed Crane Pond (located where we now have St. James and Highland Avenues). The house later became the Holy Child Guild, a home for unwed mothers run by the Sisters of Providence, and the structure was eventually demolished in the 1960s. It is now the site of Genesis House.

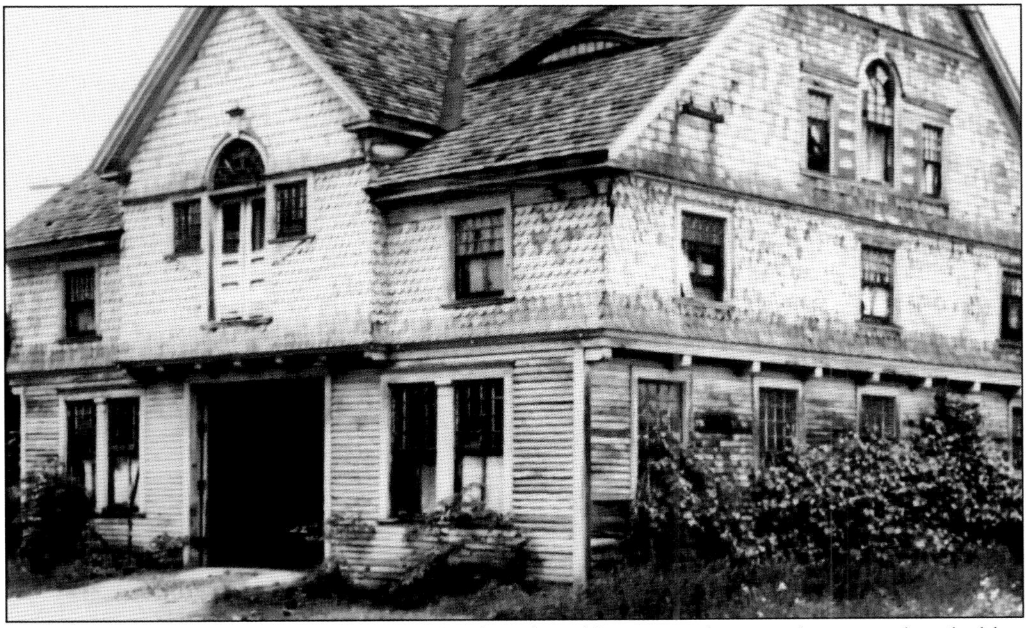

Crane Horse Stable, *c.* 1894. The Crane brothers loved horses, and racing them was their hobby. They built a .5-mile track toward the Western Avenue side of the meadow and constructed a big, red horse barn in the rear overlooking the pond. Horses were brought from miles around for training, and the Crane's prize stallion, Cronus, commanded a very high fee for stud. One of the stables, located at 17 Brookline Avenue, is shown above. It was taken down in 1949 and is now the location of Bemben's Greenhouse showroom.

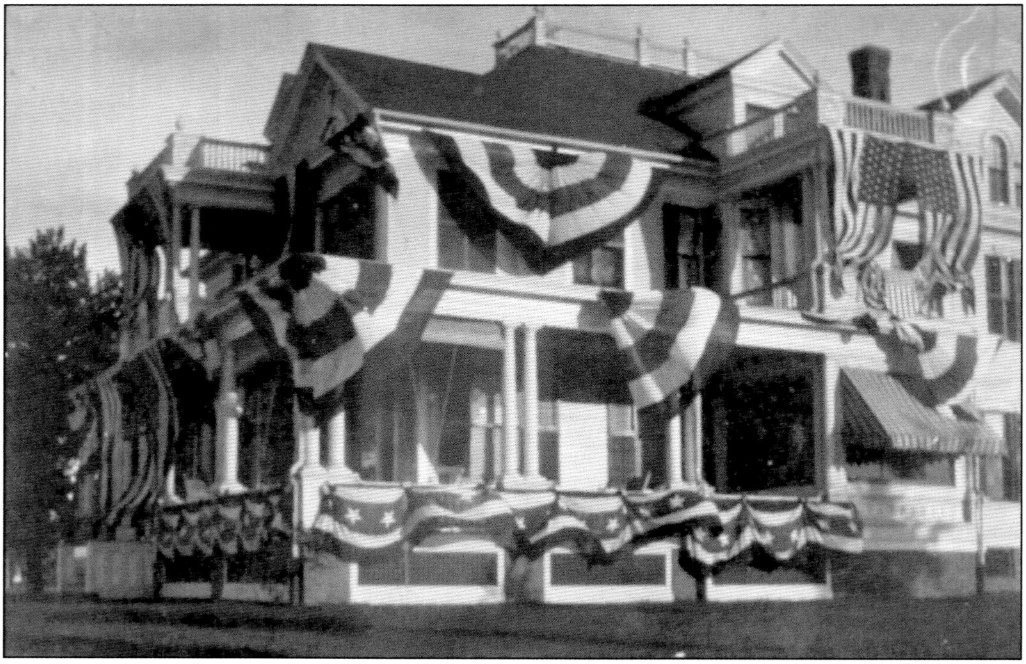

Ralph Gillett home on Tekoa Terrace. In the late 1800s, Ralph Gillett began his career with a real estate business in this home. In 1899 he built an office building at 100 Elm Street, which became known as the Gillett Block. He was president of the Hampden Railroad Corporation, which was located there, and was an officer in several other businesses.

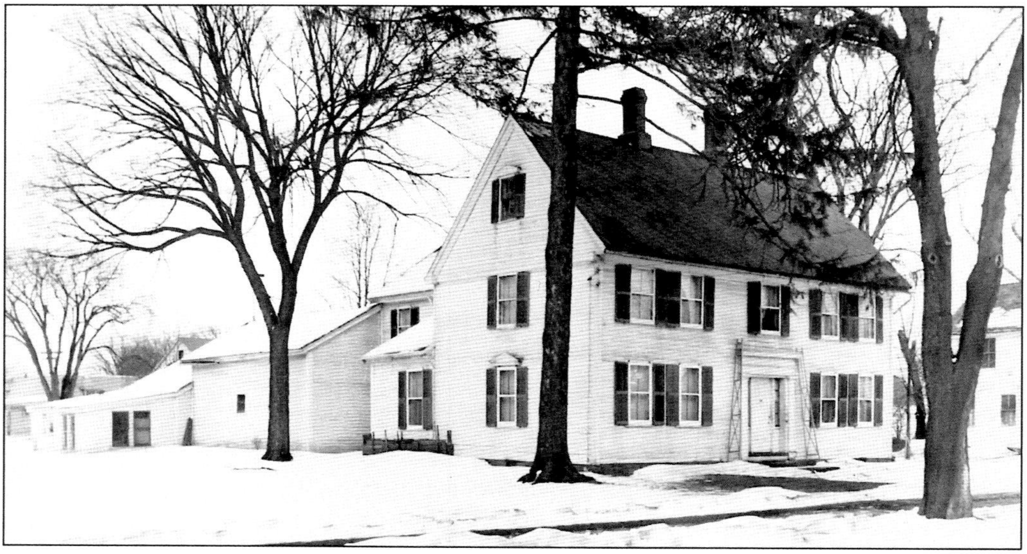

Erastus Grant Homestead, 127 Main Street (corner of White and Main), *c.* 1895. Erastus Grant was a cabinetmaker who was described as a "decided, energetic, passionate man, prompt in all his business, with an iron will, and a determination which never pauses in its purposes." He employed a large number of workers in his shop, which was adjacent to his home. Examples of his work may be seen at the Westfield Athenaeum. The house was moved in 1950 to the corner where Stanley Cleaners now stands.

Hazelhurst, 11 Mill Street, corner of West Silver and Mill Streets. This Victorian house and carriage building were built around the turn of the century. In 1923 Lorenz and Ethelyn Loud bought it from the Hazelton family and established "Hazelhurst," a maternity hospital. Ethelyn had been superintendent of the Springfield Isolation Hospital before coming to Westfield. She then ran Hazelhurst for the ten years between 1923 and 1933. The Loud family moved away in 1936 or 1937, and the house was torn down, probably about 1939. Four houses now occupy the site, two on Mill and two on West Silver Streets.

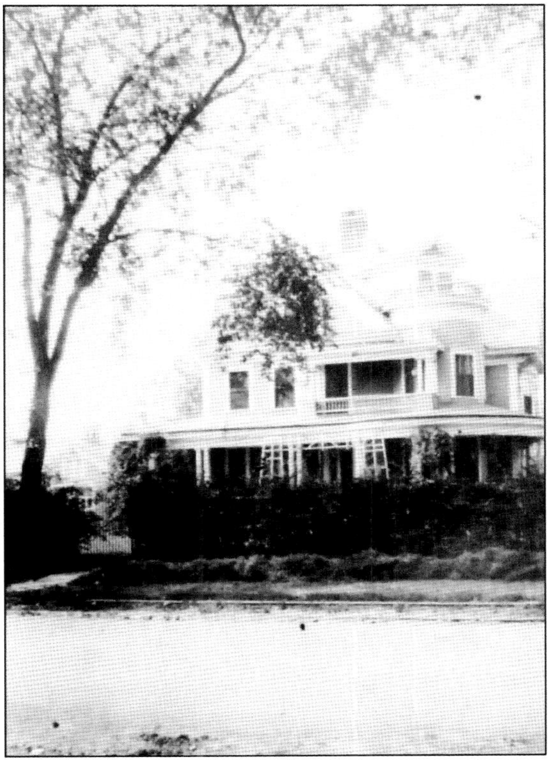

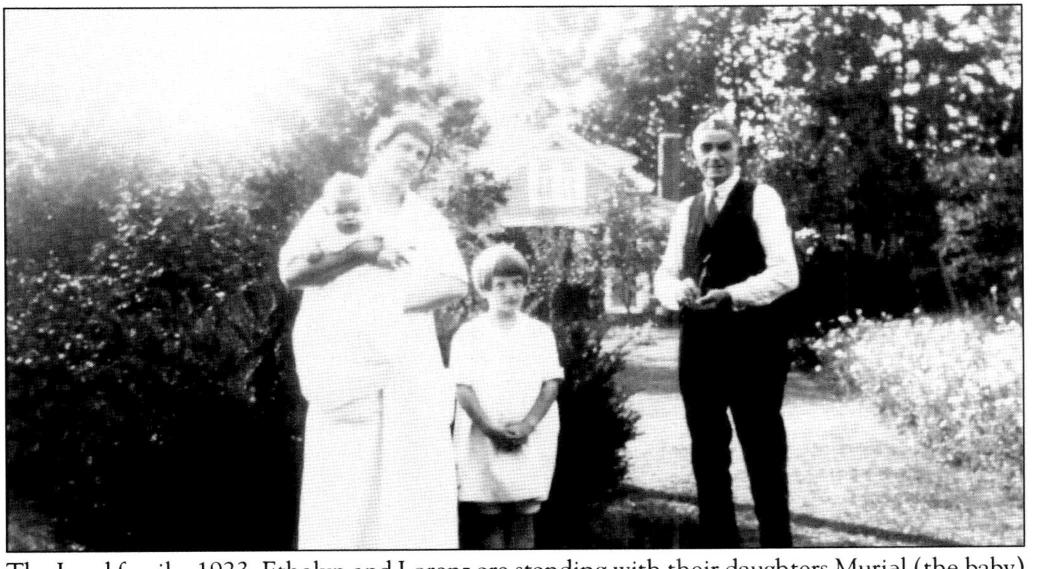

The Loud family, 1923. Ethelyn and Lorenz are standing with their daughters Muriel (the baby) and Dorothy. Muriel was born in 1923 and now lives on Martha's Vineyard. Dorothy was born in 1918 and now lives in Florida. Two years after this picture was taken, Albert was born, probably at Hazelhurst. He now lives in Longmeadow.

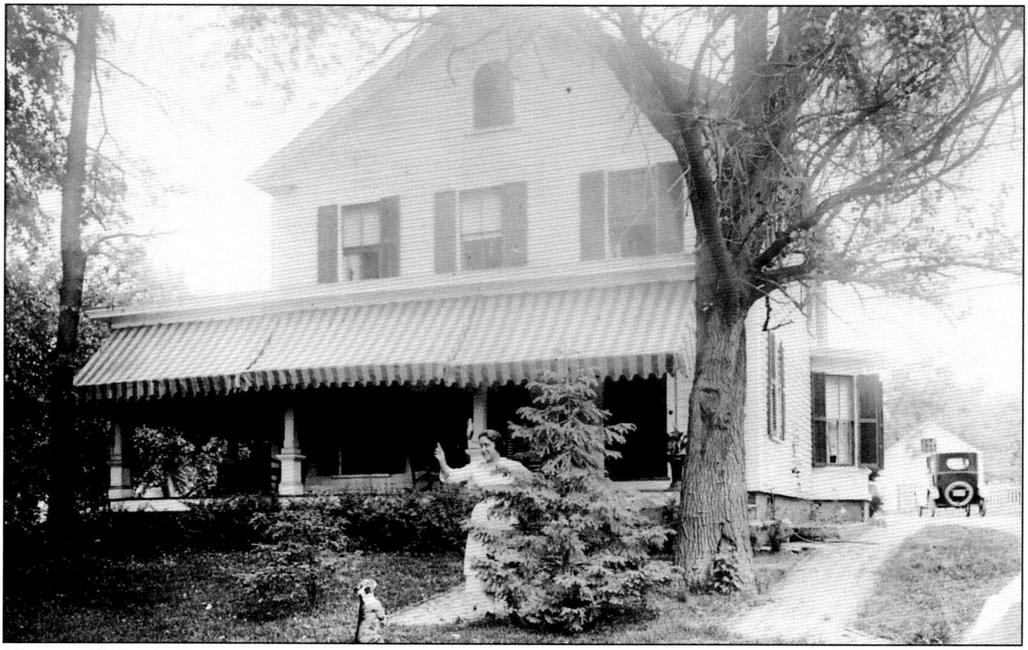

Home of Elijah Ensign, 324 Little River Road. Elijah Ensign built this house in 1918. It has a slate-covered gable roof, an Italianate-style veranda, and a round-headed window in the gable end. Awnings were added sometime in the 1920s. This picture was taken about 1928 or 1930 and shows Catherine Freed Ensign with her bulldog Trixie. This home is still occupied by the Ensign family.

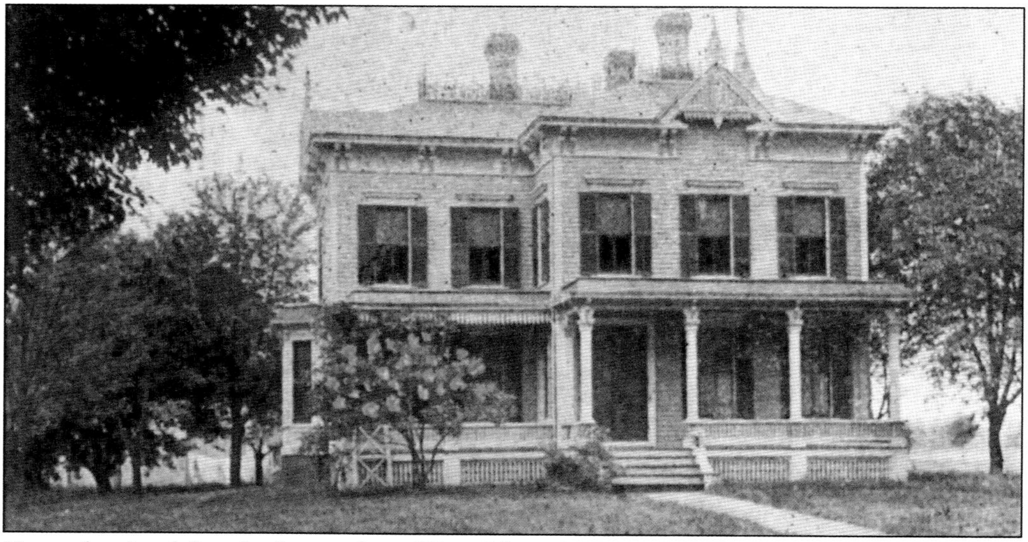

Home for Aged People. Located on West Silver Street, it was formerly the home of V.W. Crowson, treasurer of the Westfield Savings Bank. It was used as a home for the aged from 1904 to 1908. The home was then purchased by Louis Keefe (mayor of Westfield from 1923 to 1926 and 1929 to 1931). Mr. Keefe's daughter, Anna Keefe, was a teacher at Westfield High School for many years. The house was eventually razed to make room for the present post office on West Silver Street.

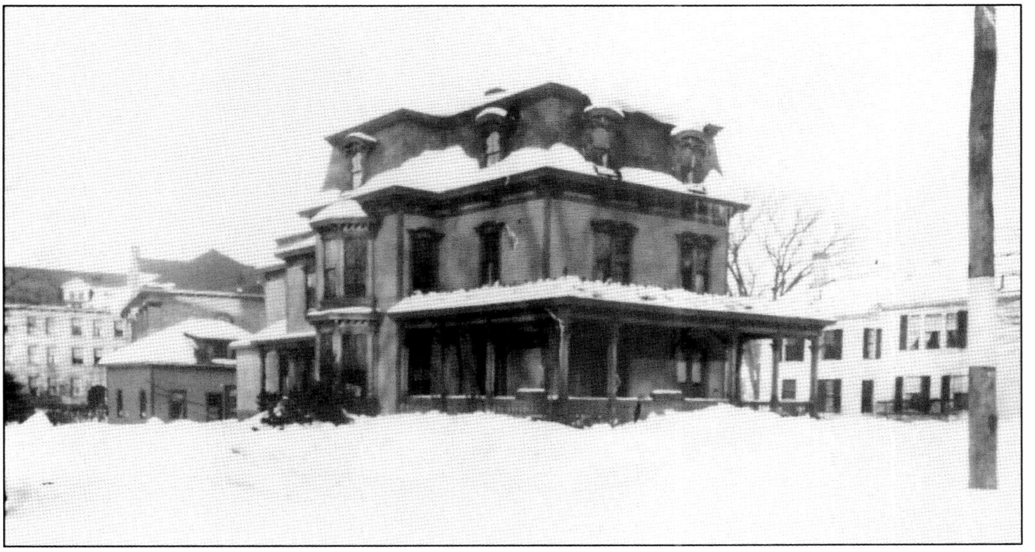

57 Court Street, *c.* 1940. This was the home of Edward Scanlon, president of Westfield State Teachers College. Because of low enrollment, the college was threatened with closing; however, the college received a temporary reprieve by the arrival of 157 U.S. Signal Corps trainees, who took over Dickinson Hall, the college dormitory. The young ladies then moved into the Scanlon Residence.

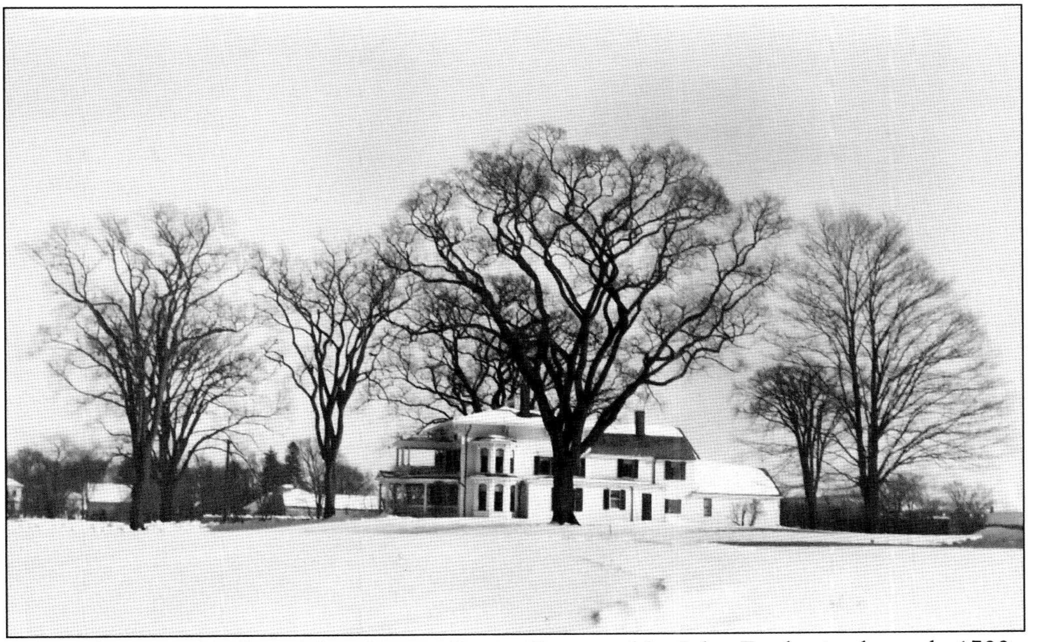

Salmond House, 30 West Silver Street. Originally started by John Fowler in the early 1700s, the house received many additions and renovations throughout the years. The picture above shows it as it was in 1948 when owned by Herbert and Eloise Fowler Salmond. The house was eventually torn down, and the middle school was built on the site.

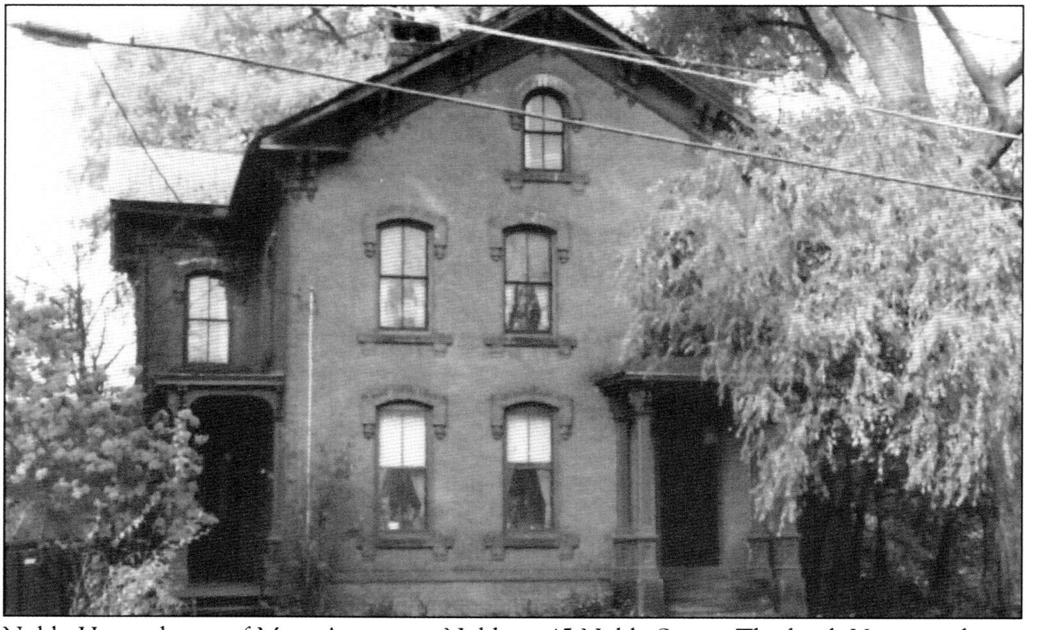

Noble House, home of Mary Angenette Noble at 45 Noble Street. The brick Victorian home dates back to about 1878. In recent times the house belonged to Attorney Mary Angenette Noble, daughter of Dr. Angenette Noble. She was a lifelong resident of Westfield, graduated magna cum laude from Bryn Mawr College, and received a doctorate of law from Northeastern University School of Law. Upon her death in 1988, the home was left to the Westfield Housing Authority. After standing vacant for several years, the house was damaged in a fire in 1997 and had to be torn down.

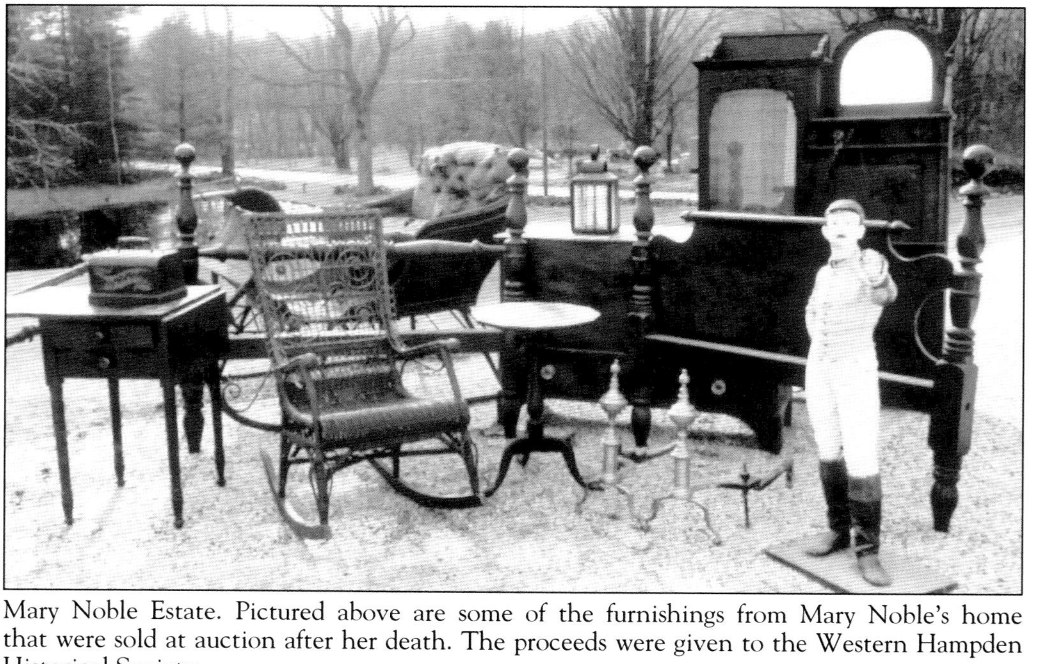

Mary Noble Estate. Pictured above are some of the furnishings from Mary Noble's home that were sold at auction after her death. The proceeds were given to the Western Hampden Historical Society.

Four

Business and Industry

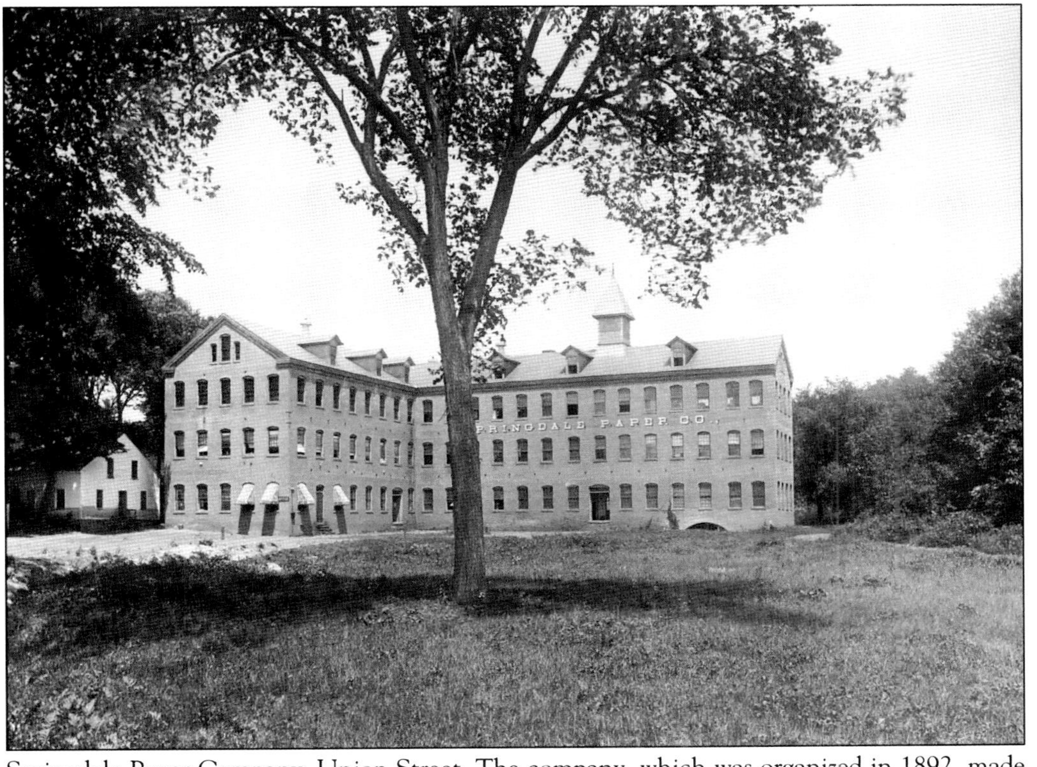

Springdale Paper Company, Union Street. The company, which was organized in 1892, made fine writing papers. Springdale Paper was located on the site of the Jessup & Laflin "Woronoco" ledger paper mill, 1.5 miles east of Westfield. It was situated on a 100-acre tract of land with tenements, a boarding house, housing for the superintendent, and two stock houses along with the plant. The president was J.E. Taylor.

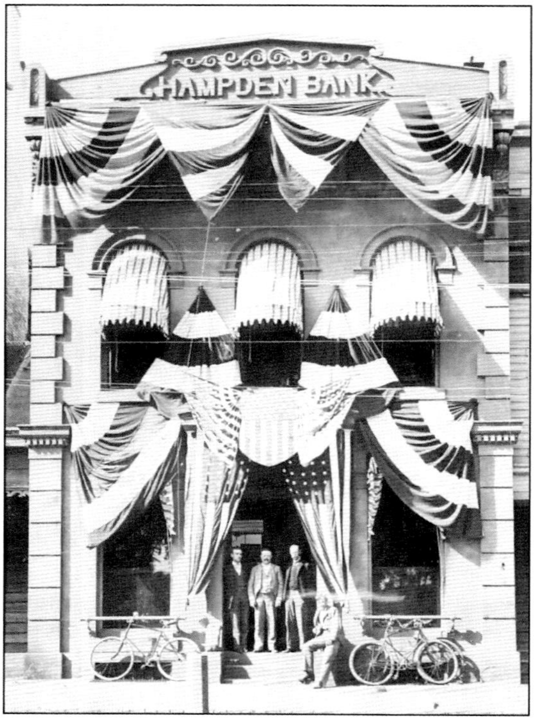

Hampden National Bank, 6 Main Street. This is one of the oldest commercial buildings in the city. In 1825 "Squire" James Fowler provided the site for the building and served as its president until 1842. The original bank structure was Greek Revival with four freestanding columns. In 1853 the board of directors decided to modify the building by razing the roof and changing the front to a brownstone Italianate style. The former bank building has housed various Westfield businesses including Hampden Corporation, the law firm of Ely & Ely, and Jack's Clothing Store. It is presently the Palczynski Insurance Agency.

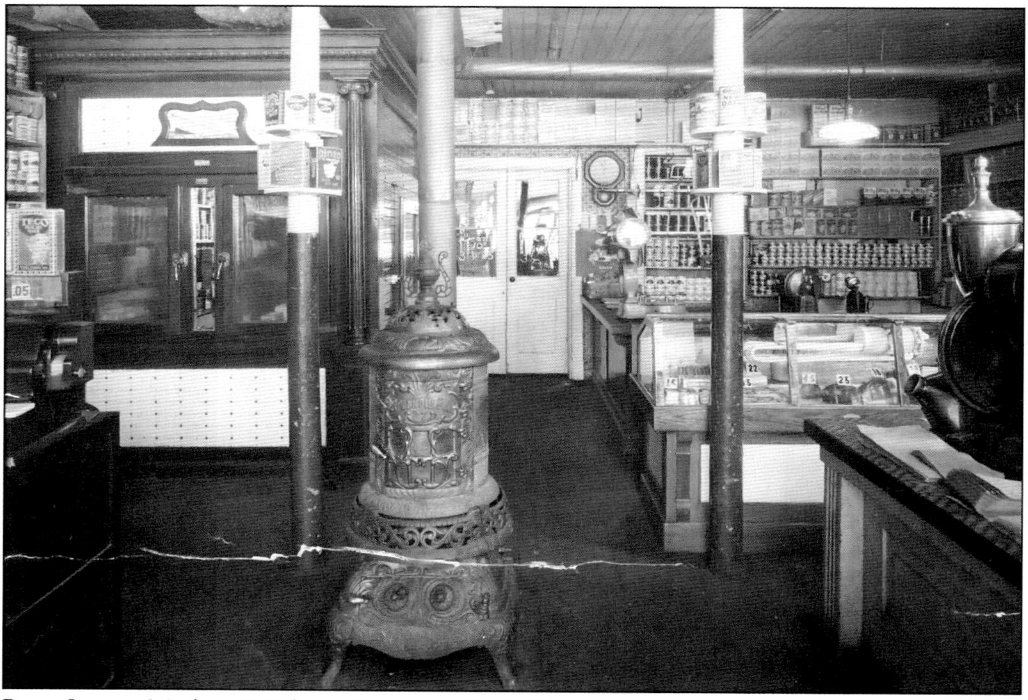

Peter Jensen Market, 9 School Street, *c.* 1890. This store became Jensen & Barnes in 1902, then Jensen & Son in 1909, with the address listed as 7 School Street. It specialized in fish and featured a full line of groceries. Eventually, the store moved to 3 Main Street.

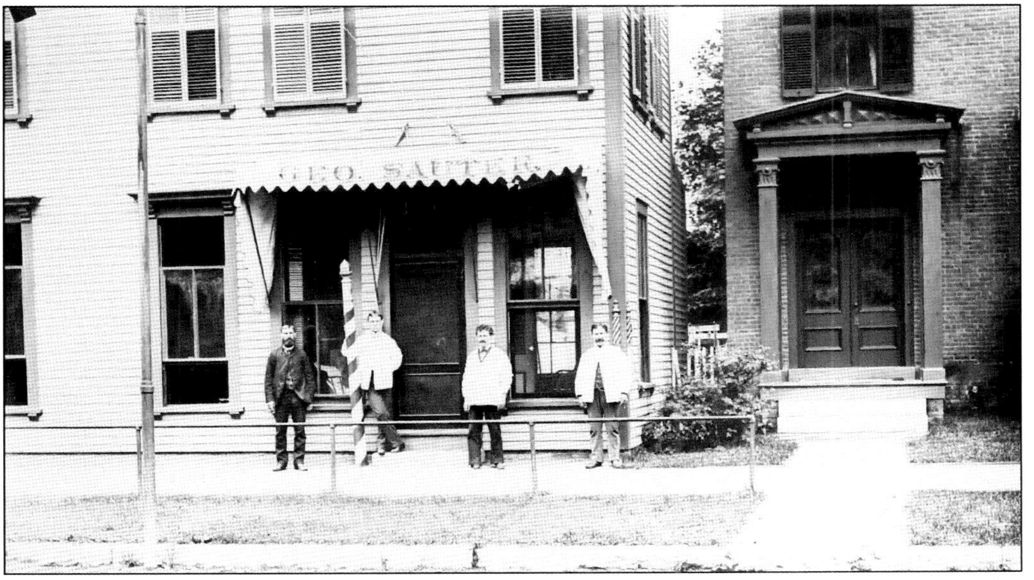

George Sauter Hairdressers. This shop was located in the Central Hotel at the corner of Elm and Chapel Streets *c*. 1890. Later, George Sauter moved to San Francisco.

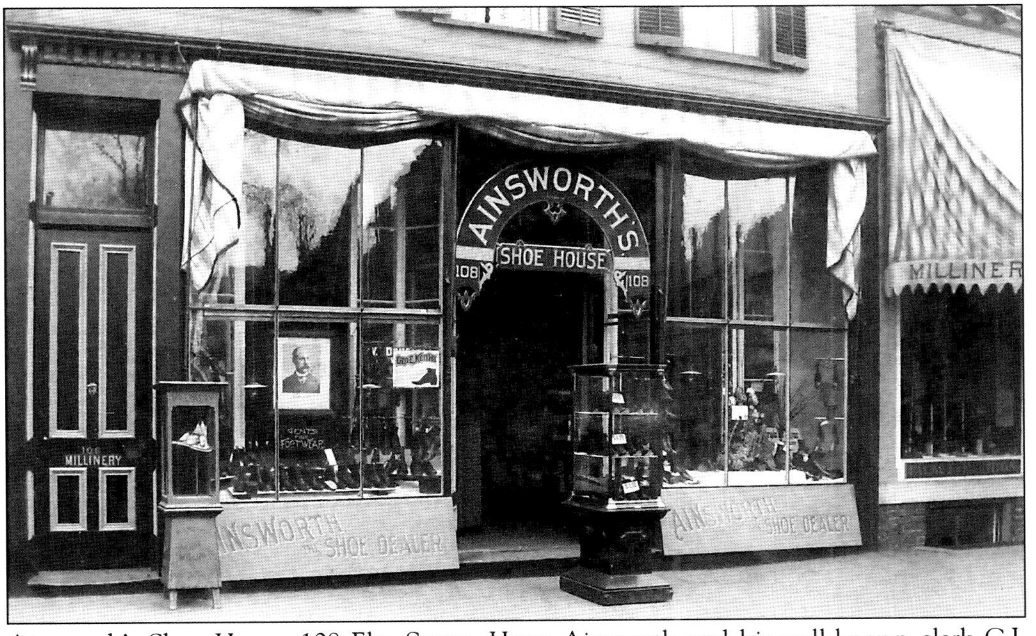

Ainsworth's Shoe House, 108 Elm Street. Harry Ainsworth and his well-known clerk C.J. Asiles sold boots, shoes, and rubbers—"fine footwear of every description." In 1902, the popular shoes were the Patrician Shoe, the Walk-Over Shoe, and the Wauk-E.Z.Y. Shoe. The store was located in the Lakin-Hall Block, which was later to become known as the Eaton Block.

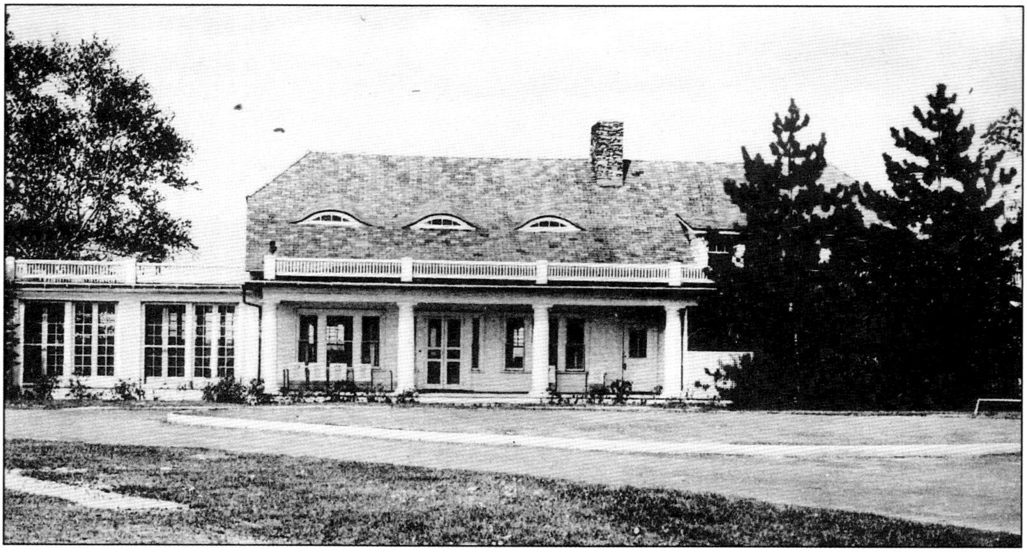

Tekoa Country Club. On September 11, 1911, the Tekoa Country Club was opened as an eighteen-hole golf course. It was on Western Avenue, currently the site of Stanhome.

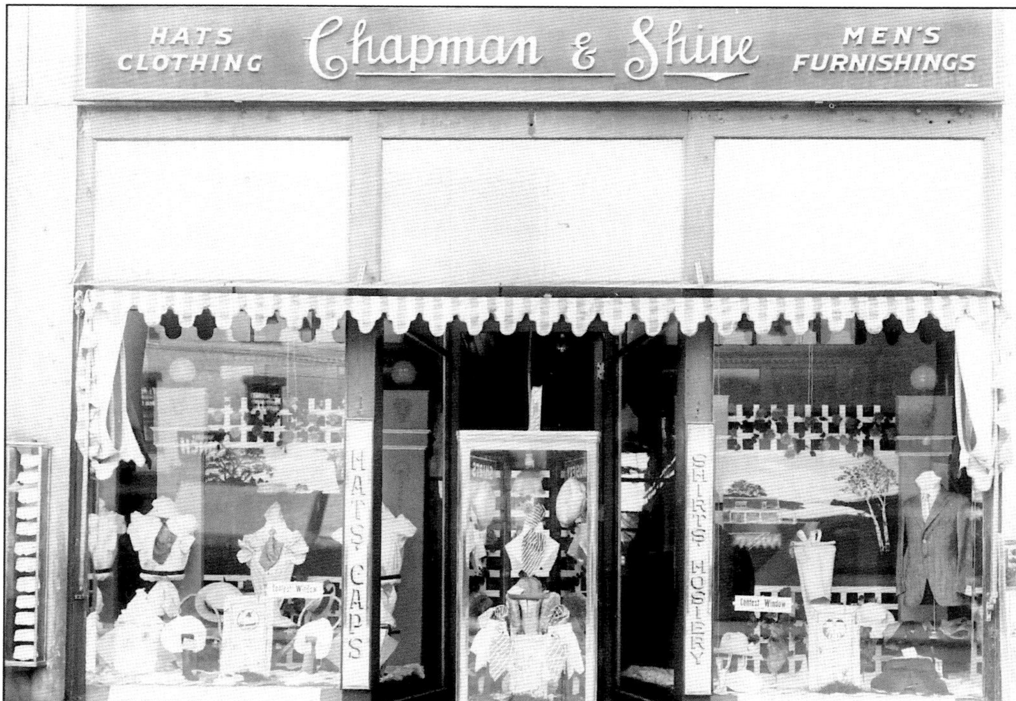

Chapman & Shine, 1914. This fine men's furnishings store was owned by William Chapman and Matthew Shine. In the summer of 1914, James Condron, a window trimmer and clerk in the store, won first prize in a contest for trimming these windows.

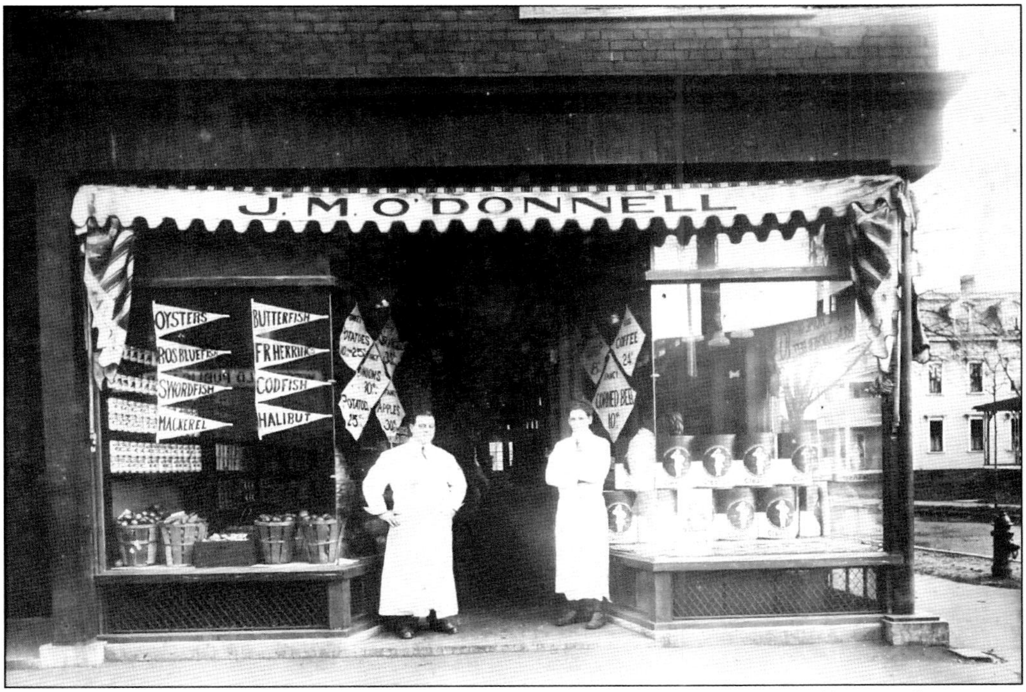

J.M. O'Donnell Market, 241 Elm Street, *c.* 1915. In 1889 John M. O'Donnell opened a grocery on 52 Meadow Street. In 1913 he moved his store to the corner of Elm and Bartlett Streets. Shown here are, from left to right: James M. O'Donnell (proprietor) and Hector LaCroix (clerk). Luther D. Cantell purchased the business in 1924.

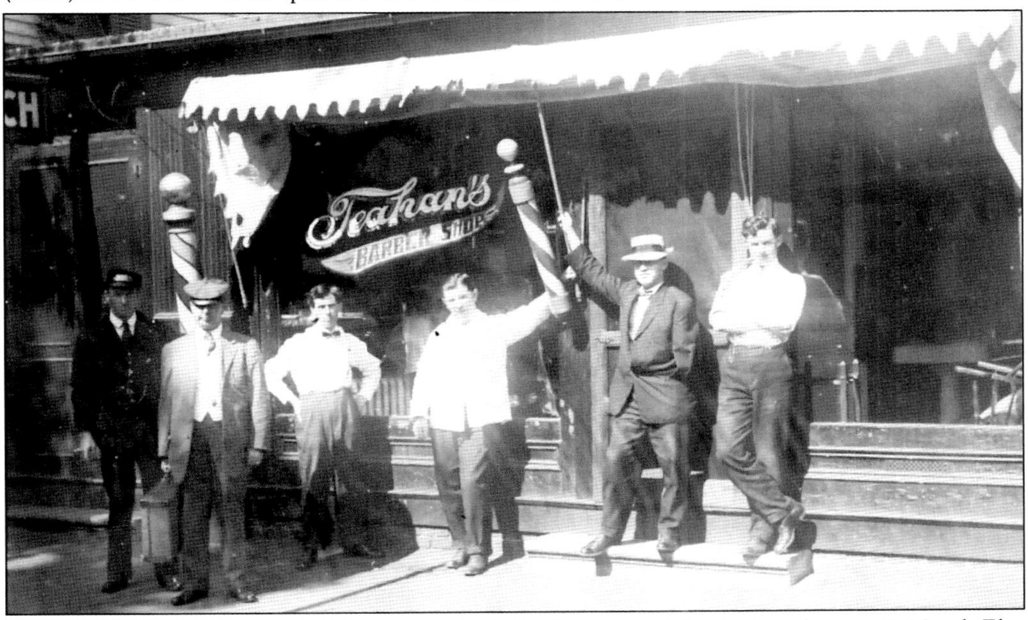

Teahan's Barber Shop, *c.* 1920. John (Jack) H. Teahan owned this barber shop at 46 North Elm Street. He is shown here with his hand on the barber pole. With him, from left to right, are: Ed Brown, Tony McQueen, Jimmy Devine, William McCauley, and Charles Marcoulier.

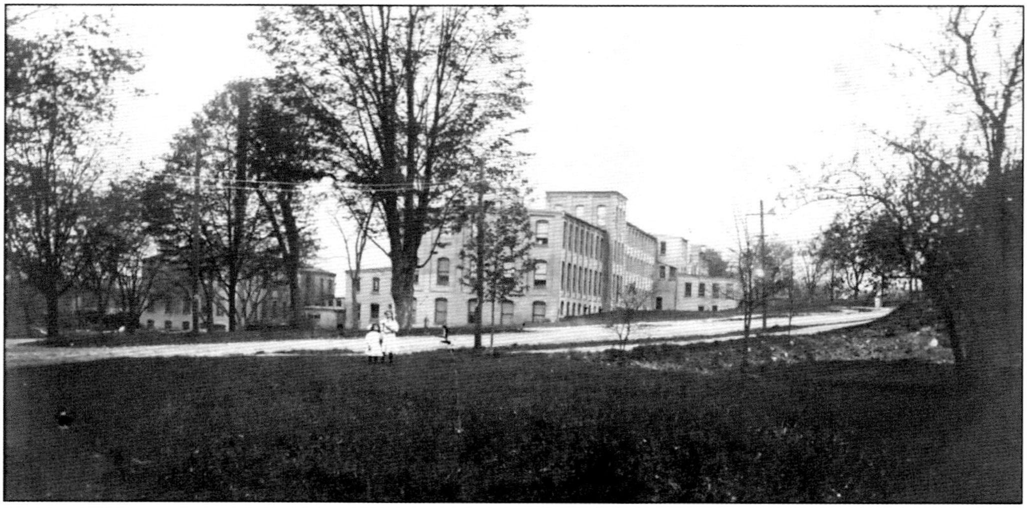

Crane Paper Mill, lower Mill Street, *c.* 1900. This business was founded in 1868 by two brothers, Robert B. and James A. Crane. They specialized in manufacturing "Linen Record," "Japanese Linen," and "All-Linen" papers. After the deaths of the original partners, the business was purchased by Crane and Company of Dalton, Massachusetts. The mill building was home to Steven's Paper Mill from the late 1930s through the late 1970s. At present, it houses several small businesses.

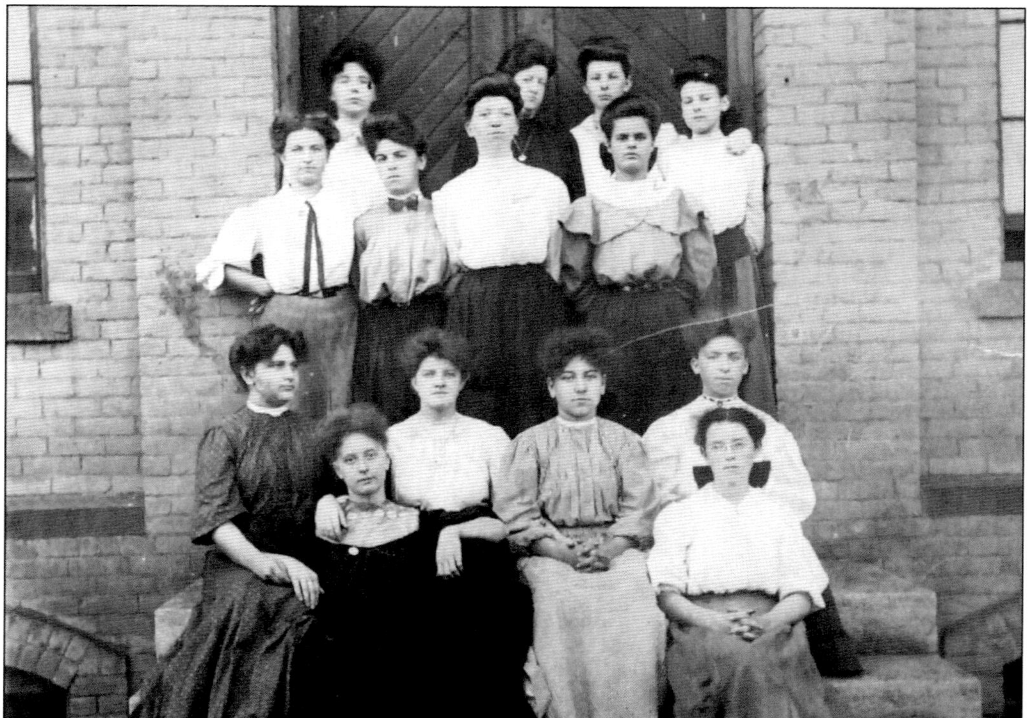

Workers at Crane Mill, *c.* 1907. Some of the young ladies in the picture above are Mabel Haskins Bush, Vida Webb Kenyon, Edith Bein Whitney, and Nel Templeton Reed.

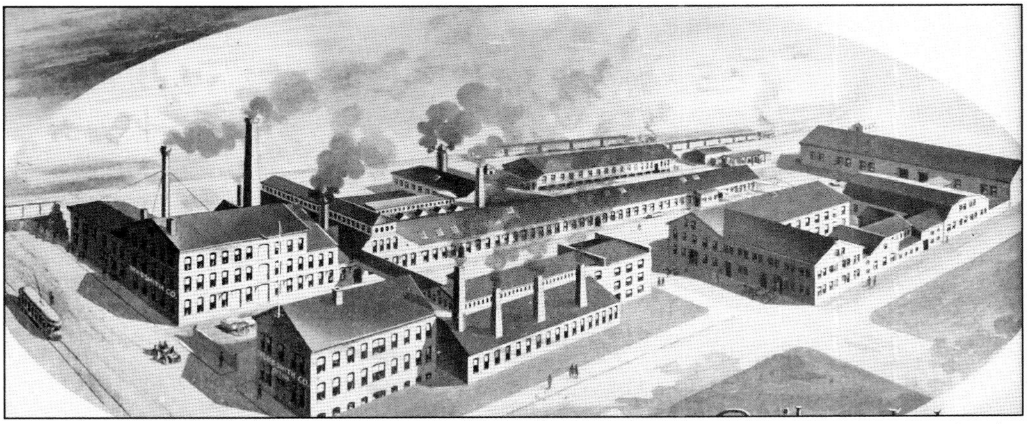

H.B. Smith Company. Founded in Westfield in 1853 by Henry B. and Edwin Smith, the H.B. Smith Company was the first to manufacture and market cast-iron sectional boilers. They were used to heat commercial and industrial buildings, schools, hospitals, churches, apartment houses, and private homes. Although the largest market for these boilers was in the northeastern United States, they were sold to every state in the union and to many foreign countries.

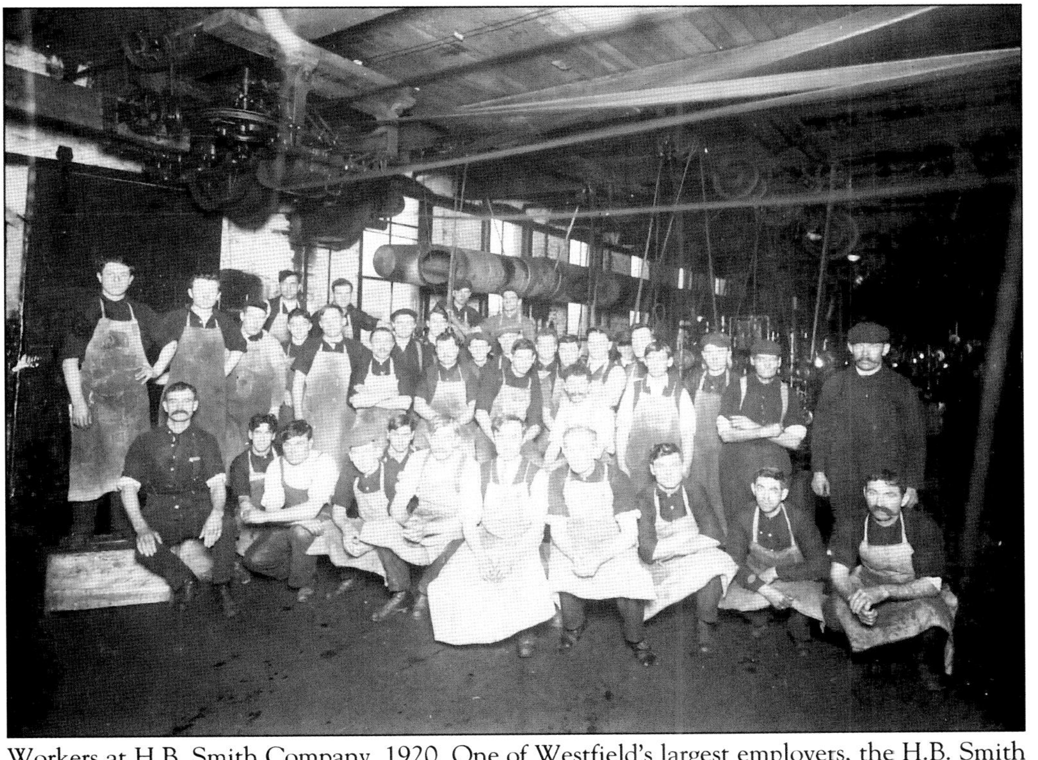

Workers at H.B. Smith Company, 1920. One of Westfield's largest employers, the H.B. Smith Company employed hundreds of workers like these on a steady year-round basis. Their policy was to employ people of almost every race, creed, and color, and as a result, the employees represented a cross-section of Westfield citizens. Many worked for the company for twenty-five years or more, and even fifty years of service was not unusual.

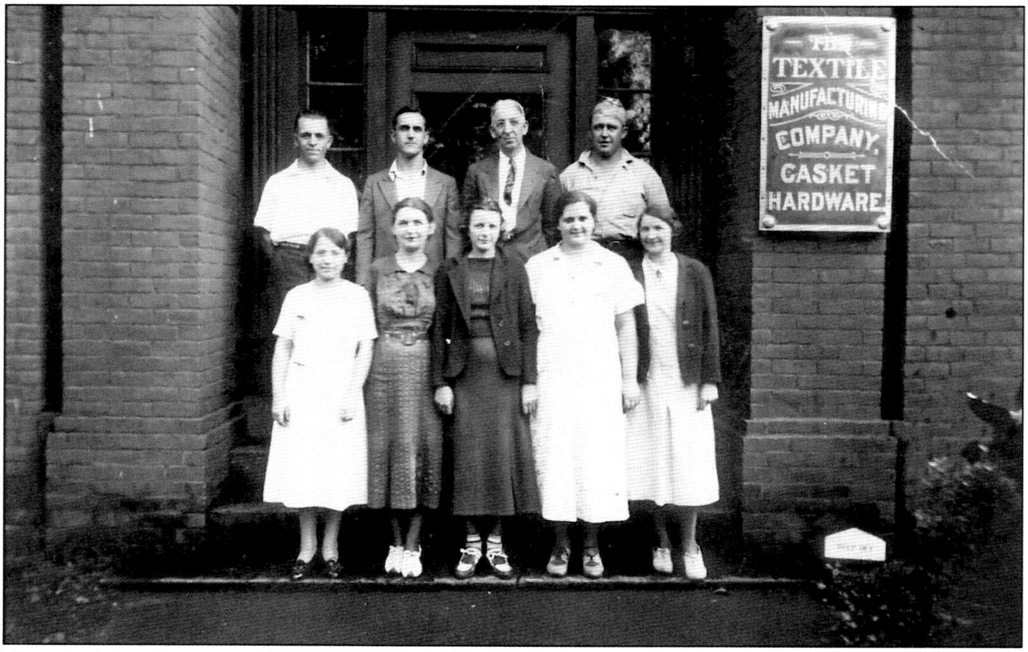

Textile Manufacturing Company, 125 North Elm Street. This company was organized in Connecticut in 1880 and did not move into its North Elm Street quarters until the early part of 1900. Their specialty was the manufacture of casket trimmings and hardware, which were sold throughout the United States. They later also made silver toilet sets and novelties, which were reported to be very beautiful in design and finish. This picture was taken about 1929 when Anthony Samson (second from left in the back row) was an employee.

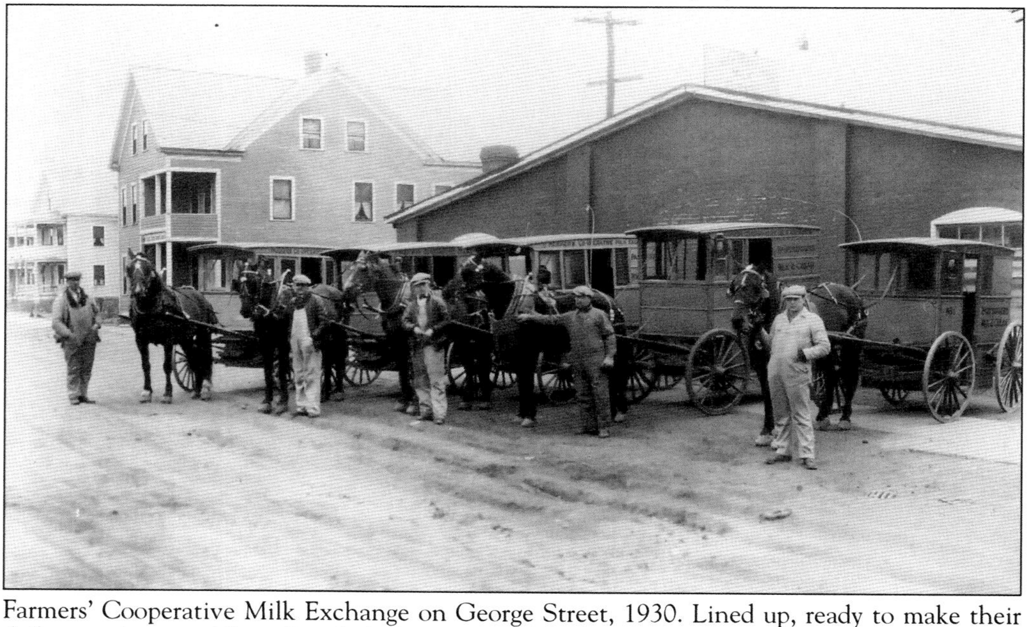

Farmers' Cooperative Milk Exchange on George Street, 1930. Lined up, ready to make their daily rounds were Albert Simchak, Lawrence Oleksak, Edward O'Rourke, George Baird, and Floyd Mallory.

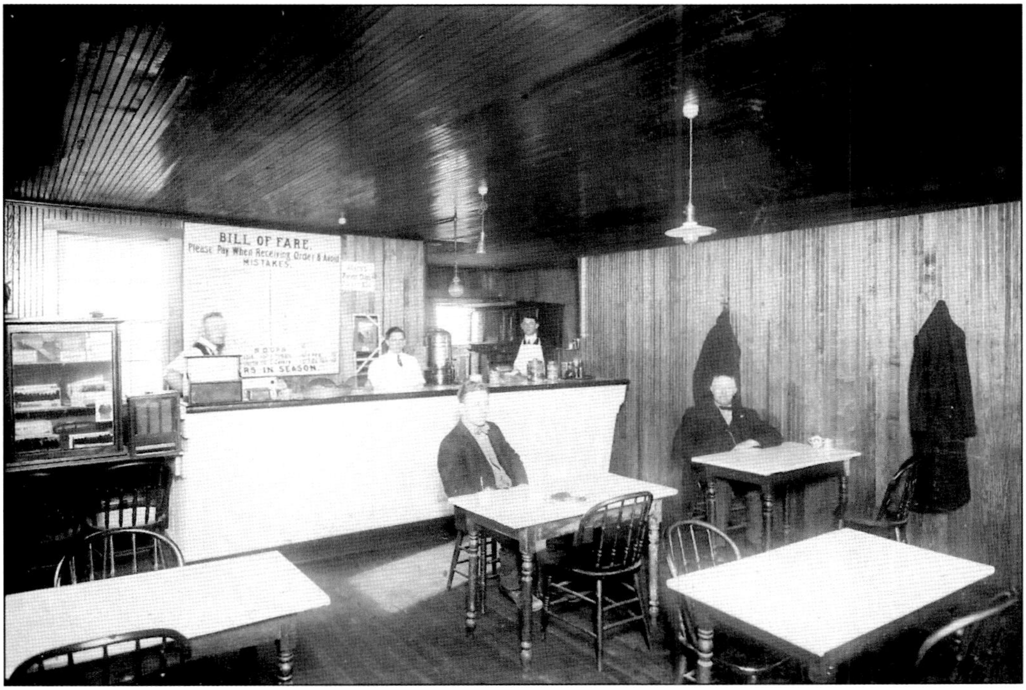

Lunch Room, Westfield Depot. There was a restaurant in the New Haven waiting room. The railroad often employed men there who had been disabled by accidents in other railroad jobs. Note that the "Bill of Fare" advertises bacon and eggs for 20¢, indicating that this picture was probably taken in the 1930s.

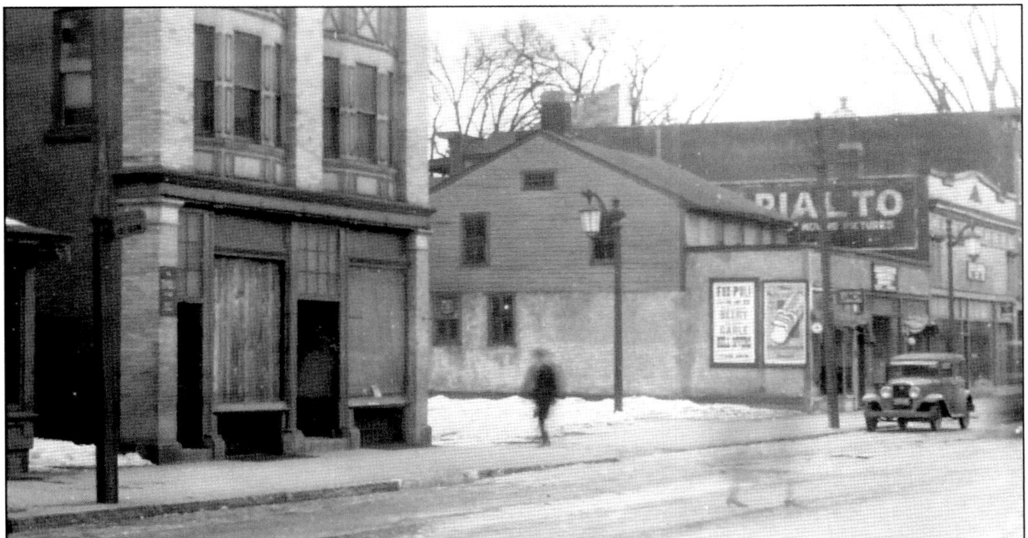

Number 271 Elm Street. Built in 1909, this building (on the left) was originally the Tivoli Hotel. There were rented rooms upstairs and a bar and billiard room downstairs. In 1938 Frank L. Parody bought the building and opened a retail fabric outlet for dress goods. He has since expanded it to a complete home-decorating business, and the Parody family will celebrate their sixtieth year in business in 1998.

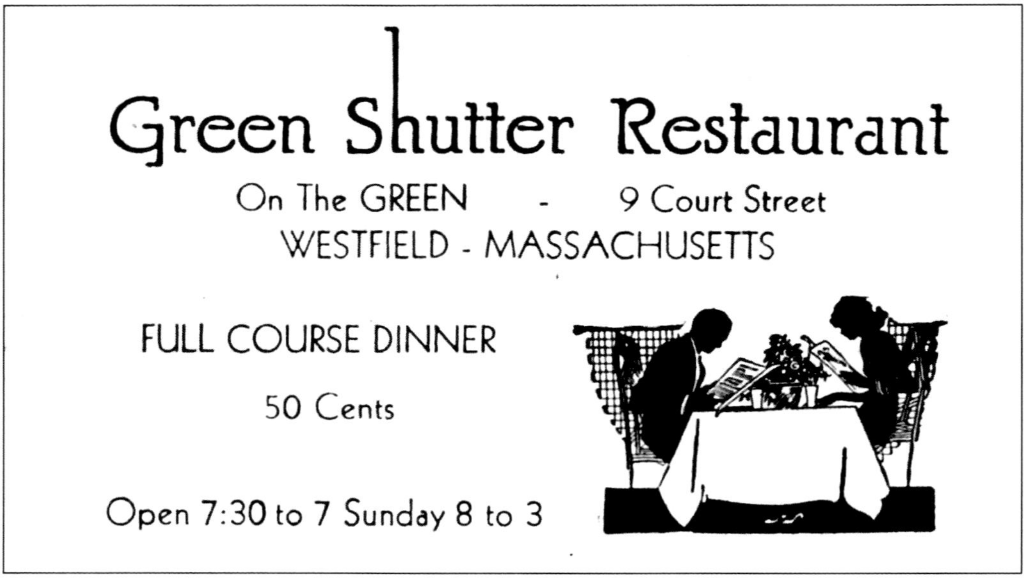

Card from the Green Shutter Restaurant. The original business card is printed in green and advertises a full course dinner for 50¢. Thomas H. Harnett was the owner, and the time was probably the late 1930s.

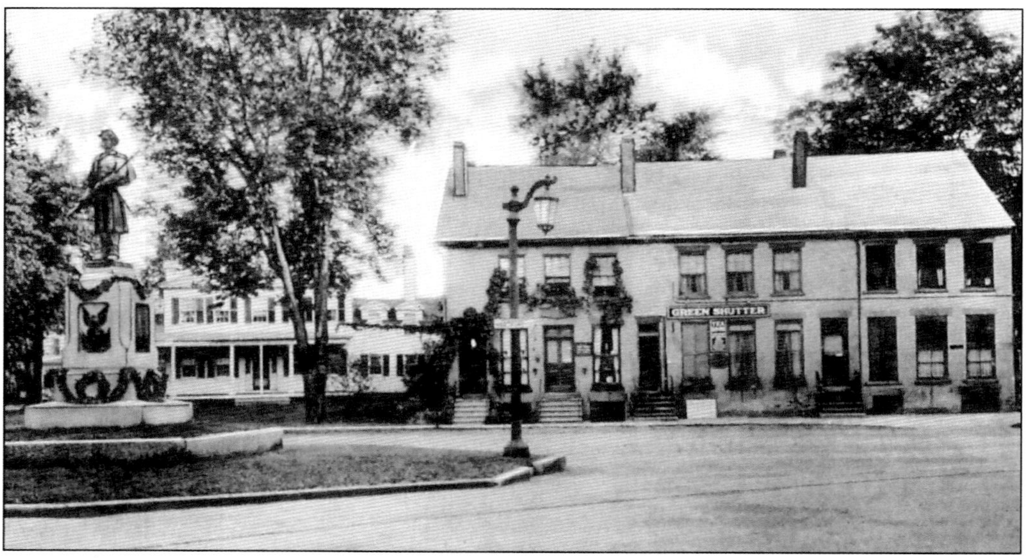

Green Shutter Tea Room. The back of this 1948 postcard advertised a special Sunday dinner for $1; steak and chicken were the restaurant's specialties. Antonio Alonzo and Gus Daes were the proprietors.

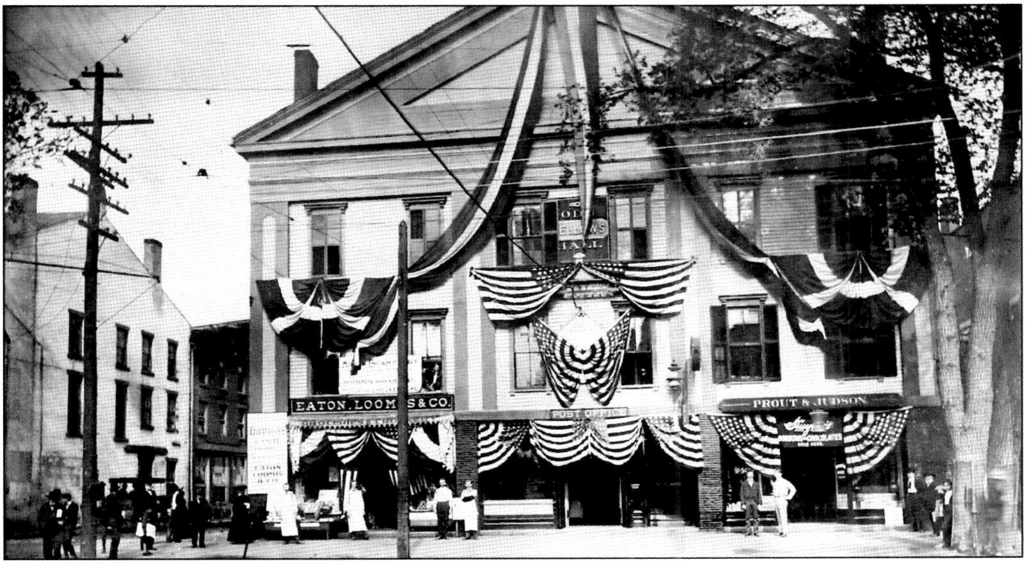

Numbers 24–26 Elm Street. This building was originally a Methodist church. The frame was built in Northampton and floated down the old canal. Since that time several businesses, primarily grocery stores, have been located in the first-floor storefronts. In 1875 the post office moved into the basement, and after that time, the building was referred to as the Commercial Block. The picture above shows the old post office between the well-known Eaton Loomis and Prout & Judson stores.

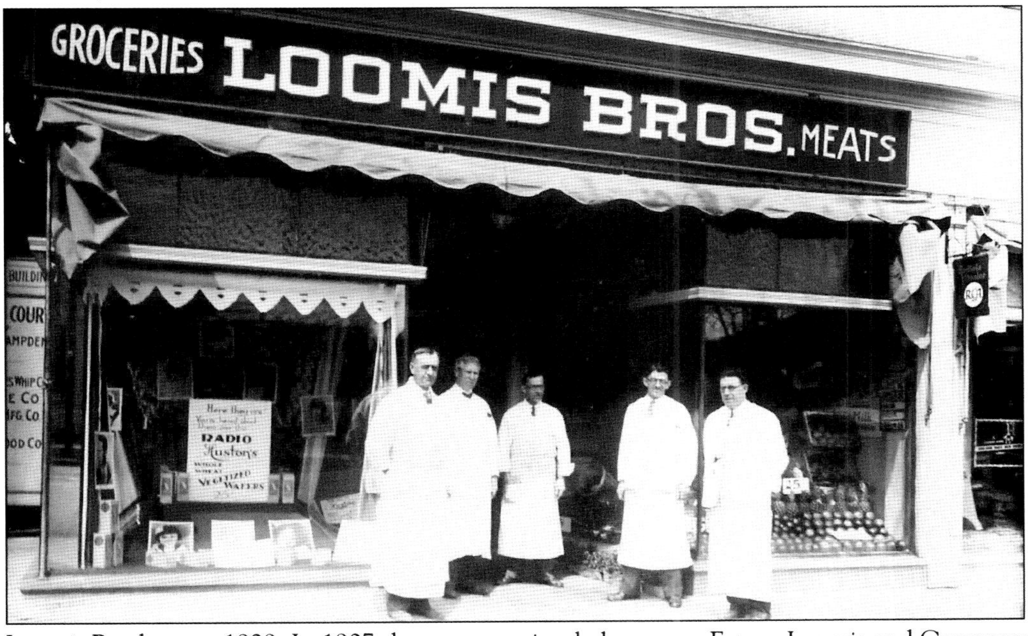

Loomis Brothers, *c*. 1929. In 1907 the store previously known as Eaton, Loomis and Company became Loomis Brothers. They were "dealers in groceries, crockery, fruits and confectionery." The store was located on the corner of Elm and School Streets until 1929, when they moved to 24 Main Street. The above picture shows William B. Loomis, Robert (Bert) C. Loomis, Denison H. Loomis, and Henry Malone.

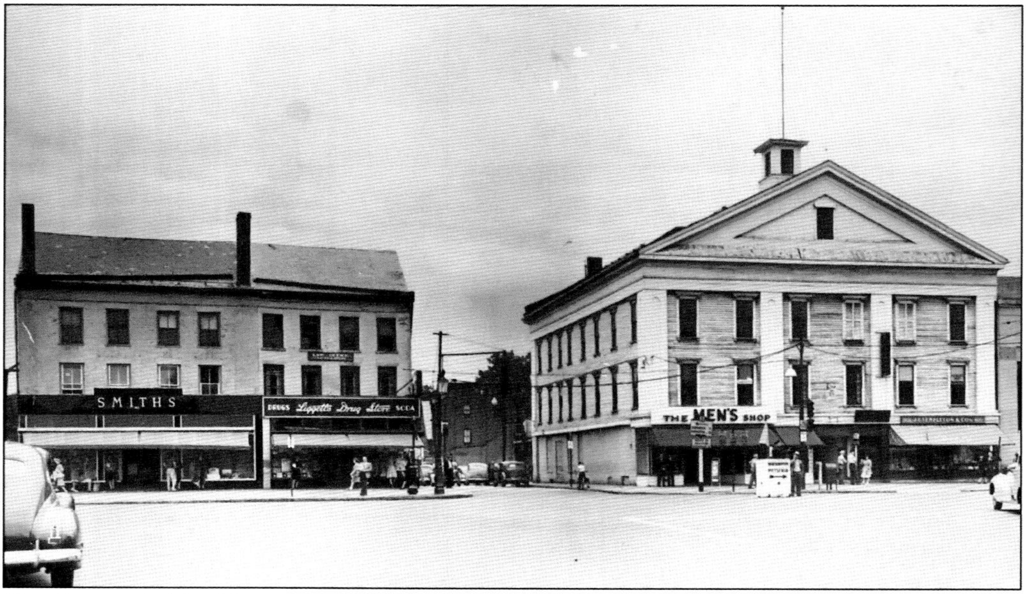

Elm Street, 1940s. These stores will be familiar to many. The Commercial Block now has a square cupola where the church steeple once had been. Further modifications were made when the roof and third floor were razed.

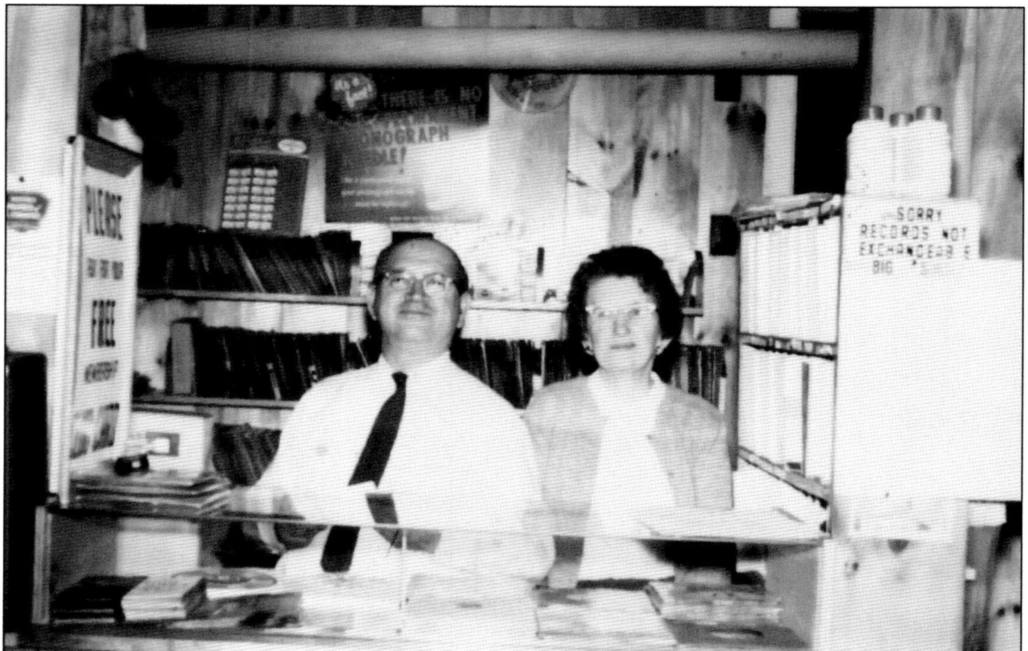

John's Music Shop, 24 1/2 Elm Street. In the 1940s John's Music Shop was located between the Men's Shop and the Templeton Drug Store. John and Mary Prystas (pictured above) were the proprietors.

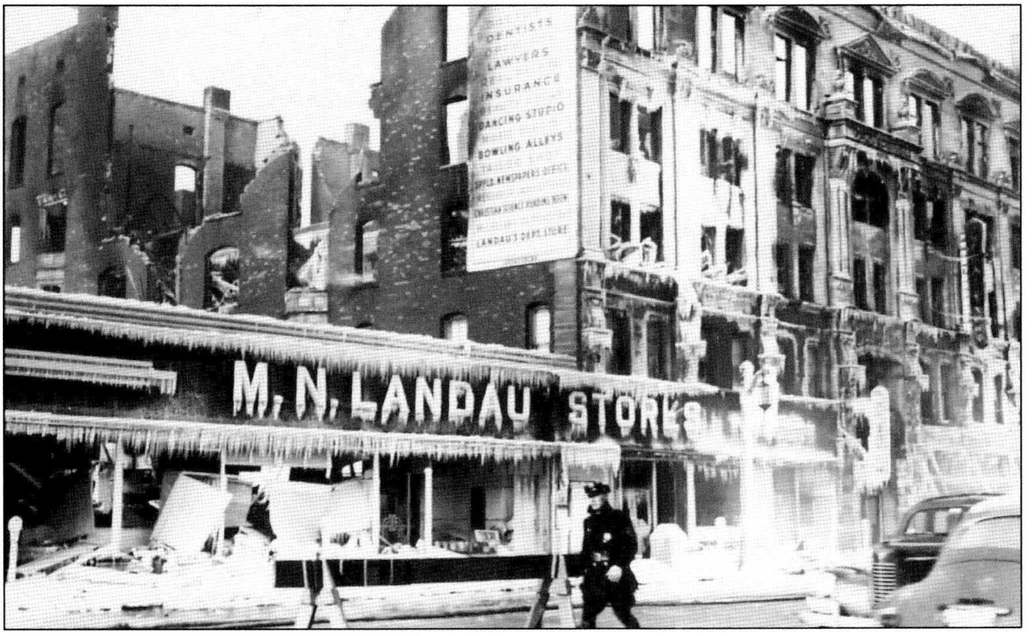

M.N. Landau Store, 1952. Landau's was closed following the disastrous Professional Building fire in 1952. They temporarily located directly across the street in the Columbus Building. The Landau Store was promptly rebuilt and reopened in the original location with their complete stock and staff.

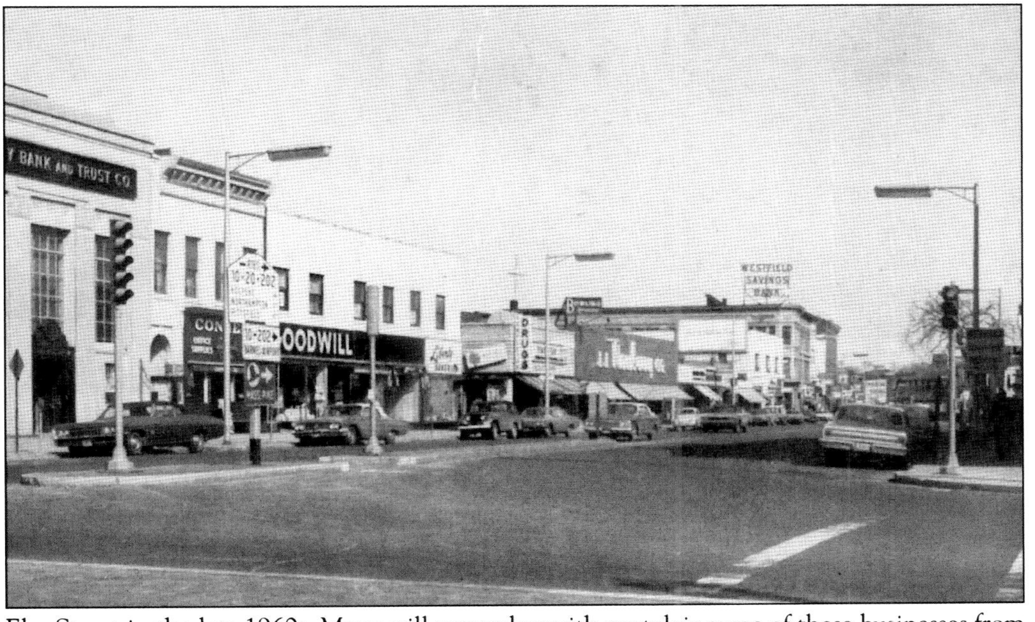

Elm Street in the late 1960s. Many will remember with nostalgia some of these businesses from the late 1960s. Note that Newberry's is now where Landau's used to be. It opened in Westfield in 1960 and claimed to be "Westfield's only complete department store." It burned in 1986 and never again reopened in Westfield.

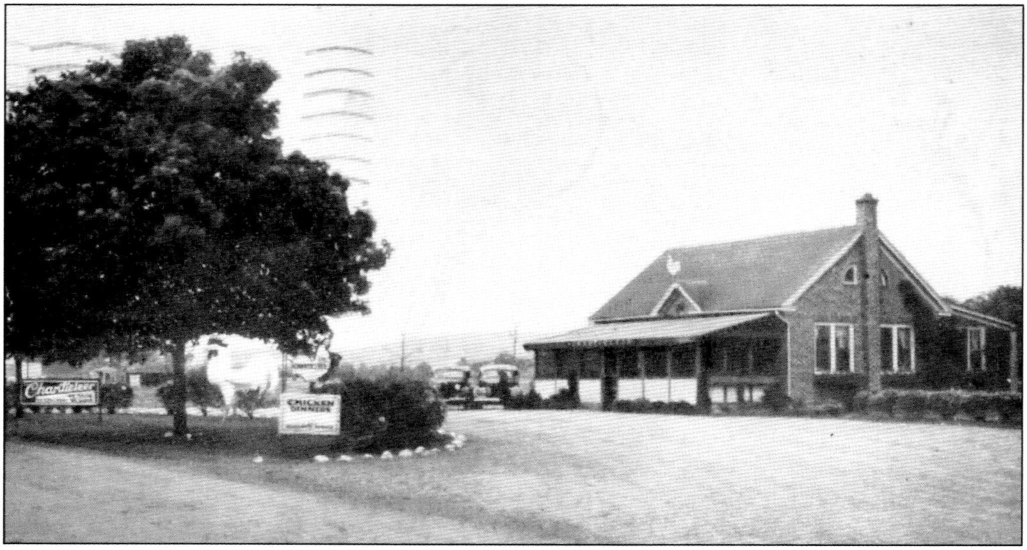

The Chanticleer, College Highway, 1941. The large Chanticleer rooster became a familiar landmark to those passing by on Route 202 and 10. What started as a poultry farm owned by Max Axelrod in the 1930s later grew into a popular restaurant and short golf course.

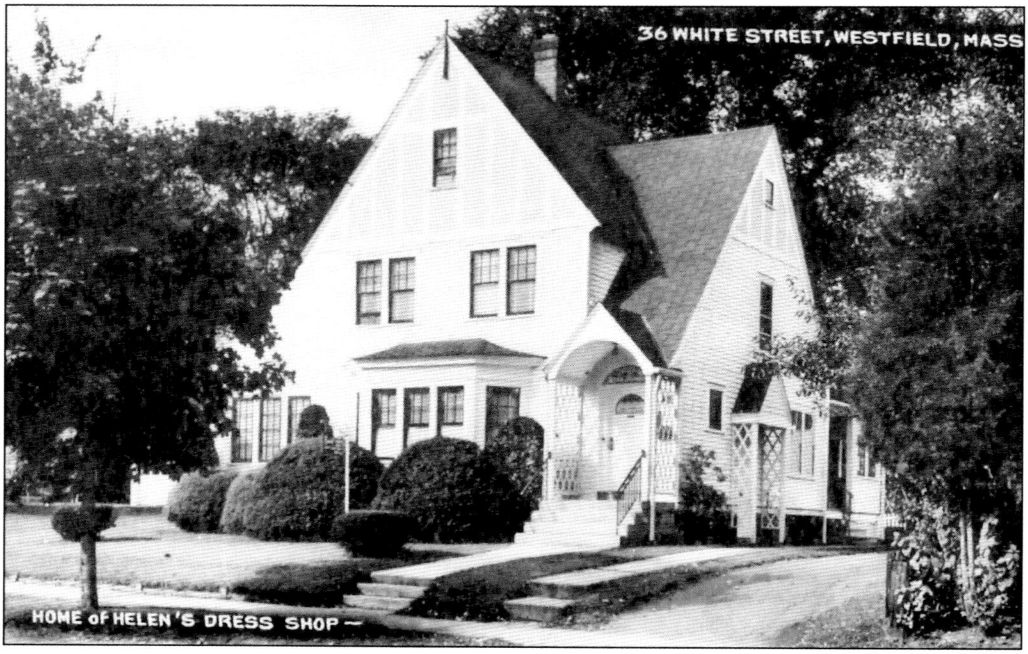

Helen's Dress Shop, 36 White Street. Most women who grew up in the Westfield area are familiar with Helen's. It has always been the place to find a wedding gown or bridesmaid's dress. Originally owned by Helen Sadowski many years ago, her daughter-in-law now owns the business.

Five

Fire and Floods

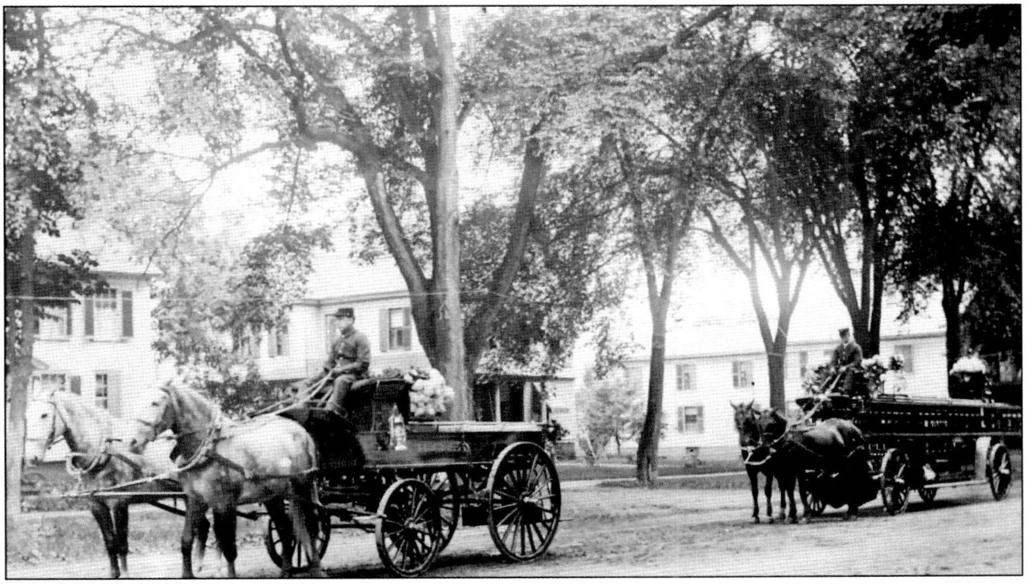

Horse-drawn fire apparatus, 1905. The Westfield Fire Department purchased its first pair of horses, Kittie and Nell, a pair of mahogany bays, in 1895. These horses, along with drop harnesses purchased in 1894, greatly improved fire response time. By 1905 the department owned nine horses.

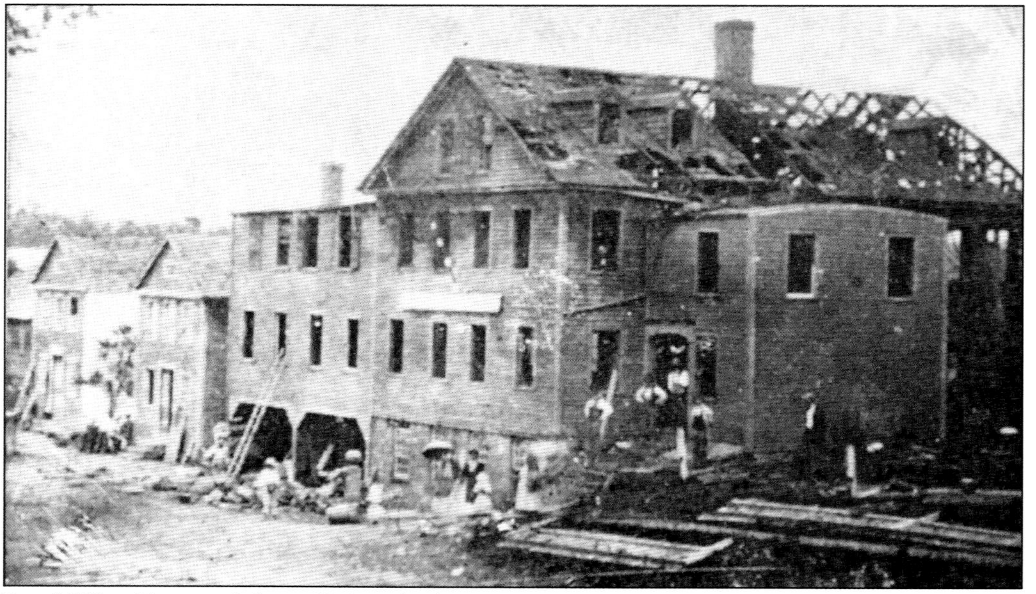

Rand Whip Factory, July 1853. Fire broke out in the stocking and rounding room of the whip factory, and "as soon as the pitch caught fire, the flames spread with fearful rapidity." The Rough and Ready Company used water from the "old canal" to quench the flames. Occupants of the building were Rand & Company (whip makers), N. Chapin (plane and tool makers), E. Goodrich & Company (whip mounters), and Halladay & Dickerman (machinists).

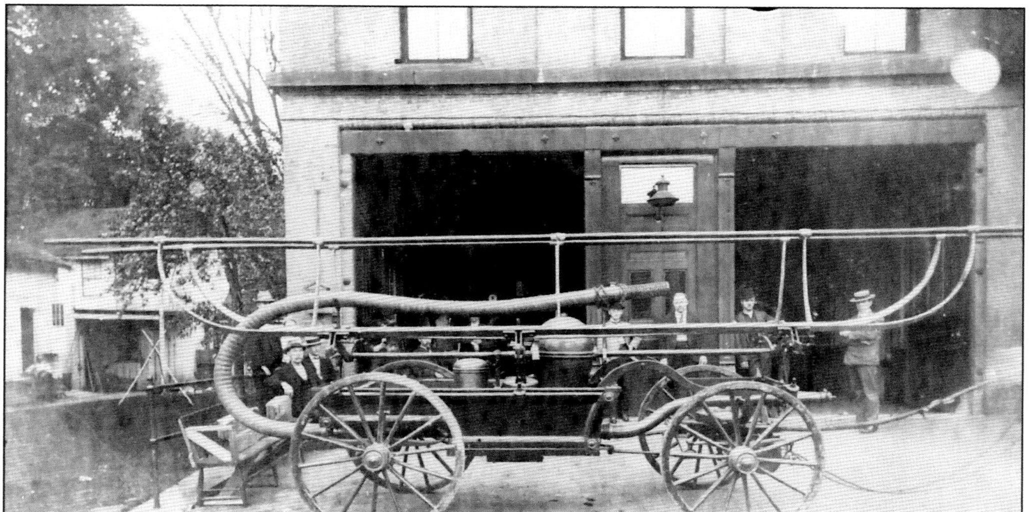

E.R. Lay Veteran Firemen's Association's "Hand Tub." The Rough and Ready and the Bay State were suction-type fire engines, like the one pictured above. In the event of a fire, the firemen would go to the engine house, drag out the "tub," and run to the fire. When they found it and a water supply, they would then begin pumping the water onto the fire.

Officers of the Rough & Ready Fire Engine Company, No. 1, 1856. In the center is E.T. Johnson (foreman). From the top, moving clockwise, are: Charles B. Whipple, Addison Noble, Terry S. Noble, Dwight Kellogg, Jefferson Green, David Noble, George D. Smith, and Sela Randall. Westfield had two all-volunteer fire companies from the mid-1800s to the 1870s—the Rough and Ready on Main Street and the Bay State on North Elm Street.

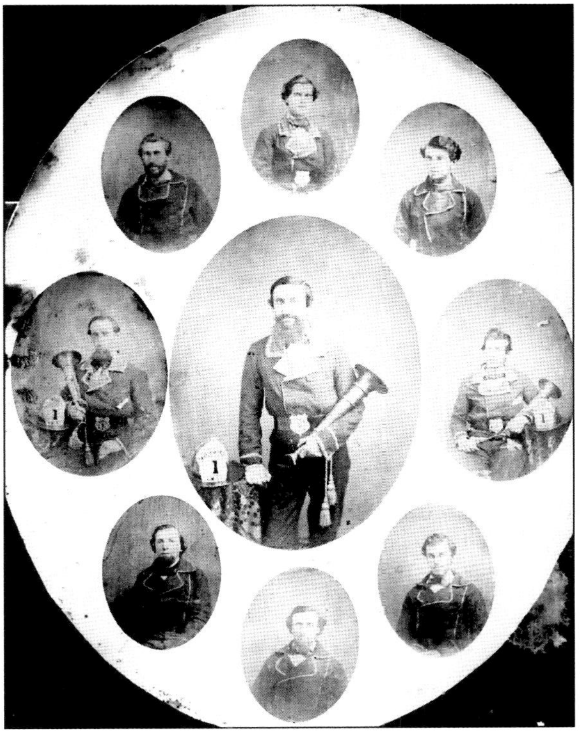

Steamer No. 1. Purchased for $4,000 in 1871, Westfield's first and only steamer was the "pride of the citizens." More powerful than hand engines, it could send a horizontal stream up to 248 feet with a large enough water supply. The steamer became obsolete in 1874 when the town installed a gravity system of water supply from the Montgomery Reservoir and fire hydrants came into use.

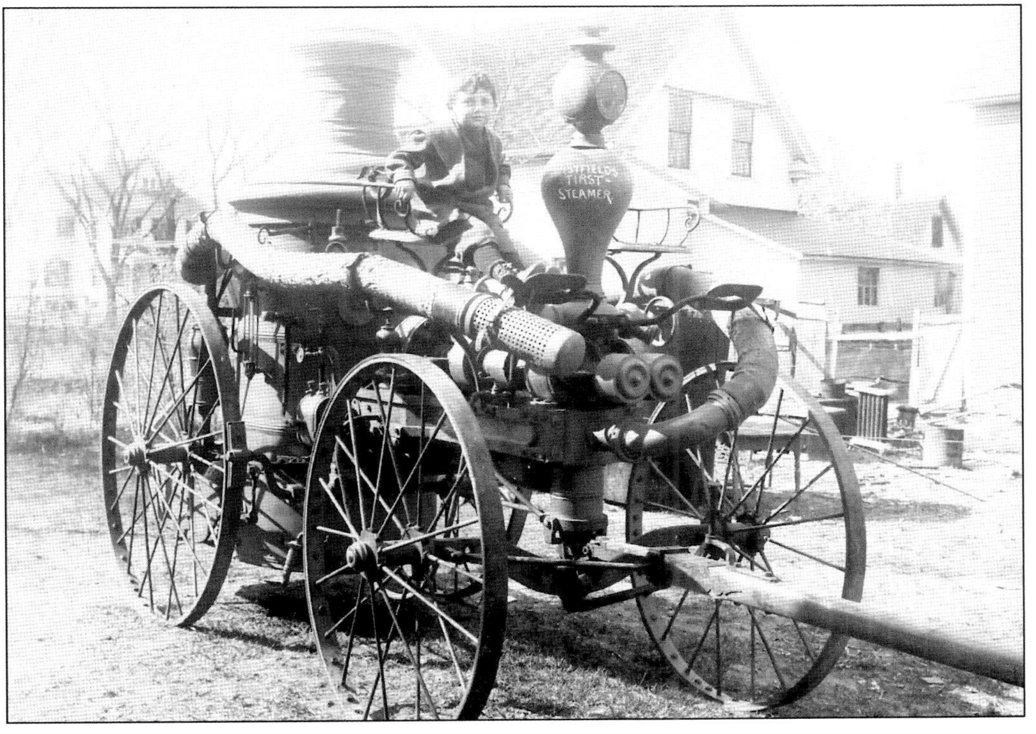

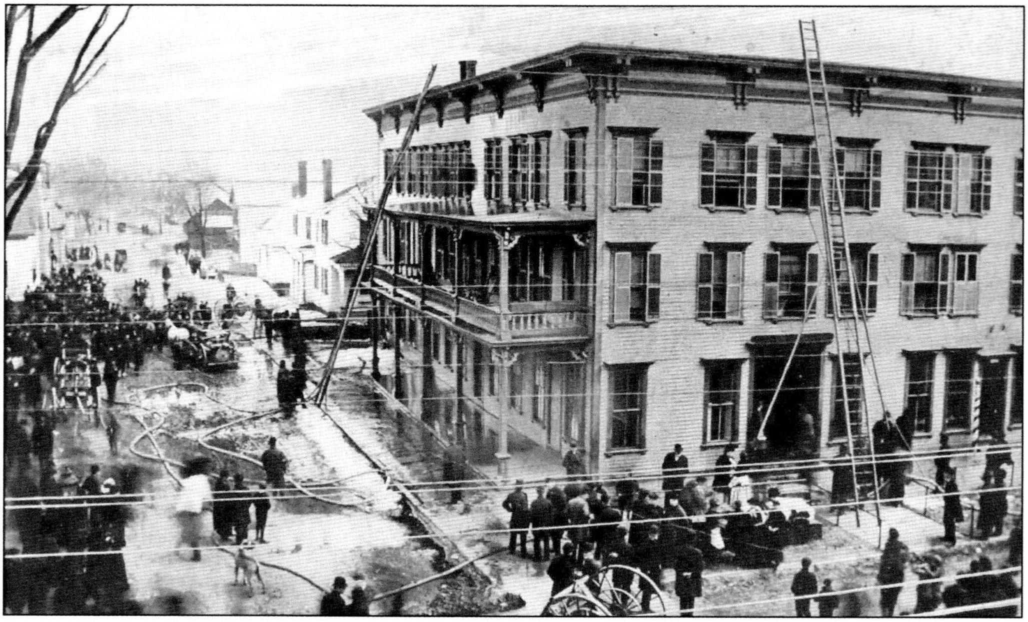

Central House fire, April 18, 1891. The Central House Hotel on the corner of Elm and Chapel Streets suffered partial damage in a fire which started in the oil room. The building was owned by H.J. Smith.

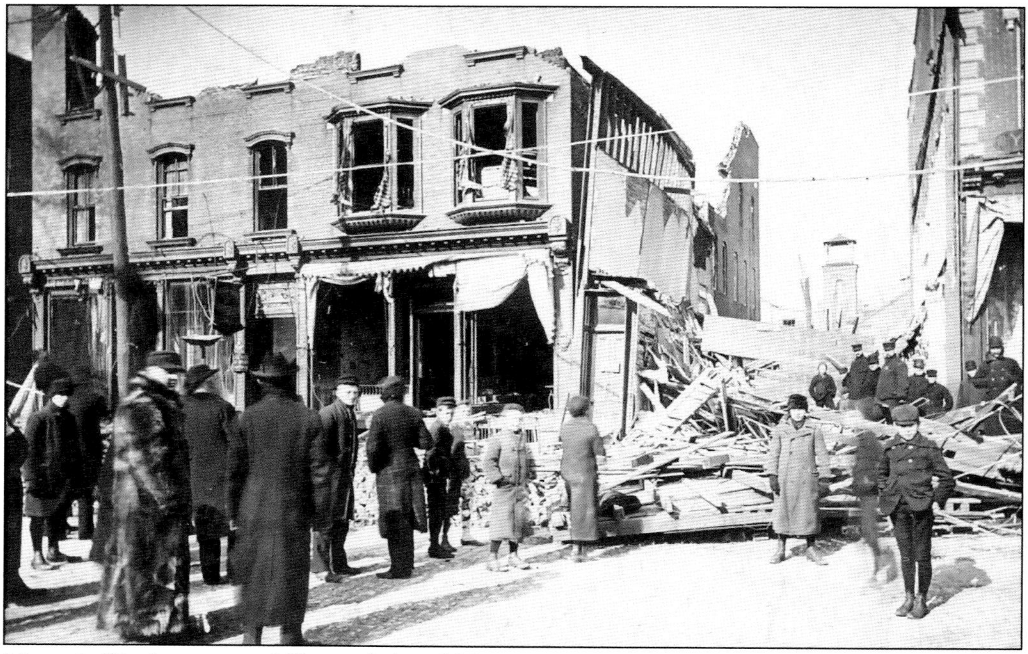

Masonic Block, corner of Elm and Arnold Streets, 1896. On March 11, 1896, a fire broke out in the basement of W.R. Smith's shoe store. The fire spread through the building. The firemen kept the fire from spreading to other buildings, and after ten hours of the "hardest kind of labor," they had the fire out. The Masonic Lodge, D.L. Gillett Dry Goods, and others all relocated, and the building was torn down.

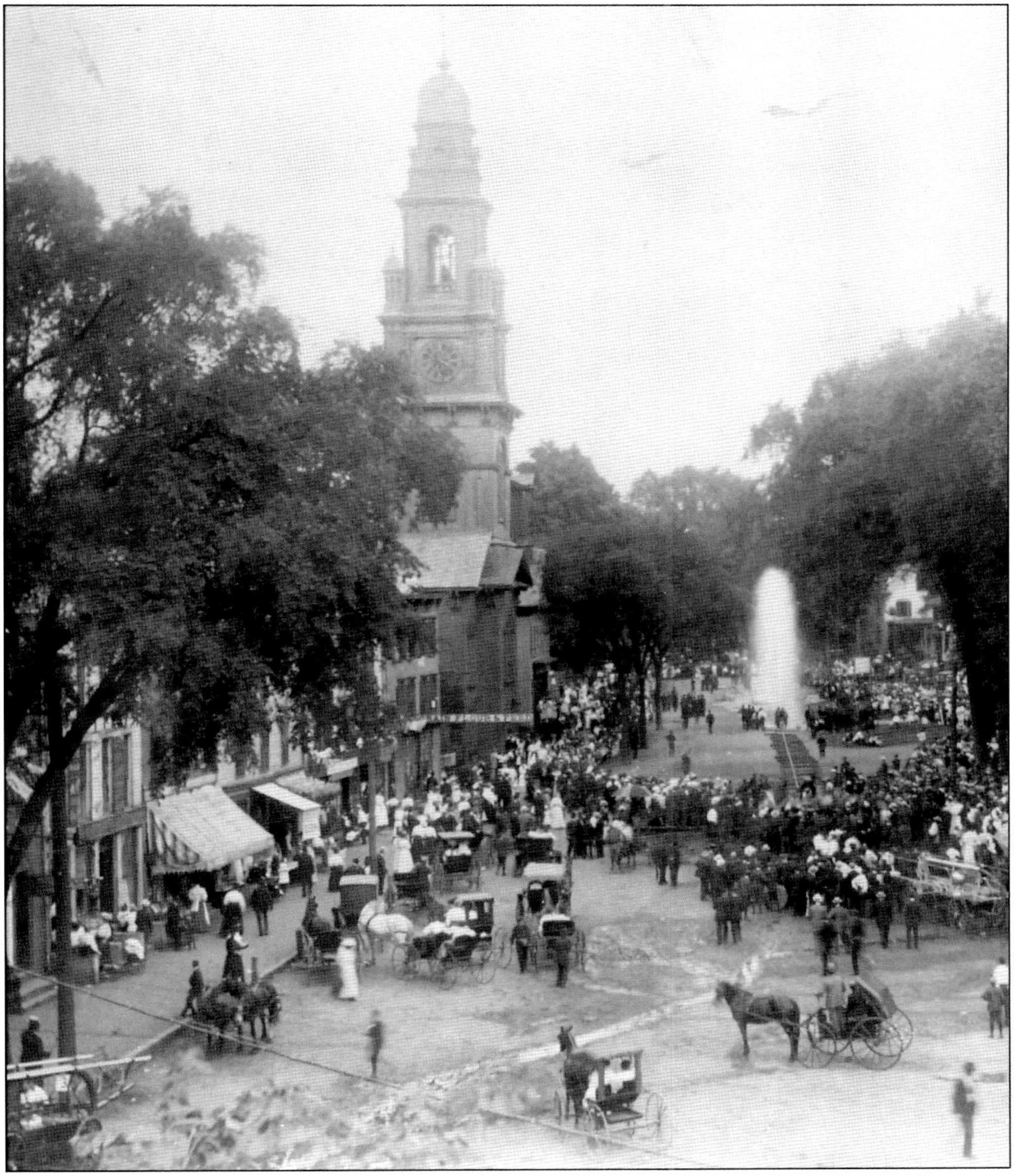

Firemen's Muster on Broad Street, late 1800s. Firemen's musters were competitions between fire companies to determine who could throw a stream of water the highest and the farthest. Believed to have started in New England, the tradition spread across the country. The fire companies of Westfield participated in many musters. Just before the Rough and Ready was sold, the company got together for one last time at a muster in Fitchburg, Massachusetts. G.D. Smith was in command of the sixty-eight veteran firemen enrolled, with M.D. Searles and A.E. Beldon as his assistants. According to the *Westfield Newsletter*, the Rough and Ready "took the first prize of $400 in a play of 222 feet. They came home on the owl train and were met at the depot by their friends with torches and martial music. The boys went away hopeful and came back with banners flying. There is not a hand engine in the country that can beat her when she is well manned." Fifty dollars of the prize money was donated to the Chicago Relief Fund.

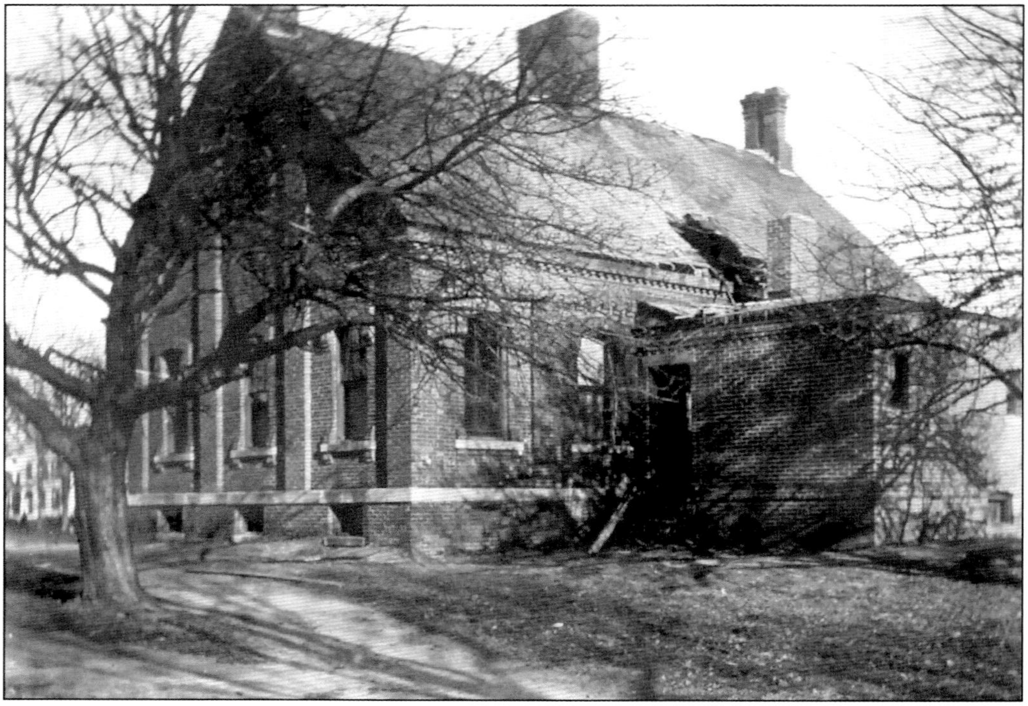

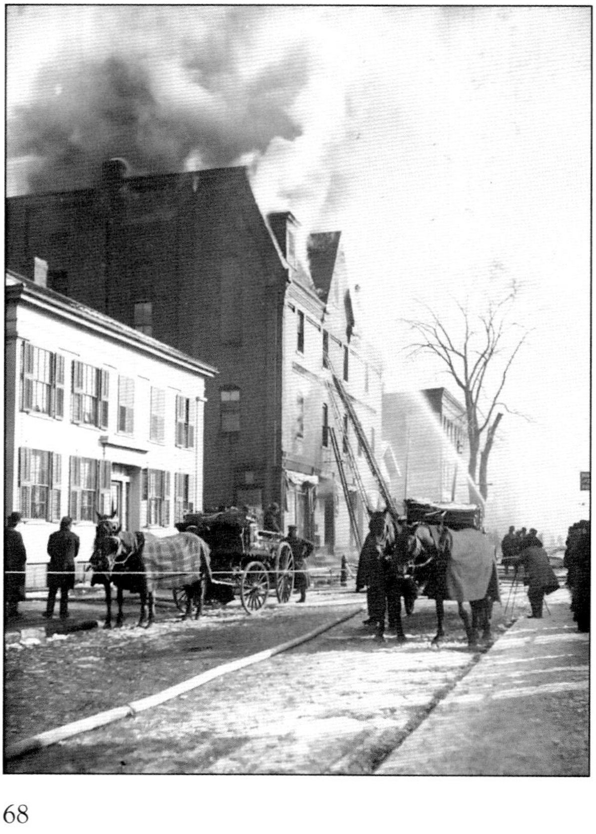

Silver Street Schoolhouse, December 16, 1901. Badly burned roof timbers and extensive flooding were the results of a furnace fire and the subsequent efforts to put it out. The Silver Street Schoolhouse was erected in 1867 after fire destroyed a wooden schoolhouse in the same place. The two-room schoolhouse had four grades in 1901, and at one time it had seven grades.

Columbia Hall fire, November 15, 1904. A fire starting on the second floor of Hearn & Company severely gutted the building owned by Fred Schmidt on School Street. The third floor was used for public social events.

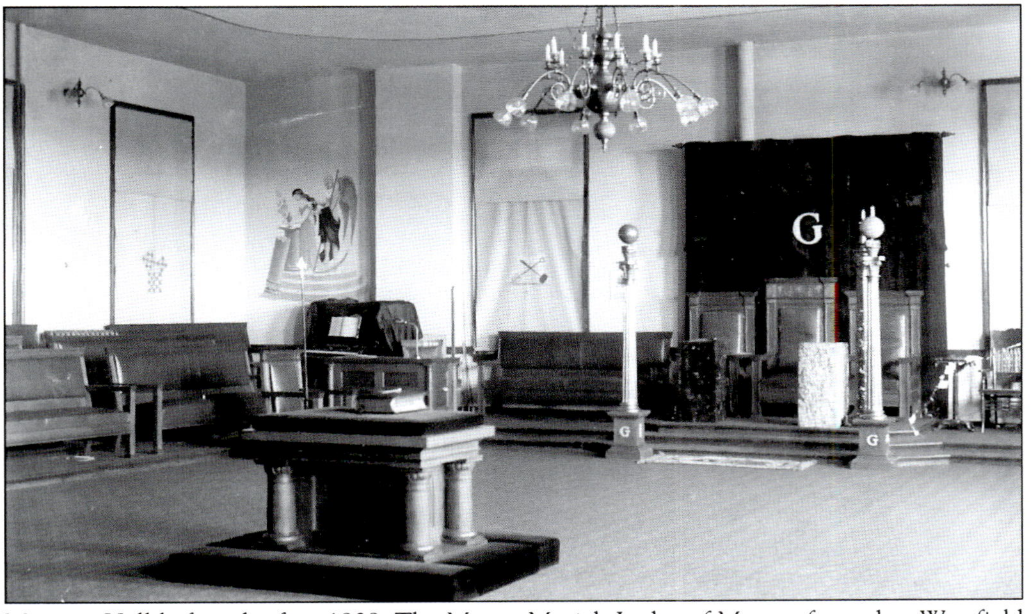

Masonic Hall before the fire, 1908. The Mount Moriah Lodge of Masons formed in Westfield in 1856. After their building burned down in 1896 (see Masonic Block fire, page 66), the lodge met in the Lane and Loomis Block for about one year before moving into the Parks Block on Elm Street.

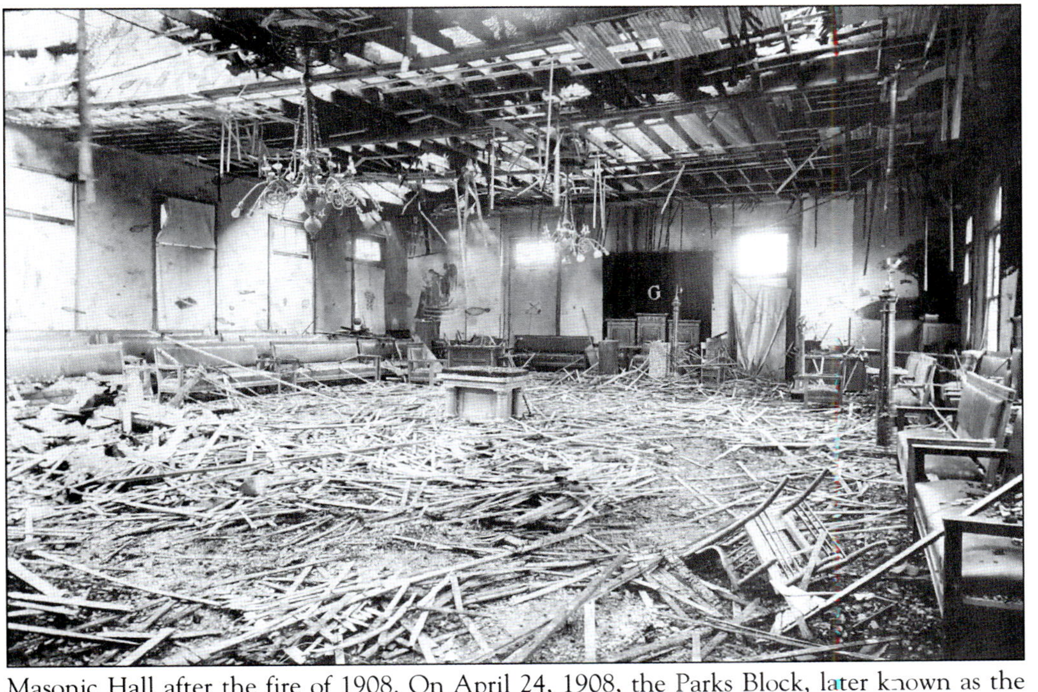

Masonic Hall after the fire of 1908. On April 24, 1908, the Parks Block, later known as the Professional Building, caught fire. The fire, the second one in this building, seemed to be worse over the Masonic Hall. The Masons were able to salvage some of the regalia shown in this picture, and it is still in use today in their Broad Street location.

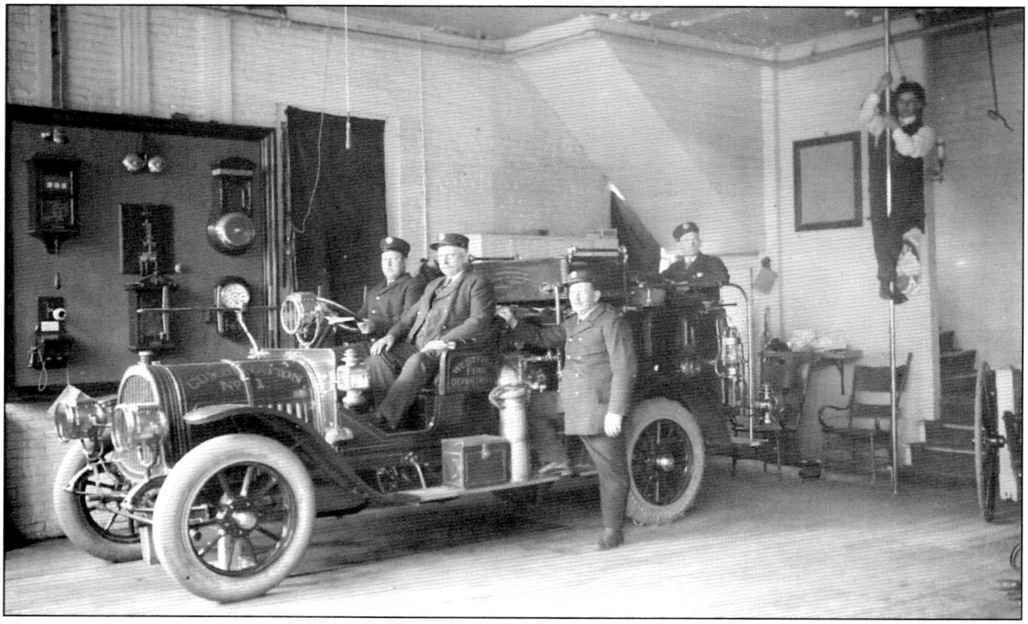

Combination No. 1 at the Arnold Street Engine House, 1909. Installed in 1909, this "motor driven apparatus" was a vast improvement over the horse-drawn engine. It gave "better protection to the outer districts, and covering two thirds more territory than the horse, can get to a fire much quicker, is more reliable, practically tireless and has to be fed only when worked."

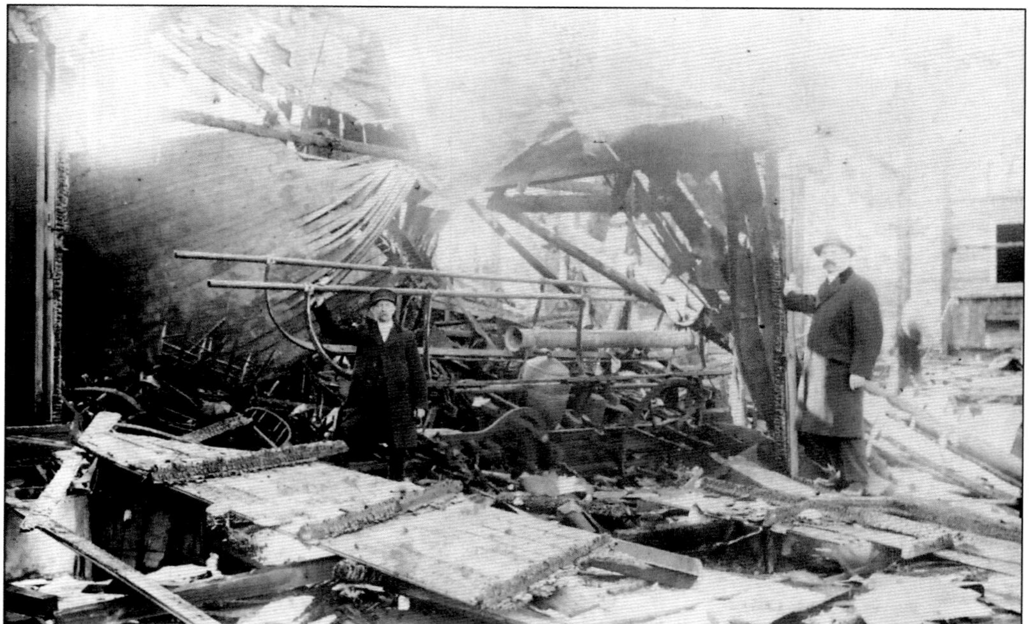

Elm Street garage fire, Dewey's Court, December 10, 1912. At 6:40 am, a fire broke out in the building once known as the Gem Opera House, shooting flames above the tree tops and causing gasoline explosions. The building was a total loss. Twenty-two cars stored in the building and the E.R. Lay Veteran Firemen's Association's hand tub (shown in this picture) were destroyed.

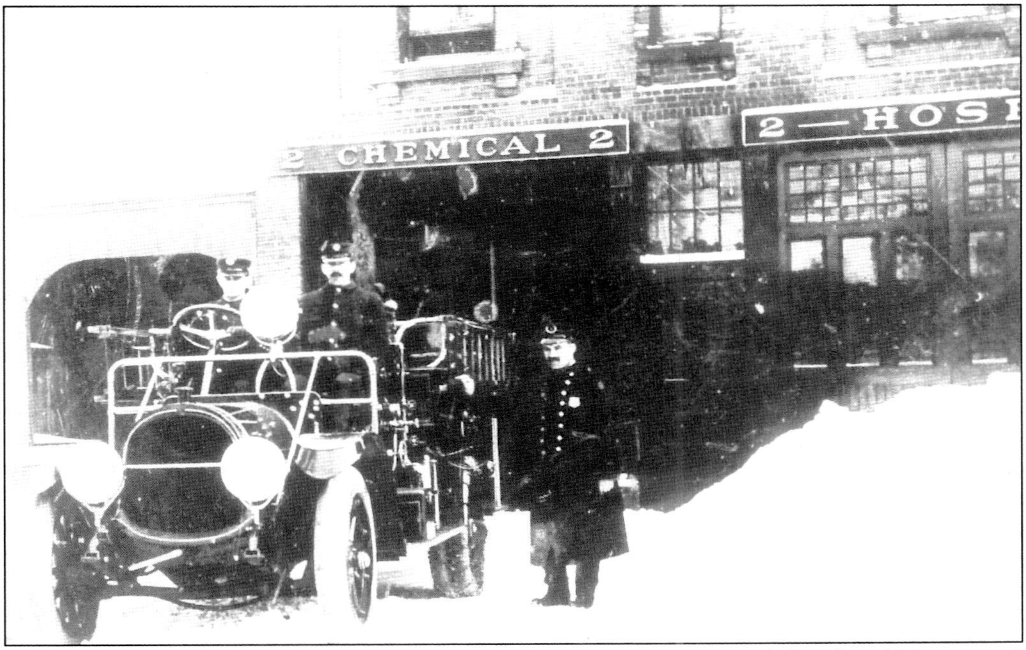

North Elm Street Engine House, 1920s. Police Officer Pat Coffee stands beside Bill Tupen and John Griffin in the fire engine. The shed on the side of the building was where the horses' hay was kept. It was later used for storing sand.

1-2 Court & Holland Ave.
1-2-3 Court & Washington St.
1-2-4 Court & Bates St.
1-2-5 Court & High St.
1-3-2 Sanatorium
1-3-6 Jr. High School
1-4 Broad St.
1-4-1 Broad & Bush St.
1-4-2 Broad & Silver St.
1-4-3 Peck's Lumber
1-4-5 Strathmore Paper
1-4-6 Foster Mach.
1-4-7 First Cong. Church
1-5 H. B. Smith Co.
1-5-1 Main & White St.
1-5-3 Main & Cross St.
1-5-7 Noble St. Project
1-7 Ashley St. & State
1-9-5 Joseph Ave.
2-1 Montgomery & Notre Dame
2-1-2 Notre Dame & Crown St.
2-1-3 Montgomery & Pine
2-1-4 Pochassic St.
2-1-5 Adam St.
2-3 Montgomery St. School
2-3-1 Blessed Sac. Parish Cen.
2-3-2 Clay Hill Holyoke Rd.
2-3-4 Holyoke Rd.
2-3-5 Box Makers Inc.
2-3-6 Savage Arms
2-3-7 Dry Bridge Sandy Hill Rd.
2-3-9 Rosedell Dr.
2-4 Oakdale Ave.
2-4-1 Airport
2-4-3 Prospect St.
2-5 Depot Sq.
2-5-1 Anderson & Son
2-5-2 Stanley Home N. Elm
2-5-3 N. Elm Westminster St.
2-5-6 Union & N. Elm
2-5-7 Whites Quaint Shop
2-5-8 Old Colony
2-6 Union Dartmouth St.
2-6-1 Moseley School
2-6-2 American Abb. Co.
2-6-3 Union Carpenter St.
2-6-4 Westfield Metal Products
2-6-5 Westfield Chem. Corp.
2-7 Col. Pine Acres
2-7-1 Burek Oil Co. Arch Rd.
2-7-2 Woodside Ter. & Rogers Ave.
2-7-3 Southampton School
2-7-4 O'Connor Lumber
2-8 Meadow Brook Lane
2-8-1 Buresh NonWoven
3-1 Hanover & Meadow
3-1-2 St. Paul St.
3-1-3 Meadow & White
3-1-4 Meadow & Fredrick
3-2 St. Mary's School
3-2-1 Bartlett Cor-Mech.
3-4 Elm & Cowles Court
3-4-1 Elm Bartlett St.
3-4-2 Westfield Grinding Wheel
3-4-3 Holy Trinity School
3-5 Franklin Washington
3-5-1 Franklin & Shepard
3-5-2 Franklin & Allen Ave.
3-5-3 Franklin Ellsworth
3-5-4 Russell Rd.
3-5-6 Putman Drive
3-5-7 Berkshire Dr.
3-6 Maple & Morris St.
3-6-1 Orange & Sackett St.
3-6-2 Orange & Kellogg St.
3-6-3 Orange & Shepard St.
3-6-4 Franklin Ave. School
3-6-5 Gas House Sibley Ave.
3-7 Lowell Ave. Western Ave.
4-1 Elm & Arnold St.
4-2-1 Washington & Church
4-3 Cherry St.
4-5 Elm & Franklin St.
4-6 W. School & Hampden St.
4-6-1 Dickson Hall
4-7 Elm & School St.
4-8 Jefferson & Madison St.
4-9 Jefferson & Allen Ave.
5 Noble Hospital
5-1 Mill & Silver St.
5-1-2 Pleasant & Pearl St.
5-1-3 Harrison Ave.
5-1-4 Southwick Rd.
5-1-5 Holy Child Guild Mill St.
5-1-6 Vadnais & Mill St.
5-2-1 Ely St.
5-3 Day Ave.
5-3-1 High School
5-3-2 Loomis Ave.
5-3-4 Trade High School
5-4 Holland & Woronoco Ave.
5-4-2 Abner Gibbs School
5-6 South Maple St.
6-1 Cleveland Ave.
6-2 Main & Noble St.
6-2-1 Lindbergh Blvd.
6-4 E. Silver & Lozier Ave.
6-5 King Grand & Bates St.
6-7 West Silver & Dudley Ave.
6-8 Silver & Cross St.
7-1 Highland Ave. & Wilson
7-2 Western Ave. & Lloyd's Hill
7-2-3 Loring Lane
7-3 Granville Rd.
7-4 Overlook Drive
7-4-3 Westwood Acres
7-4-5 Western Circle
7-5 State Teacher's College
7-5-2 Southern Slopes
7-6 Bates Cor Donald
7-8 Western Ave. & Tekoa Ter.
8-1 Main & Tonelli's Inn
8-1-2 Ridgecrest Manor
8-1-4 Little River & Shaker Rd.
8-1-6 Falley & Alquat
8-1-7 Cornish & Steiger
8-2 Glenwood Dr.
8-3 E. Main Oleksak's Lumber Yd.
8-5 Adam's Nursery

SPECIAL CALLS

1 Supt. of Alarms
2 Fire All Out
3 Curfew
7 Headquarters
3-3-3 No School
4-4-4 Military
2-2-2 Civil Defense

If not near fire alarm box, use telephone, dial 2-2329 or 2-2320. **State location of fire, street and number, and type of fire.**

Fire alarm box signals from Chapman Fuel Company calendar, 1963. In the event of a fire, the horn in the tower of the Arnold Street station would ring the signal three times to indicate the location of the fire.

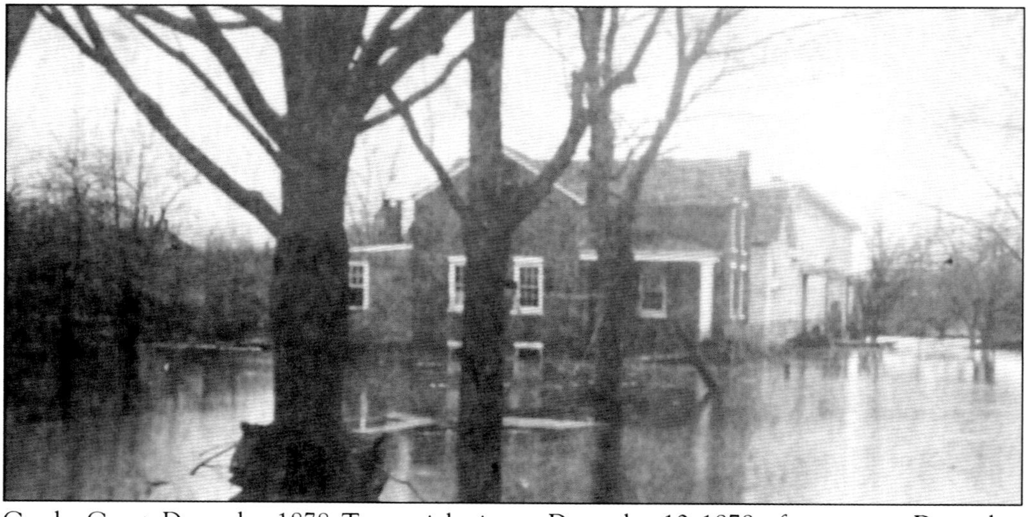

Cowles Court, December 1878. Torrential rains on December 10, 1878, after snow on December 9, led to the flood of 1878. At one point the Westfield River was rising 2 feet per hour. The water overtopped the dike, which gave way in two places—near the Great River Bridge and near Shepard Street. The river carved a new path through Westfield.

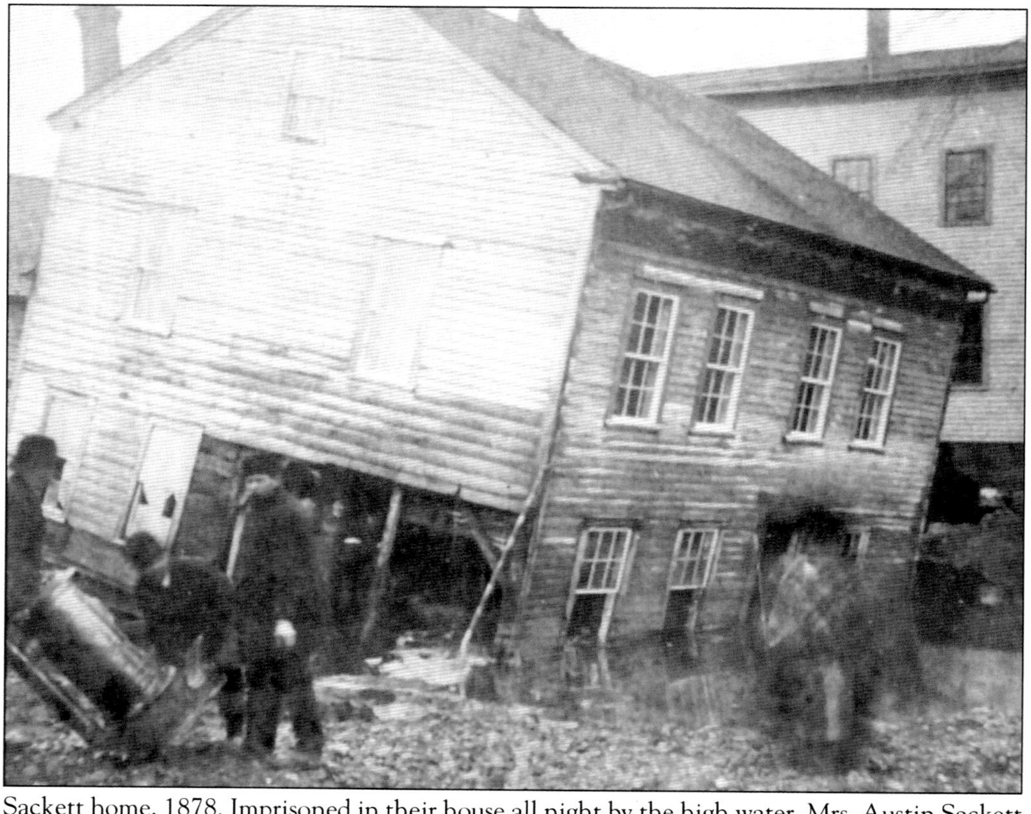

Sackett home, 1878. Imprisoned in their house all night by the high water, Mrs. Austin Sackett and her daughters were rescued at 6 am. Immediately after the rescue, the house tipped into a pit worn by the water.

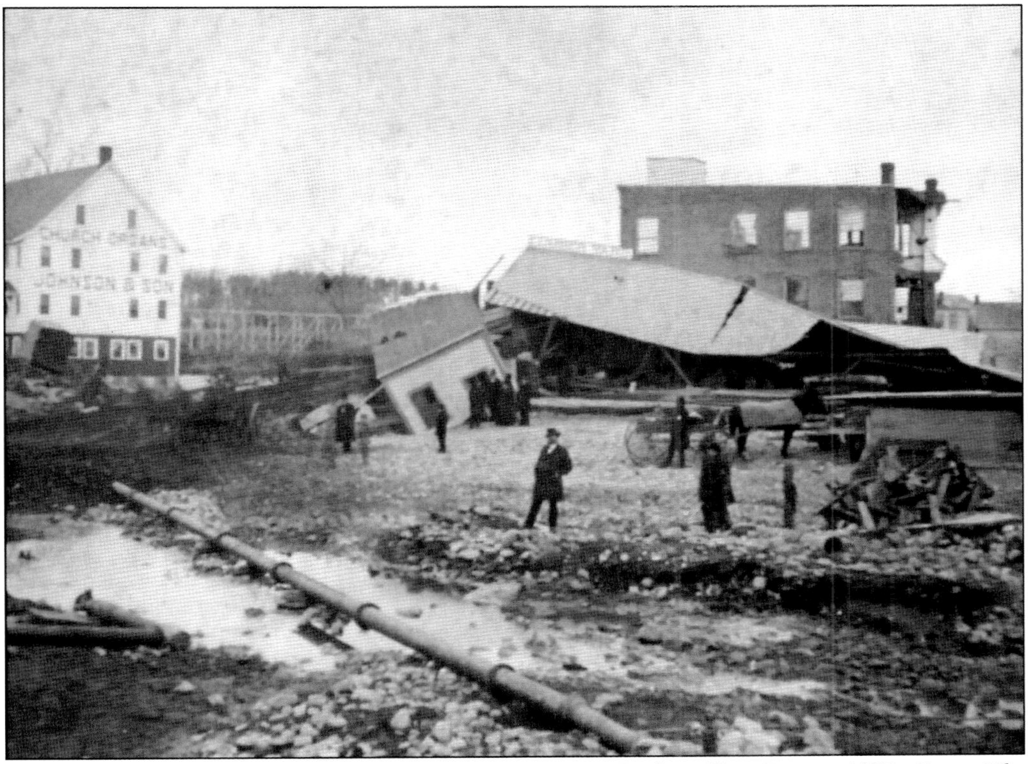

Lumber buildings and whip shop at the Great River Bridge, Elm Street, 1878. From *The Westfield Times and Newsletter*, an article states: "From Chapel Street to the Great River Bridge is the scene of greatest desolation. The street is literally torn up, drain and water pipes lay bare, buildings in ruin, sheds, dams and outbuildings piled and turned up everywhere. The scene beggars description."

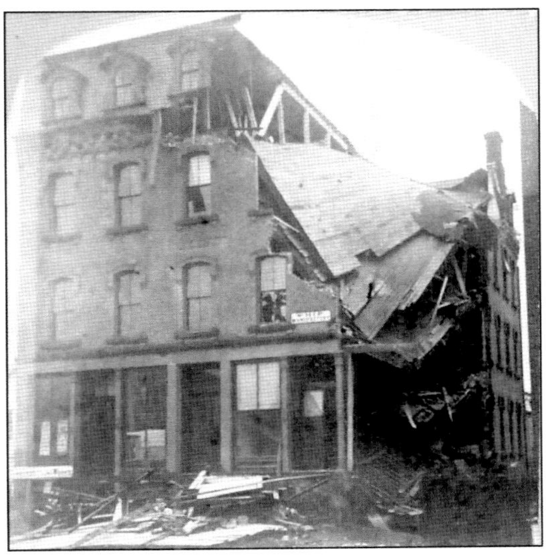

Provin Block, Elm Street, 1878. Built in 1874 at a cost of $11,000, the Provin Block was severely damaged by the flood.

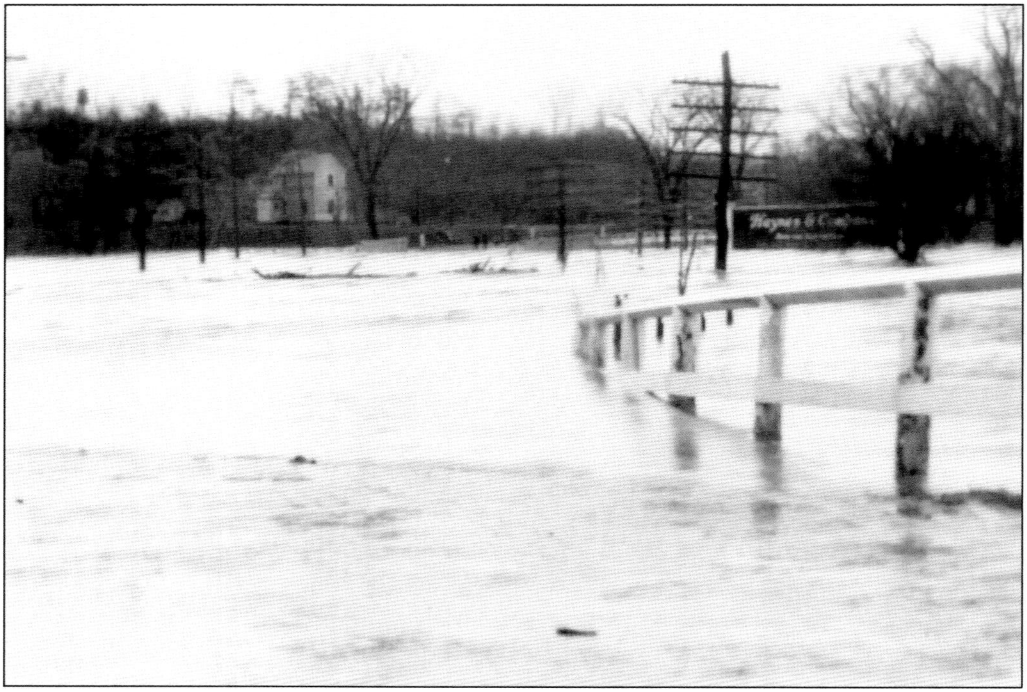

Flooding of the Westfield River near Little River Road, April 1924. The following headline appeared in the April 7, 1924 edition of the *Westfield Daily Journal*: "Westfield nearly surrounded by five foot wall of water from overflow of two rivers. Highway travel to Springfield and Huntington impossible . . . Farms and tobacco plantations suffer . . . Many building threatened . . . Golf course buried deep . . . Loss will reach thousands of dollars."

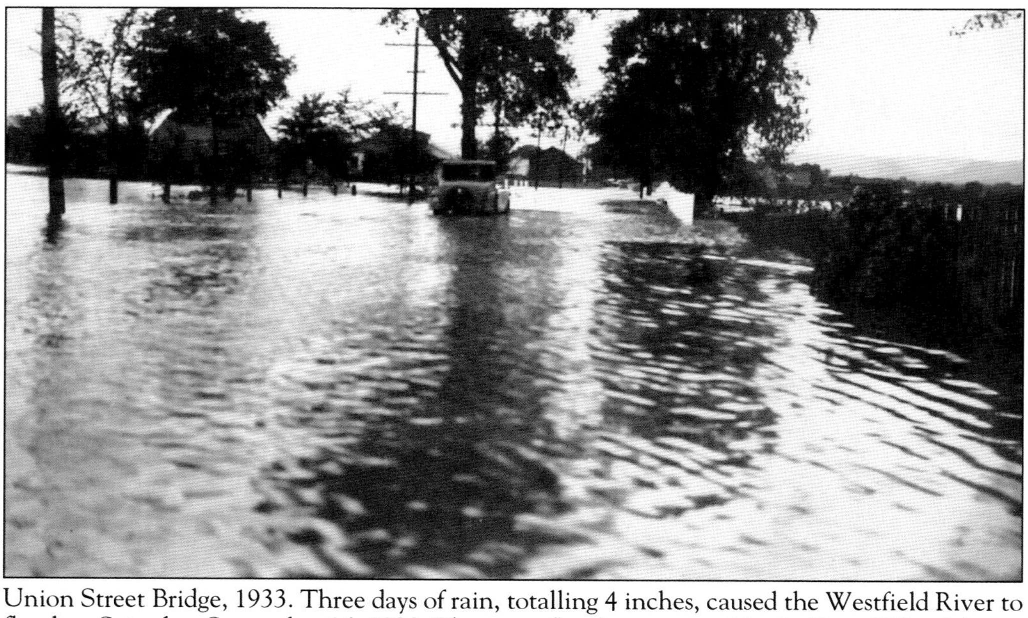

Union Street Bridge, 1933. Three days of rain, totalling 4 inches, caused the Westfield River to flood on Saturday, September 16, 1933. The worst flooding occurred in the Russell Road, lower Union Street, East Main Street, and Meadow Street sections of the city.

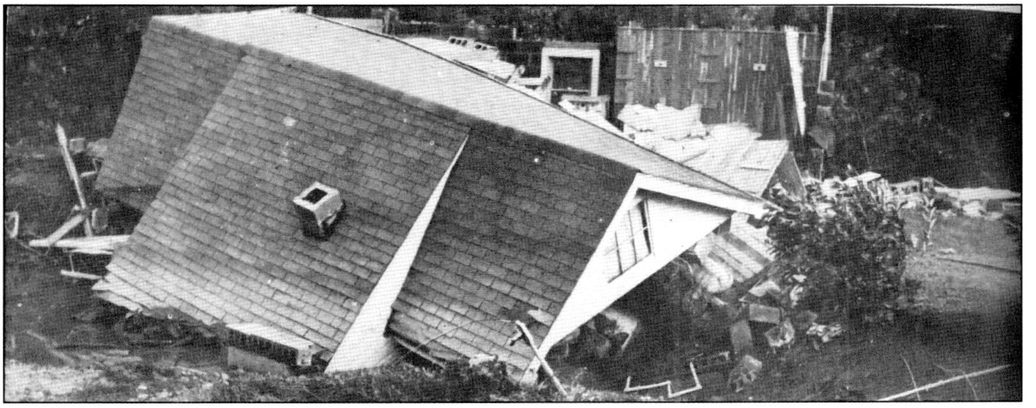

Collapsed house at the site of Burnett's Trailer Park and Sales, Springfield Road, 1955. Nineteen inches of rain fell during Hurricane Diane on August 18 and 19, 1955. This, added to the rain from Hurricane Connie a few days earlier, was far more than the rivers and streams could handle. The Westfield River, the Little River, and the Powdermill Brook all caused severe damage in Westfield.

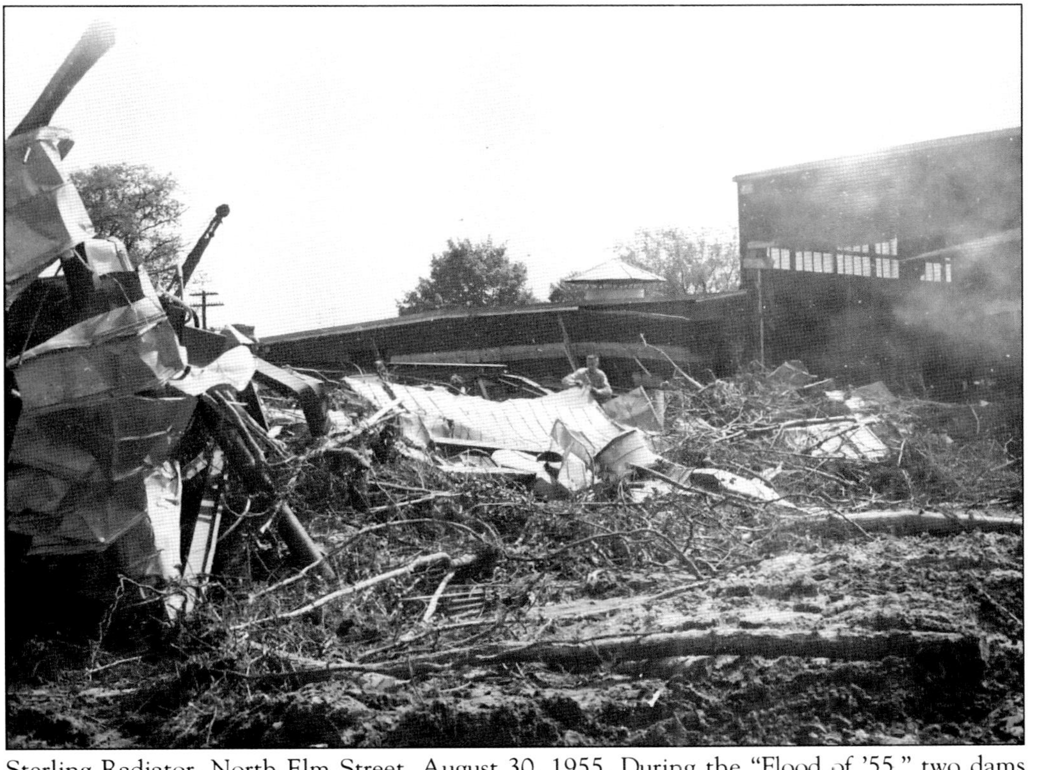

Sterling Radiator, North Elm Street, August 30, 1955. During the "Flood of '55," two dams across the Powdermill Brook broke, sending a 12-foot crest of water smashing into the Sterling Radiator plant. One building was completely demolished and the other buildings, badly damaged. When the water surged across North Elm Street, it destroyed the bridge and washed out the road.

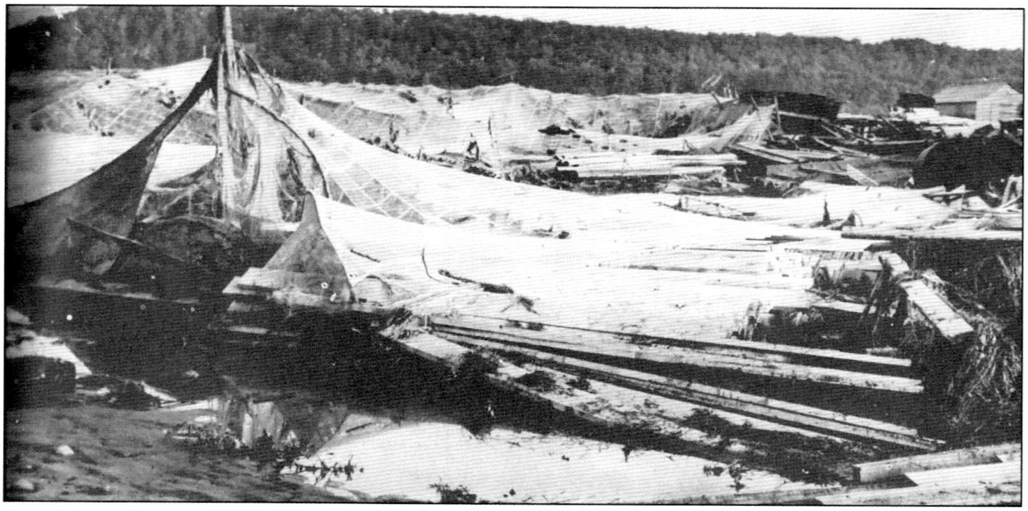

East Main Street, 1955. The lumber from the Oleksak Lumber Company of 273 East Main Street was strewn about by the floodwaters, and it flattened the netting of shadegrown tobacco plants.

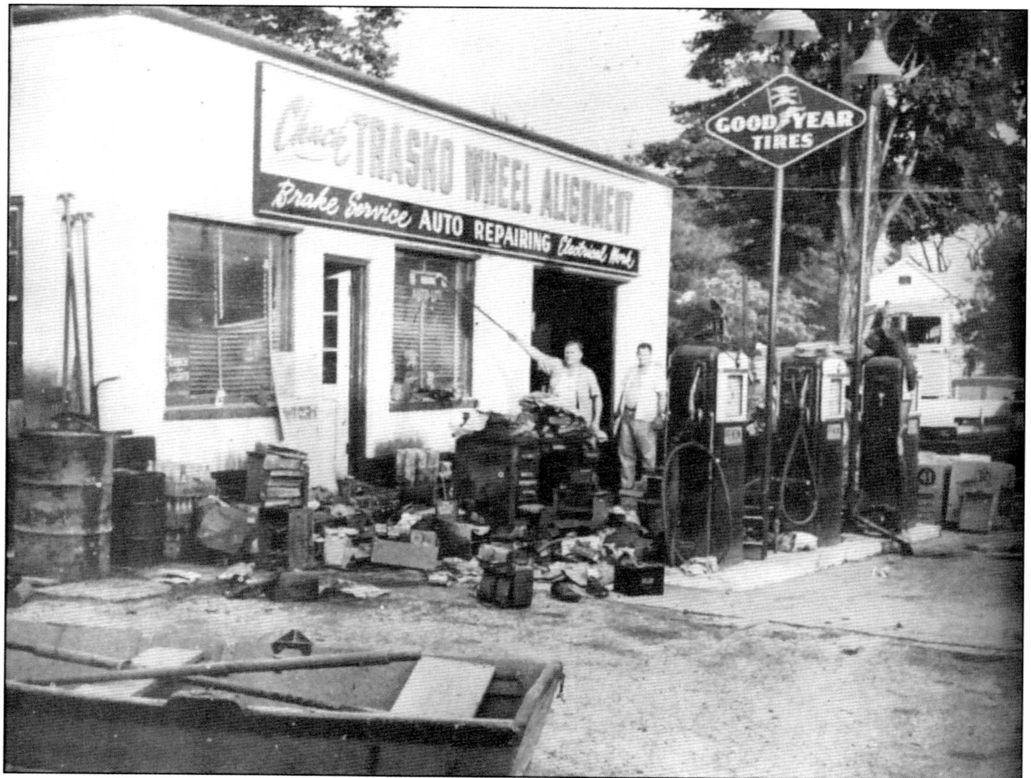

Chuck Trasko Garage, 136 Meadow Street, 1955. The man in the picture is pointing to the high-water mark on the side of the building.

Six

A Variety of Vehicles

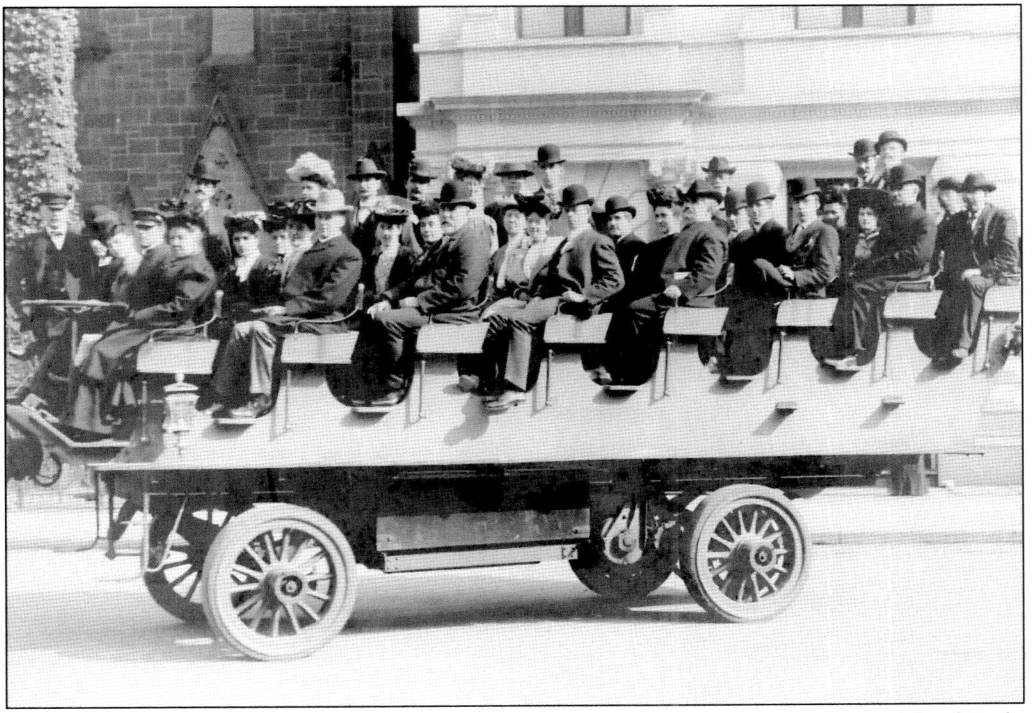

Some Westfield people on a sightseeing bus in New York City en route to Coney Island Park, about 1900.

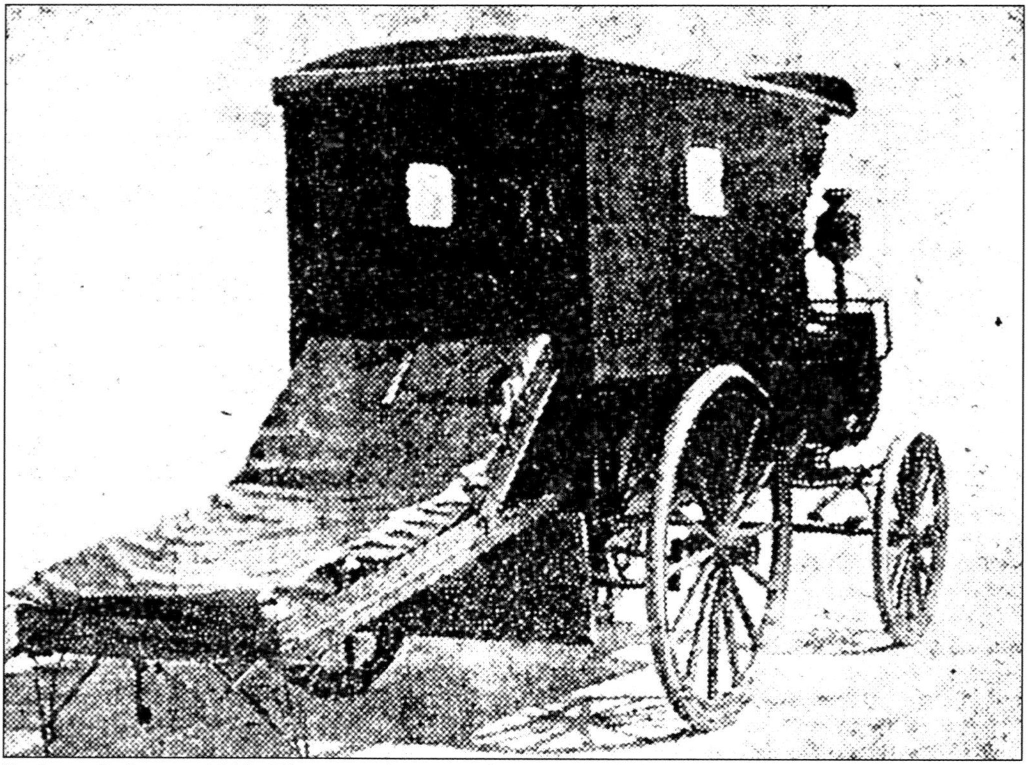

Early ambulance, 1897. This new horse and wagon ambulance, the latest convenience, was presented to Noble Hospital in July 1897. The vehicle weighed 1,500 pounds and the "bed inside is of the softest while both the head and foot are instantly adjustable to the sufferer's most comfortable position."

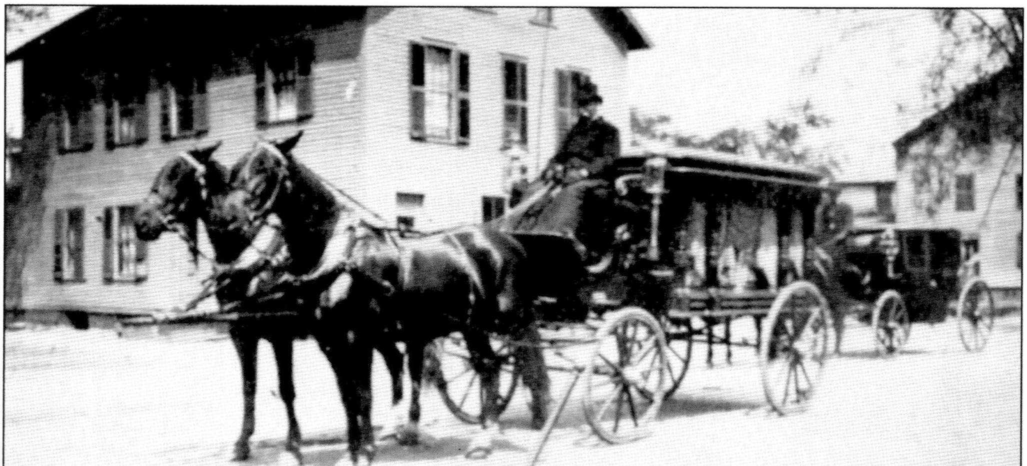

Horse-drawn hearse. Warren Parker is shown driving this horse-drawn hearse for the Healey Funeral Home in 1915. The business was started in the late 1800s in conjunction with Lambson Furniture Company. In 1944 it was moved to the Morgan House at 29 Broad Street, its current location. It is presently called the Healey-Pease Funeral Home.

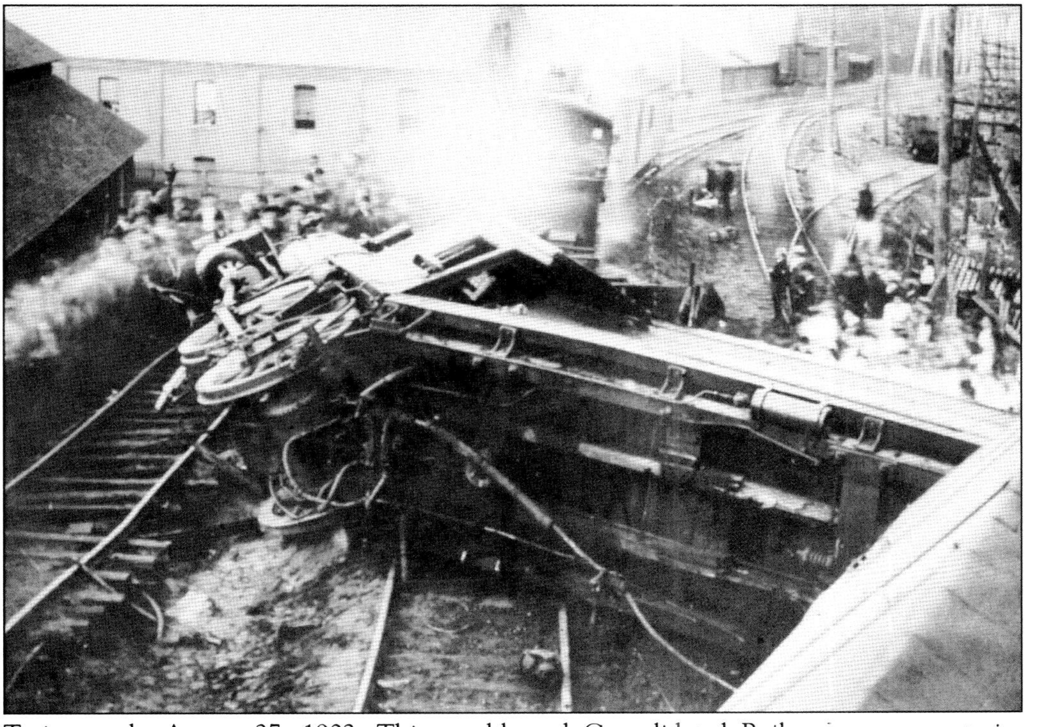

Train wreck, August 27, 1902. This northbound Consolidated Railroad passenger train, travelling from New Haven to Westfield, ran off the track on the high embankment in the rear of Cowles Court only 200 yards from the depot. The engine and baggage car were thrown on their side, while the remaining cars didn't leave the track. Fireman Archie H. Wetmore and Engineer George Van Vechten, both of Westfield, were buried in the debris. Wetmore, badly burned, was transported to Noble Hospital, but he died two hours later. Van Vechten was scalded and scratched, but luckily, his injuries were less serious.

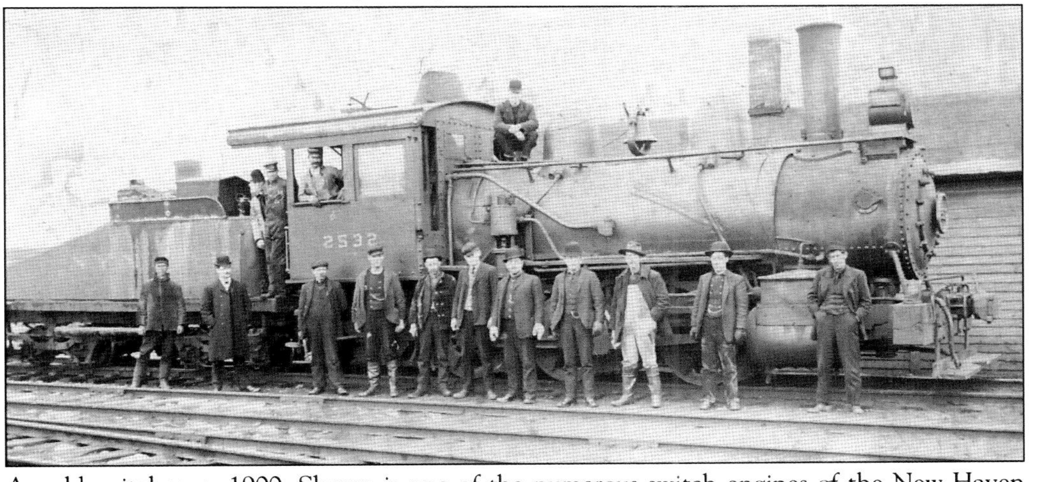

An old switcher, c. 1900. Shown is one of the numerous switch engines of the New Haven station on the North Side. Some of the men are: George Maas, Ed McCarthy, Johnnie Foley, Jack Manning, Bob McMahon, Charles O'Neil, George Alair, Jimmy Barryl, Jim Regan, Jim Elliott, and Tommy Maas.

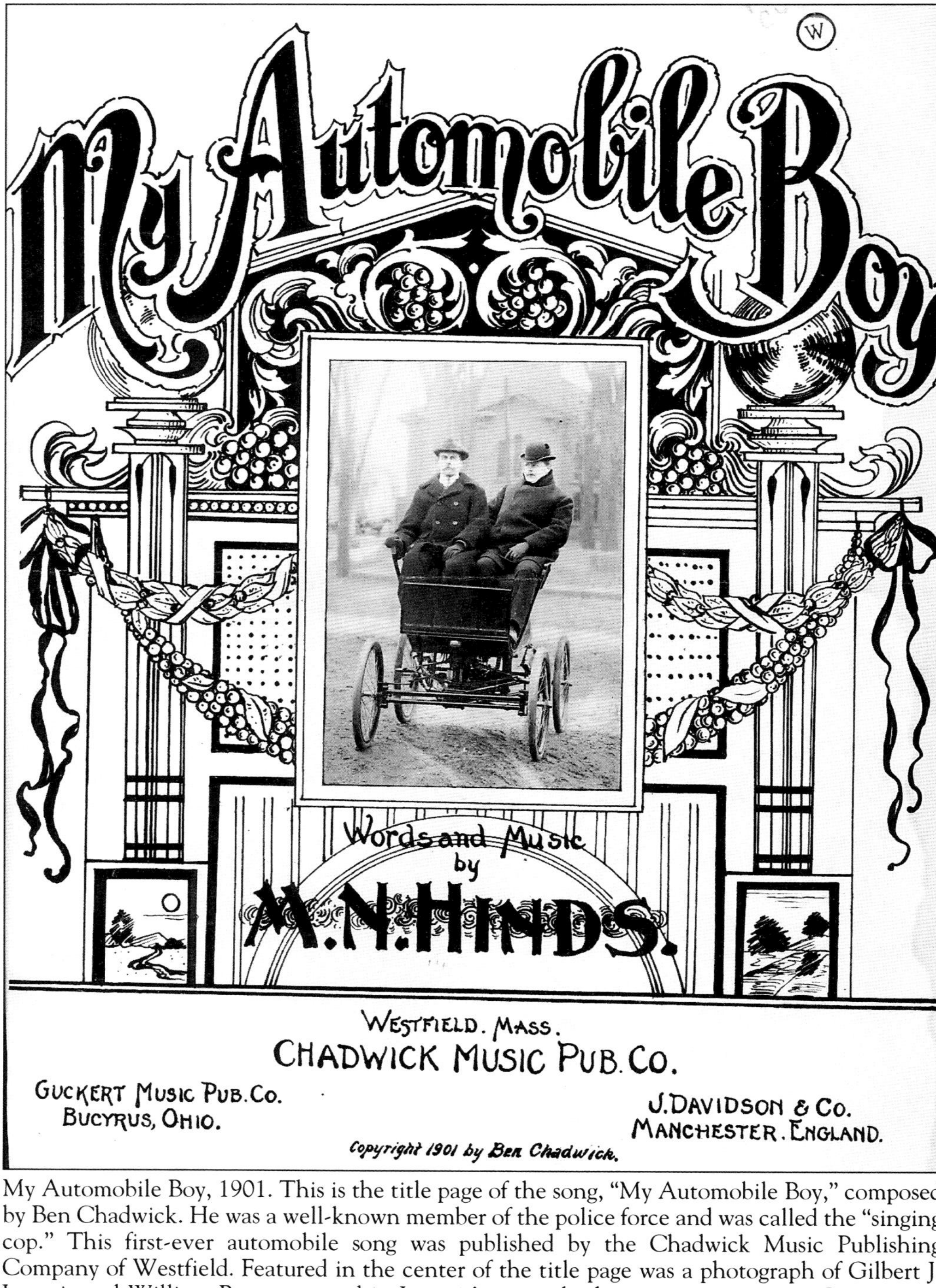

My Automobile Boy, 1901. This is the title page of the song, "My Automobile Boy," composed by Ben Chadwick. He was a well-known member of the police force and was called the "singing cop." This first-ever automobile song was published by the Chadwick Music Publishing Company of Westfield. Featured in the center of the title page was a photograph of Gilbert J. Loomis and William Barton, seated in Loomis's one-cylinder, two-passenger car. Loomis was Westfield's first builder of automobiles and a pioneer automotive engineer and designer. He was the owner of the famous automobile dog "Dandy," who always wore goggles when riding in the car, since there were no windshields in those days.

Westfield automobile, 1902. The car on the right, manufactured in Westfield, was on display at the annual automobile show in New York City. Charles J. Moore, whose plant was located on Birge Avenue, was the designer and maker of the car. Primarily, Mr. Moore was concerned with the making of automobile bodies, and, as far as is known, this was the only complete car ever made in his factory.

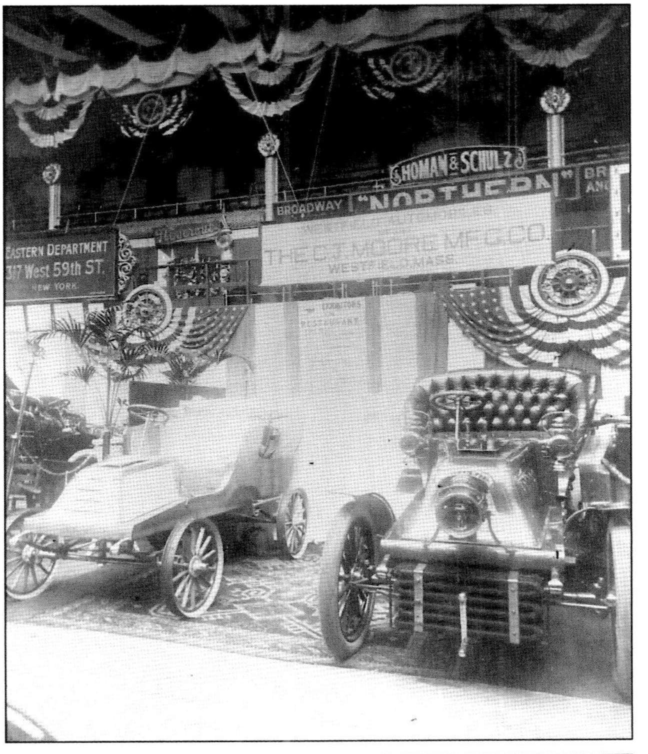

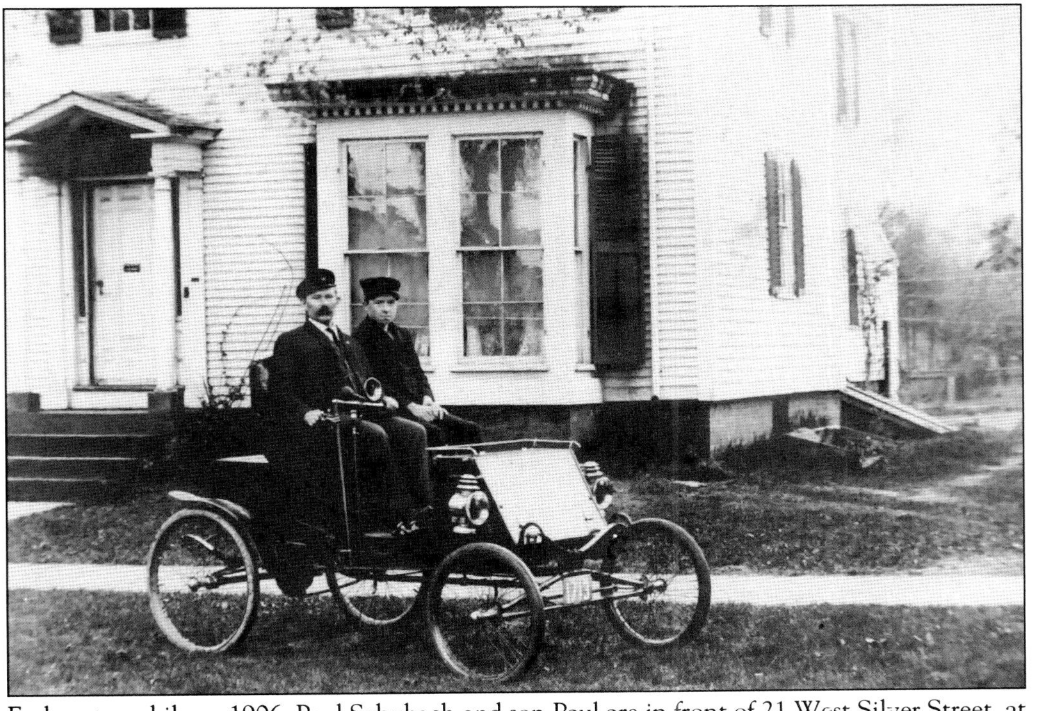

Early automobile, c. 1906. Paul Schubach and son Paul are in front of 21 West Silver Street, at the corner of Holland Avenue.

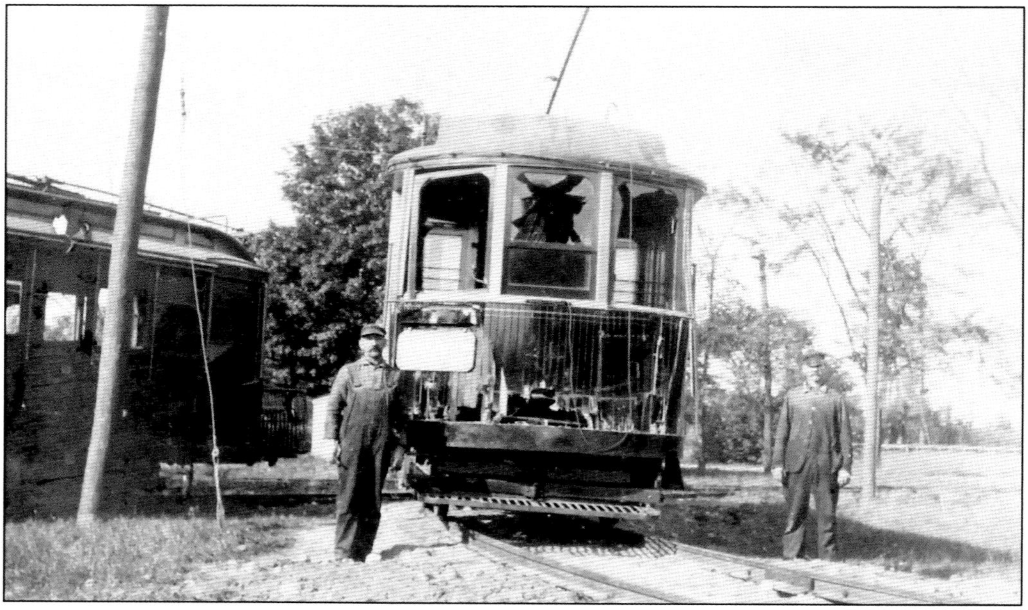

Trolley car, October 19, 1907. Passenger Car No. 379, shown here at the car barn on Western Avenue, was involved in a collision just east of the Main Street bridge over Little River as it was heading to Springfield. It ran into a work car that was standing on the track around the curve from the bridge. Motorman Wesley E. Ellis was not seriously injured. The passenger car's front vestibule was stove in and the glass broken. Pictured on the right side of the trolley is John Sime.

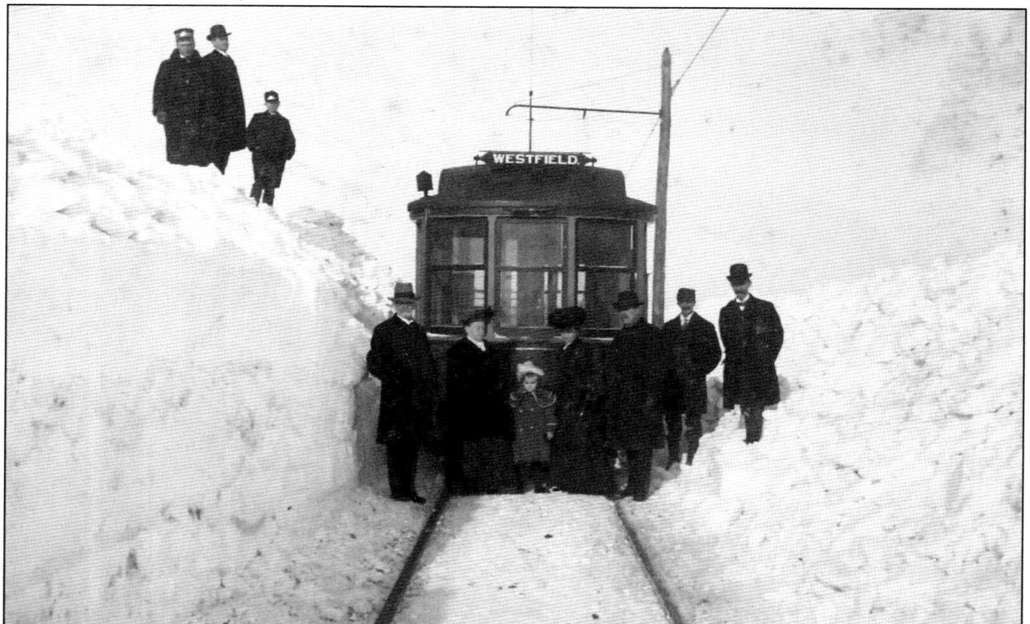

Trolley car, early 1900s. A trolley is coming from Holyoke into Westfield. Notice the high snowbanks on either side of the tracks.

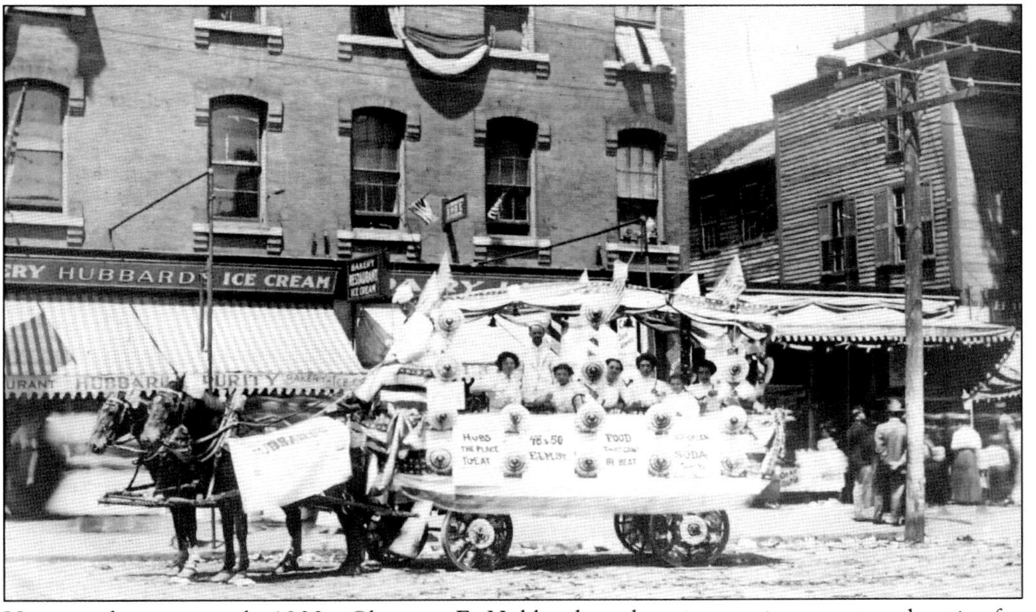

Horse and wagon, early 1900s. Clarence E. Hubbard used an interesting way to advertise for his business at 48 and 50 Elm Street. Hubbard's Purity was a restaurant, bakery, and ice-cream room. Mr. Hubbard later operated a cash grocery store on School Street.

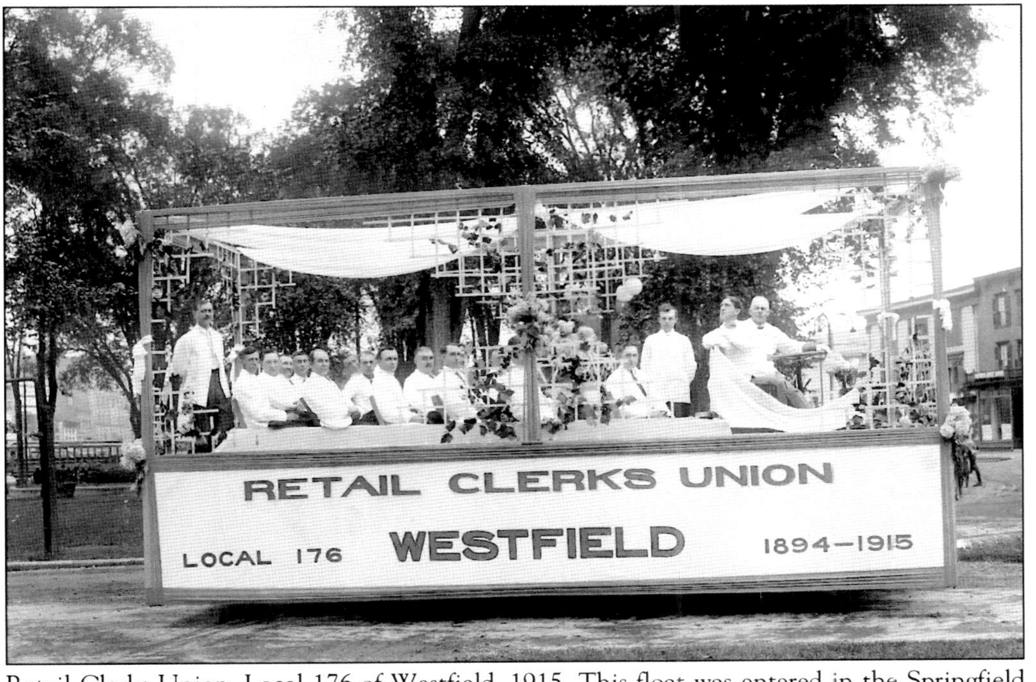

Retail Clerks Union, Local 176 of Westfield, 1915. This float was entered in the Springfield Labor Day Parade of 1915. The clerks from left to right are: Toni Fresco, Fred Killips, Eddie Frank, Anton Jorgenson, Leon Barnes, Garrett Fitzgerald, Mike Corcoran, Elmer Rust, Jim Carlin, John Heigus, Jim Condron, John McCarthy (behind the lattice), Henry Jensen, George Martin, Dick Williams, and Reuben Humphreville (owner of the truck).

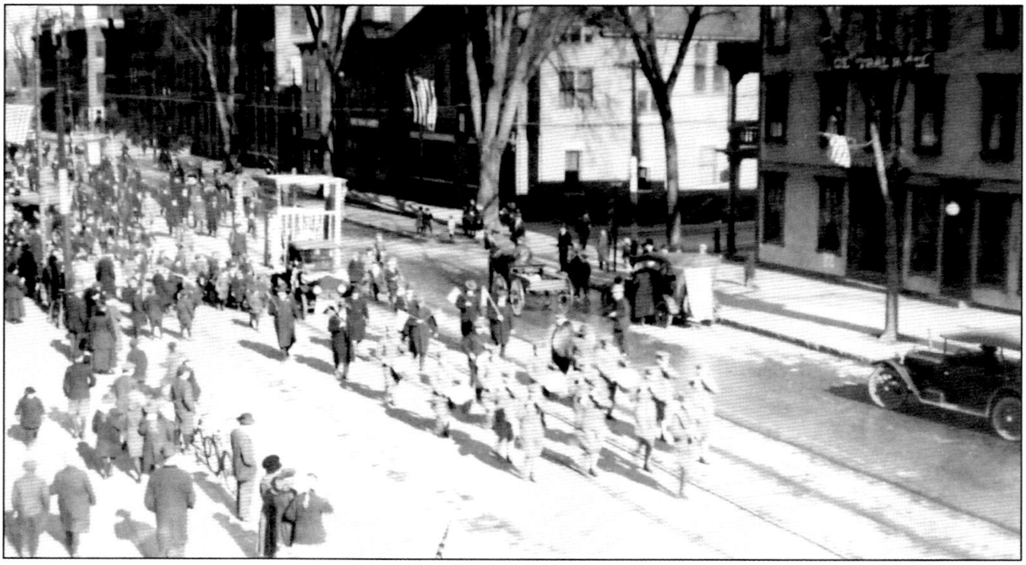

"Kaiser in a Cage," 1917. In this 1917 parade there is a "kaiser" in the cage on the Model T car. The German emperor, Kaiser Wilhelm II, was blamed for starting World War I, though historians now believe that Russia and Austria were equally guilty of starting it. Thus, we have a caged "kaiser" on display here.

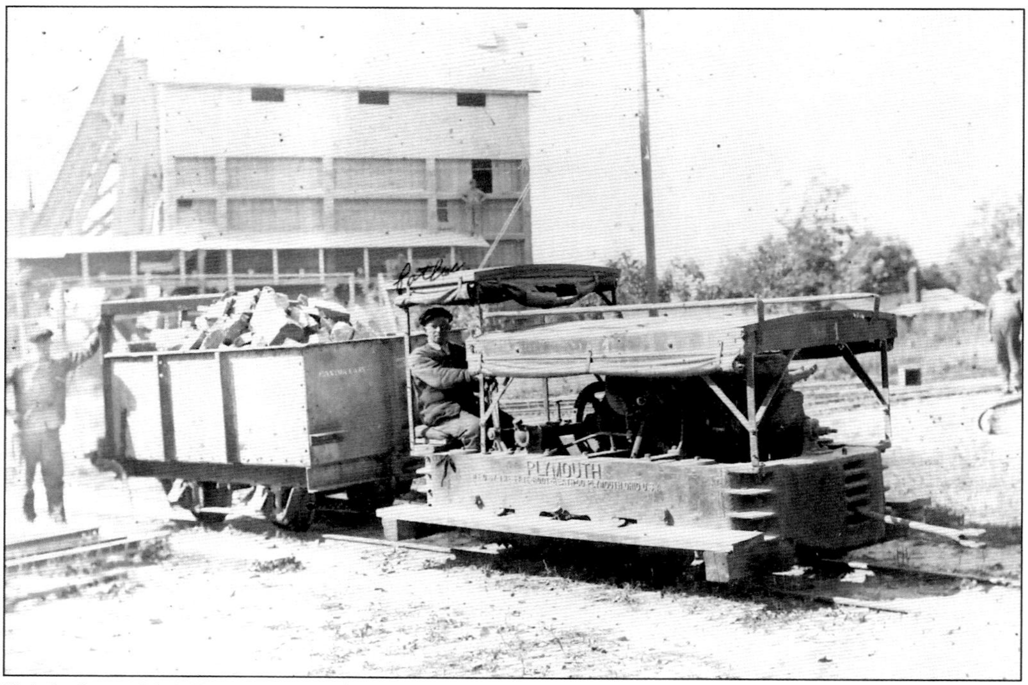

"Mule," *c.* 1926. Rocco Grimaldi is operating the "mule" at John S. Lane and Son, Inc., on East Mountain Road. Several generations of the Lane family have been associated with the company, which first started quarrying trap rock in 1894.

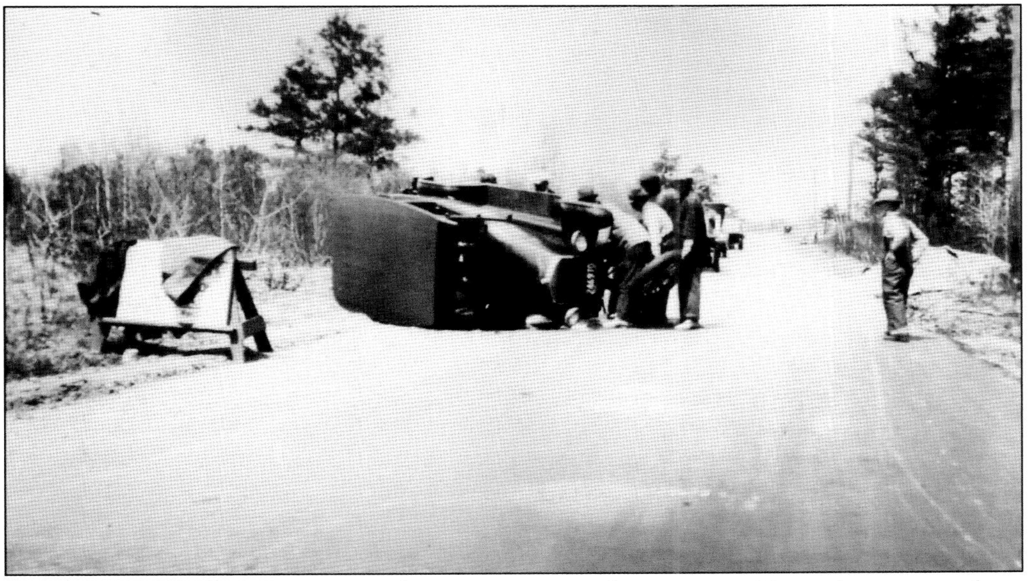

Accident, 1927. A car was tipped over onto its side in an accident that occurred on Southampton Road.

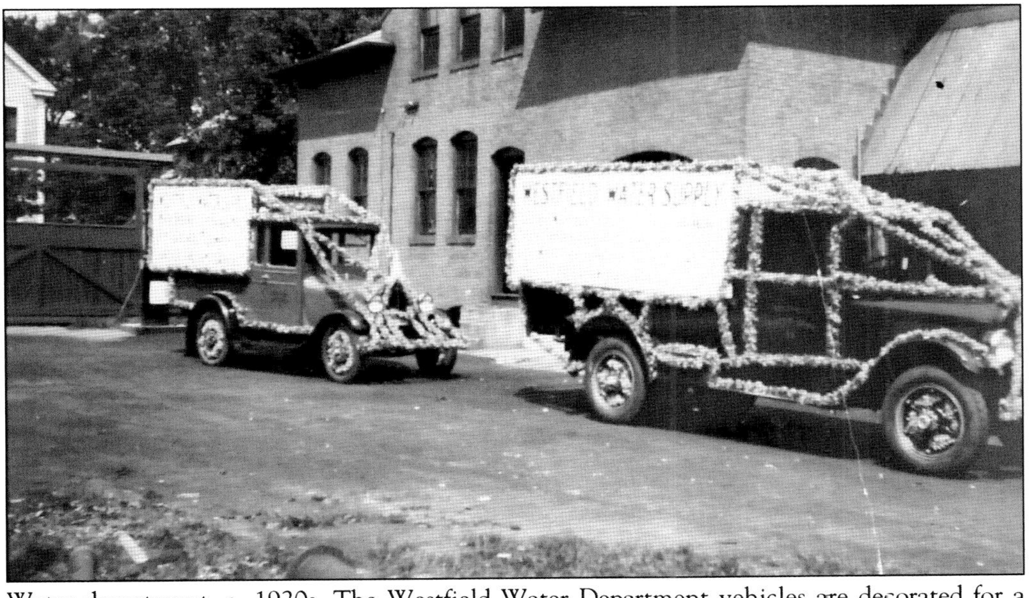

Water department, c. 1920s. The Westfield Water Department vehicles are decorated for a celebration, perhaps a parade.

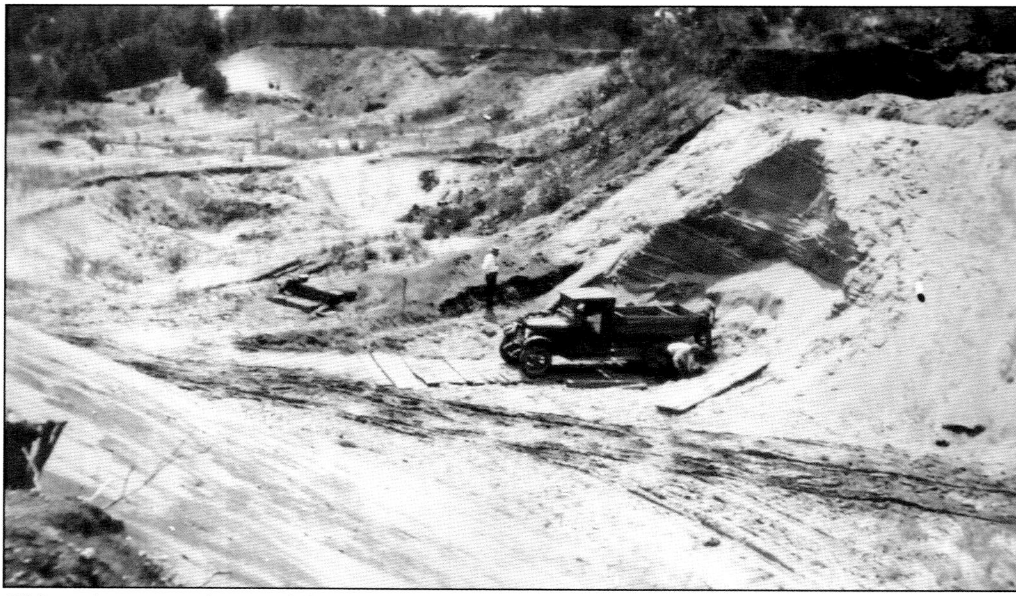

Old truck, 1927. This truck has backed up for a load of sand at the Ellis sand bank.

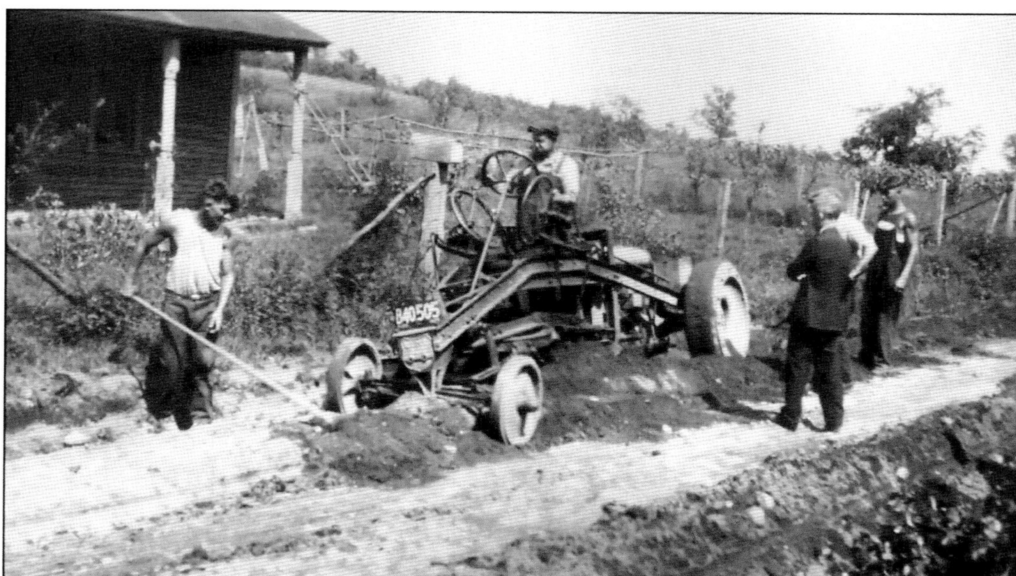

Weir grader, 1927. This is one of the vehicles that was used in road construction.

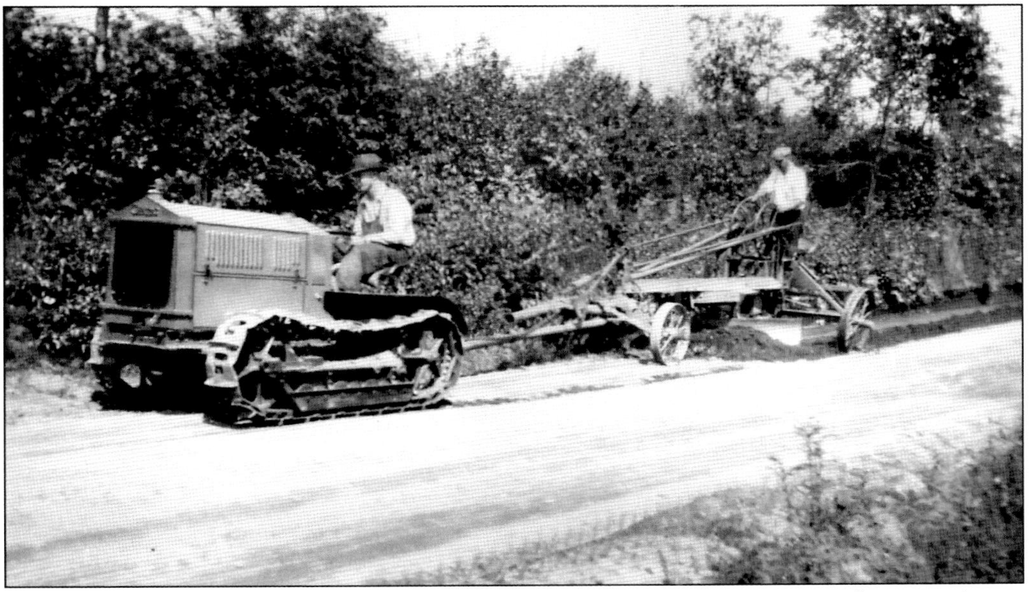

Cleveland tractor and scraper, 1927. These men are operating the tractor and scraper during another stage of the road construction.

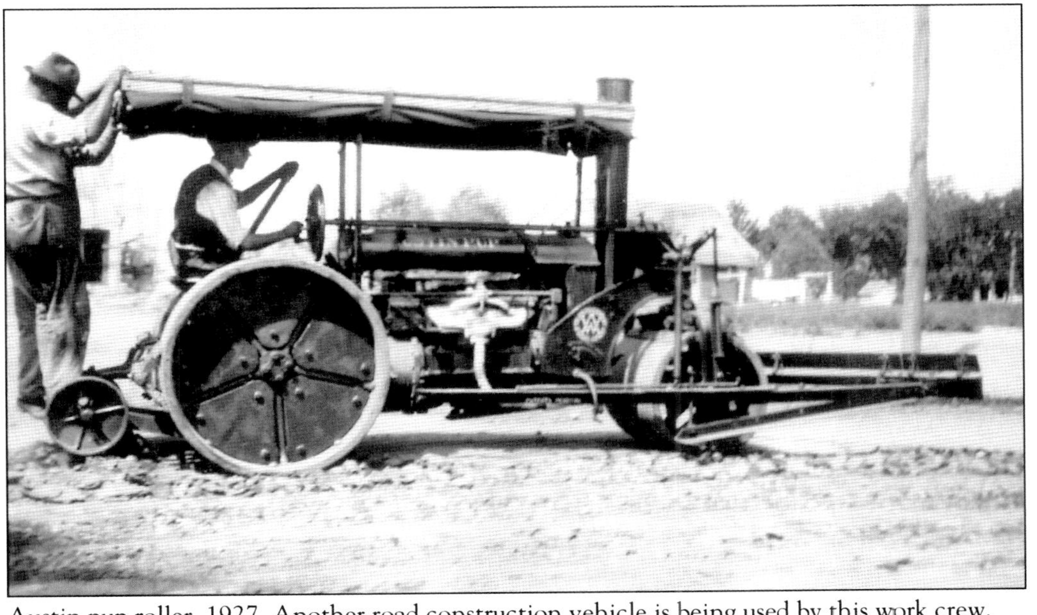

Austin pup roller, 1927. Another road construction vehicle is being used by this work crew.

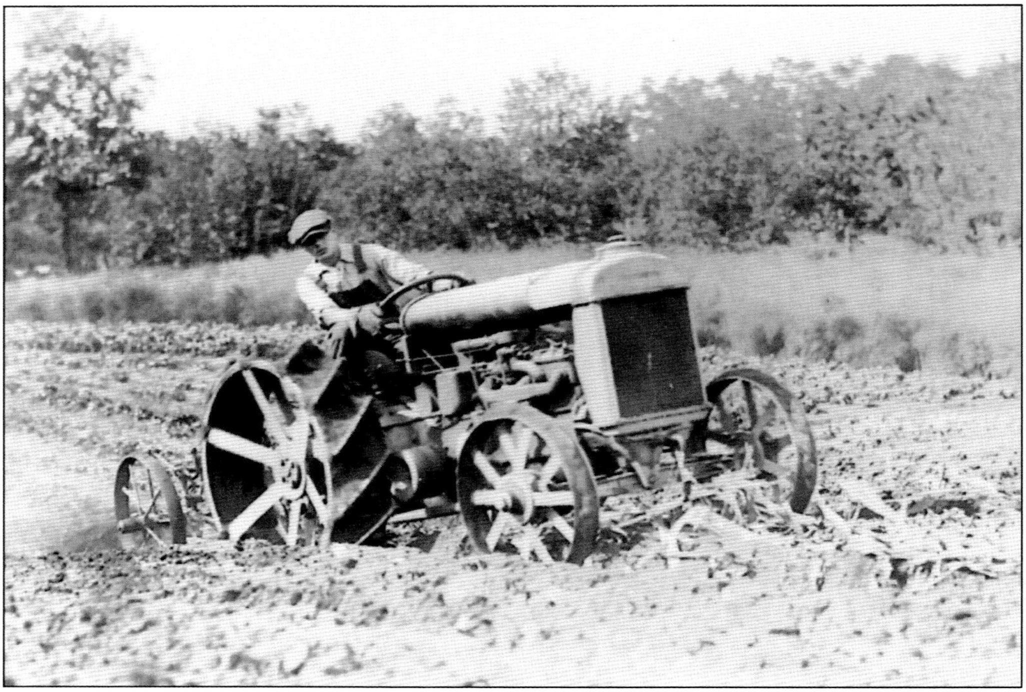

Tractor, 1927. Alfred R. Seher is shown operating a tractor on the Seher farm on Southampton Road. He still has the farm, grows vegetables and flowers, and is well known for his prize-winning gladioli.

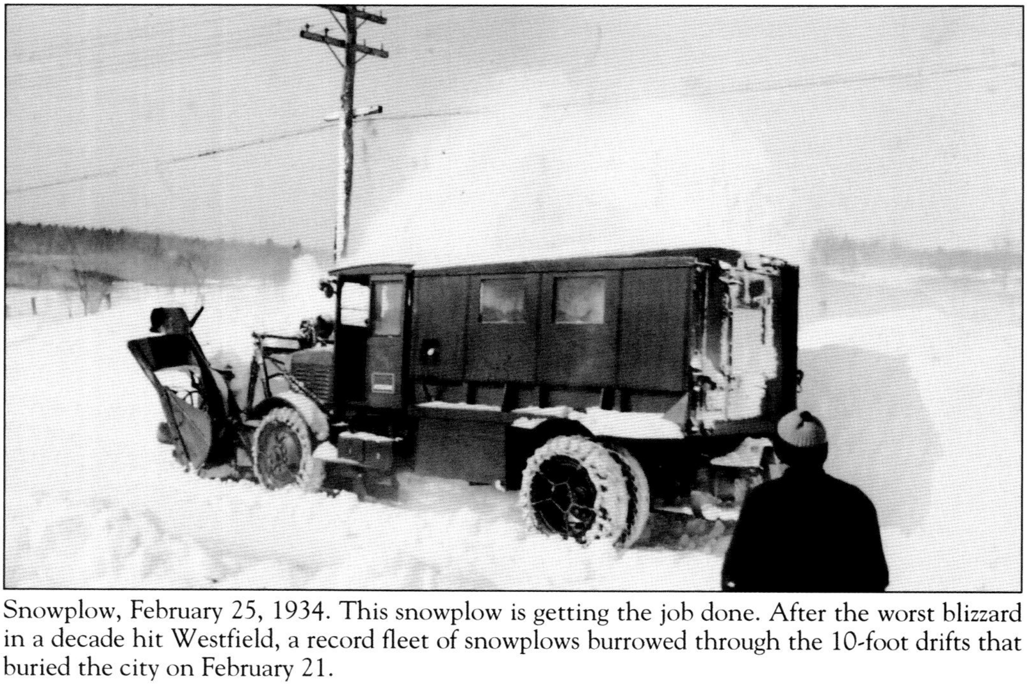

Snowplow, February 25, 1934. This snowplow is getting the job done. After the worst blizzard in a decade hit Westfield, a record fleet of snowplows burrowed through the 10-foot drifts that buried the city on February 21.

Seven

Roads and Bridges

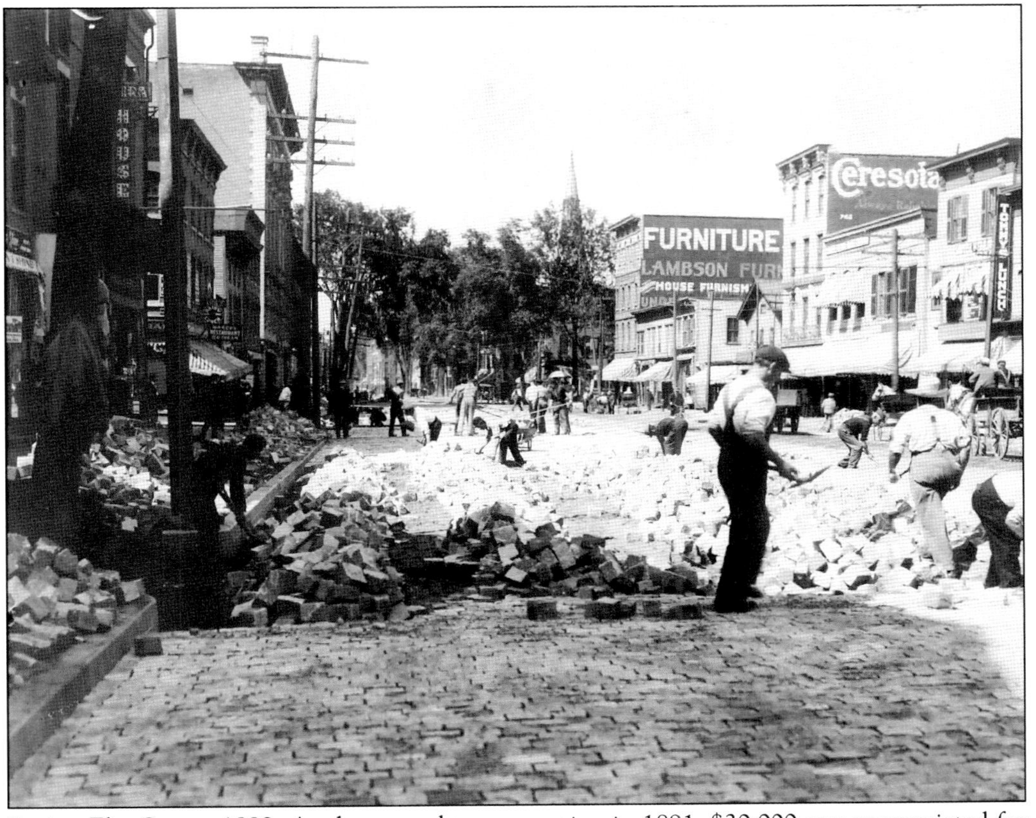

Paving Elm Street, 1892. At the annual town meeting in 1891, $30,000 was appropriated for paving Elm Street. The instructions were to "do the work as soon as practicable." The work began in the spring of 1892 and was completed in the fall of the same year.

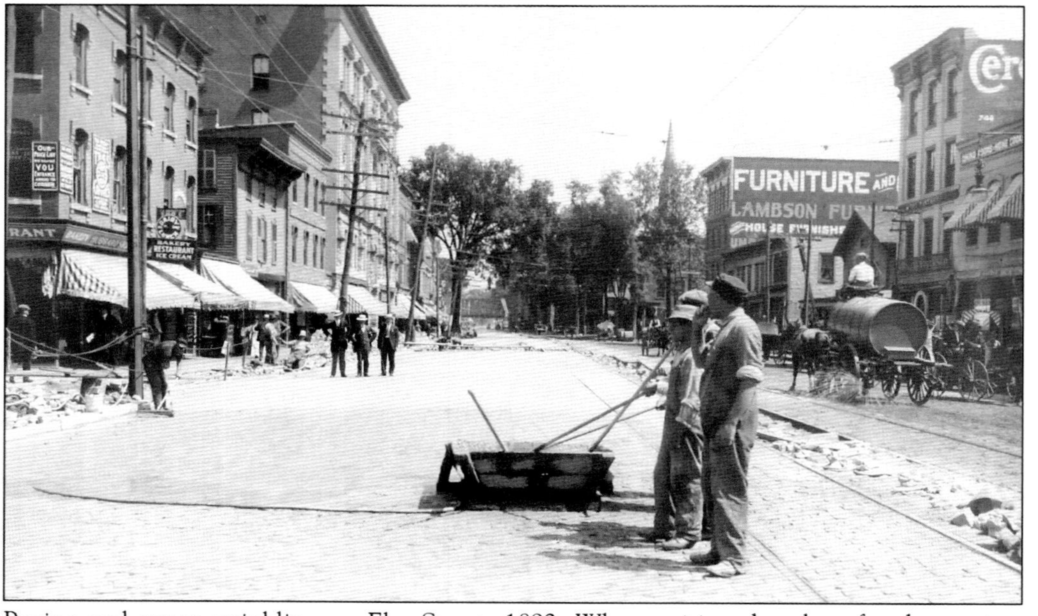

Paving and street sprinkling on Elm Street, 1892. When writing the plans for the paving, L.F. Thayer, engineer for the Town of Westfield, and the engineering department "made a survey and profile of each curbing, and cross sections of the street every fifty feet from the post office to the bridge." These plans were studied and approved by consulting engineer Henry Manley, who was an engineer for the City of Boston and president of the Massachusetts Society of Civil Engineers.

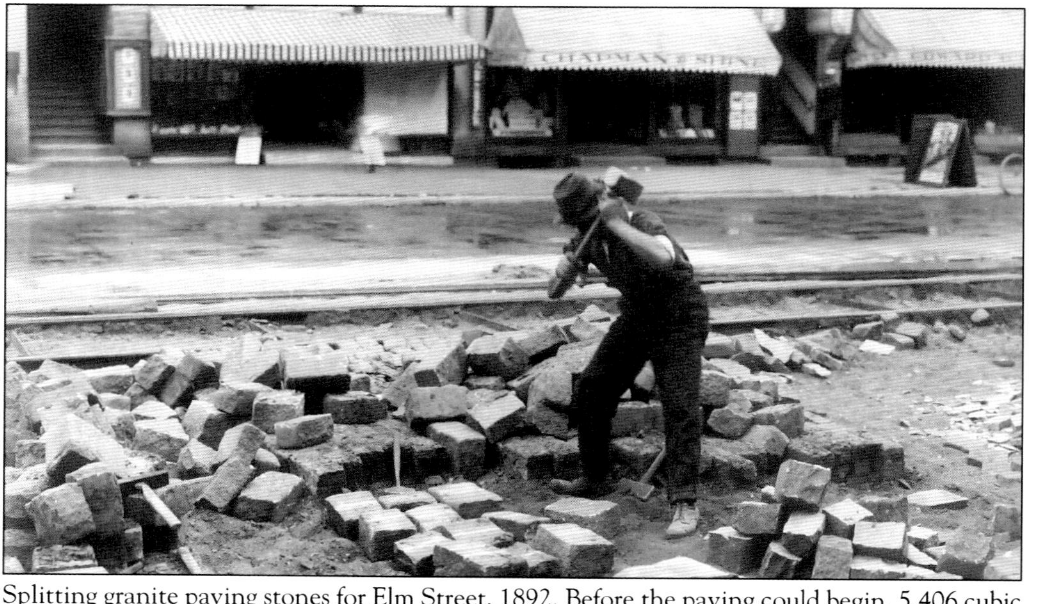

Splitting granite paving stones for Elm Street, 1892. Before the paving could begin, 5,406 cubic yards of gravel were excavated from Elm Street, and "4,300 cubic yards of sand were used for refilling" to prepare the street for the granite paving stones. The gravel removed was placed on Clinton, Phelps, Green, and Holland Avenues, along with Mechanic, Bartlett, Orange, Sackett, Arnold, North Elm, Pearl, and Grant Streets.

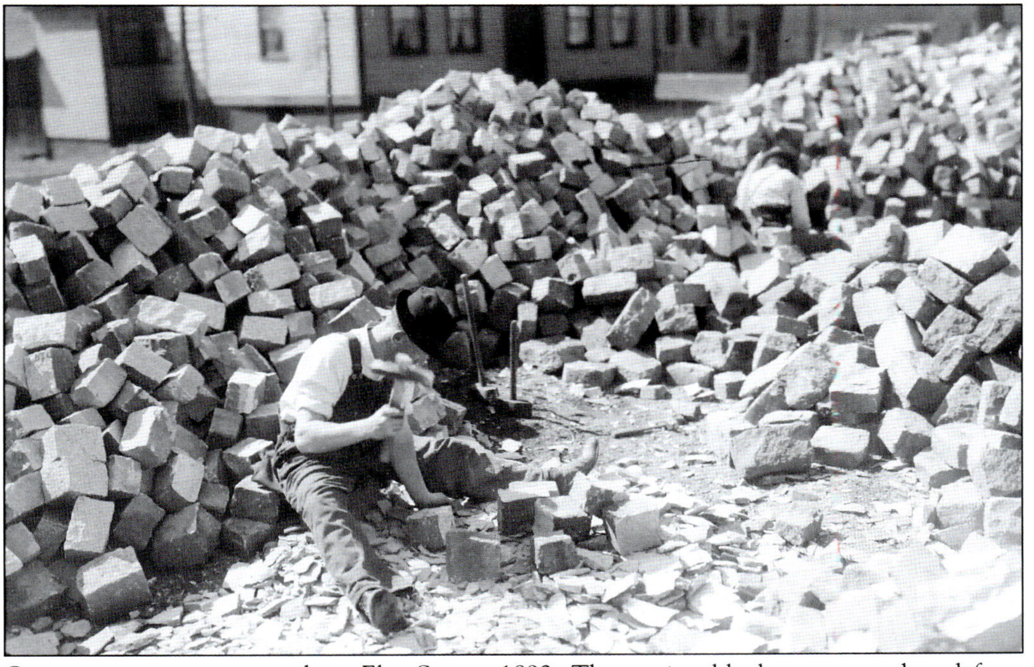

Granite paving stones used on Elm Street, 1892. The paving blocks were purchased from Hudson and Chester Granite Company for "$1.62 1/2 per yard measured in place." Laying the pavement was completed by the M.H. Mullen Company of Jersey City, New Jersey.

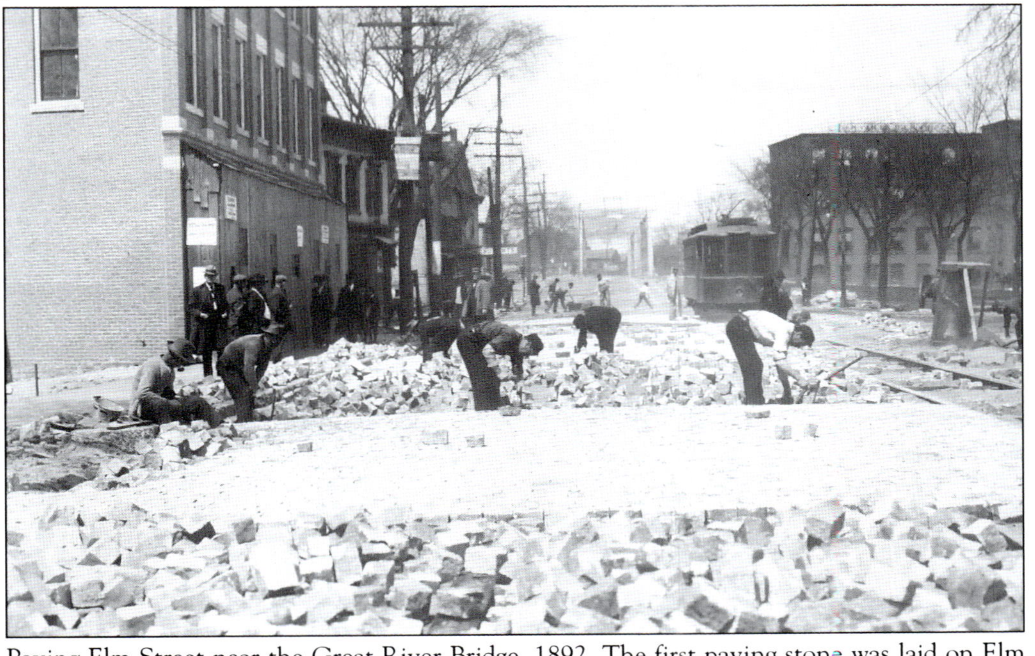

Paving Elm Street near the Great River Bridge, 1892. The first paving stone was laid on Elm Street on June 14, 1892. Six weeks later the last stone on the east side of the street railway was put in near the Great River Bridge. The pavers continued working, and the street was completed in the middle of September.

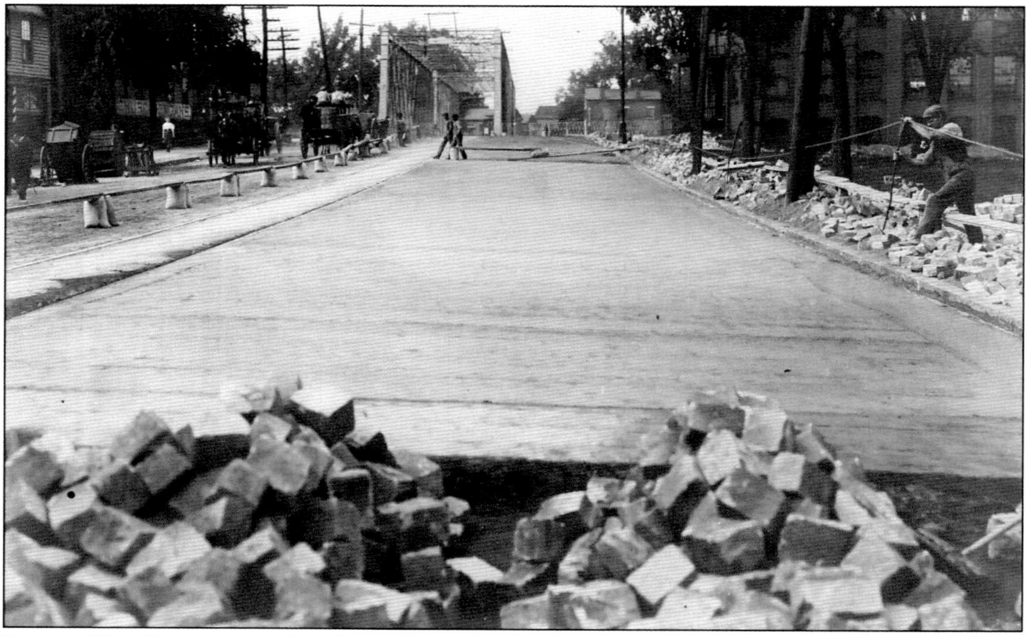

Paving Elm Street near the Great River Bridge, 1892. The waste stone from paving Elm Street was used to fill in areas of the dike which were wearing away on the west side of the Great River Bridge.

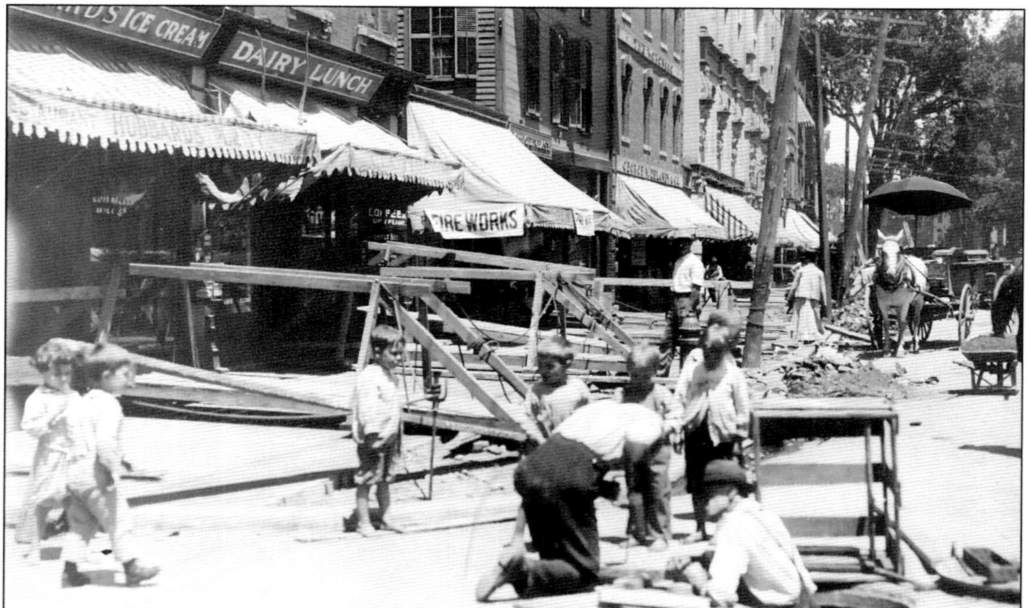

Children watching the men working on Elm Street, 1892. Along with paving the street in 1892, the Town of Westfield repaired the walks on the west side of Elm Street and laid a new concrete walk on the east side, from Meadow Street south. Also, provisions were made for the care of surface water "requiring twenty-two catch basins and the laying of about three hundred feet of extra sewer."

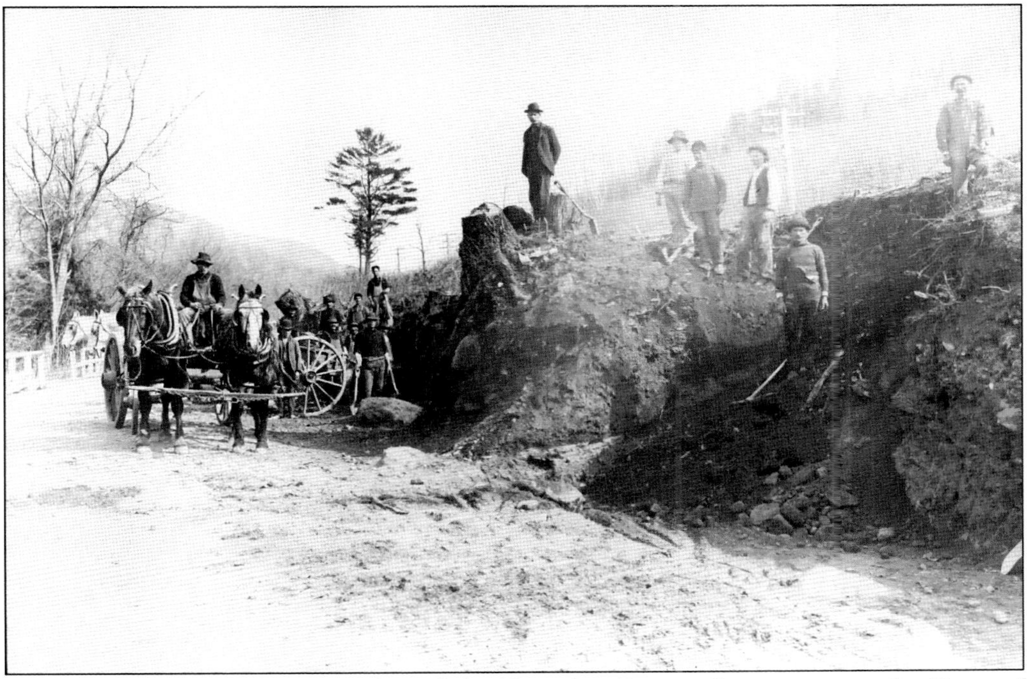

Russell Road, 1891. Following orders of the Hampden County Commissioners, the Town of Westfield made improvements to Russell Road. In 1891 this work cost the town $567.50.

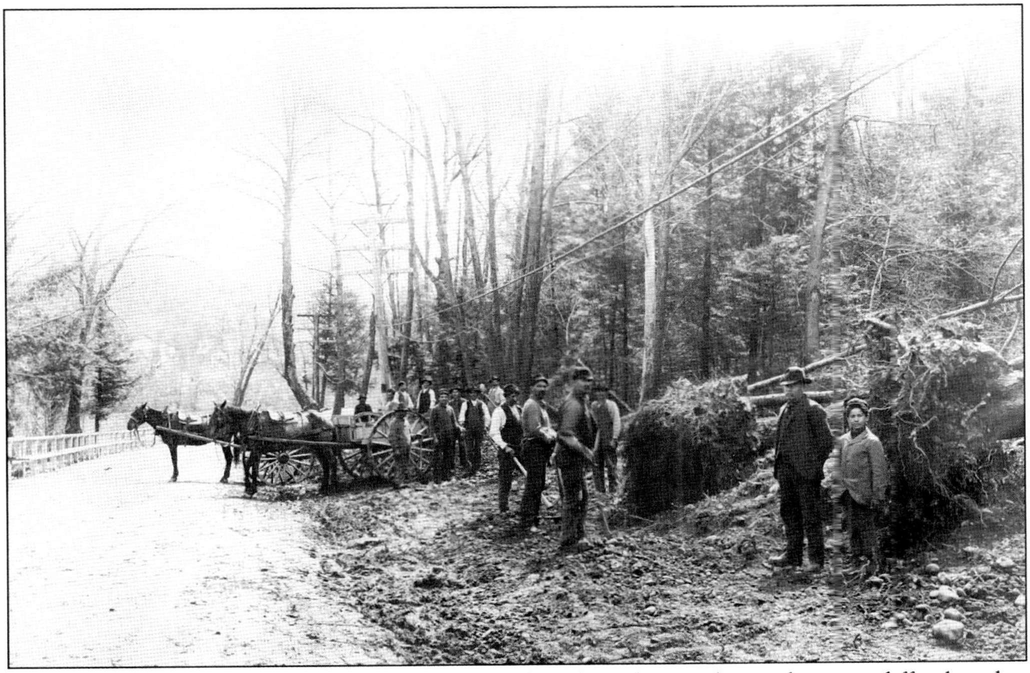

Russell Road, 1891. Trees that had to be uprooted made widening the road a more difficult task.

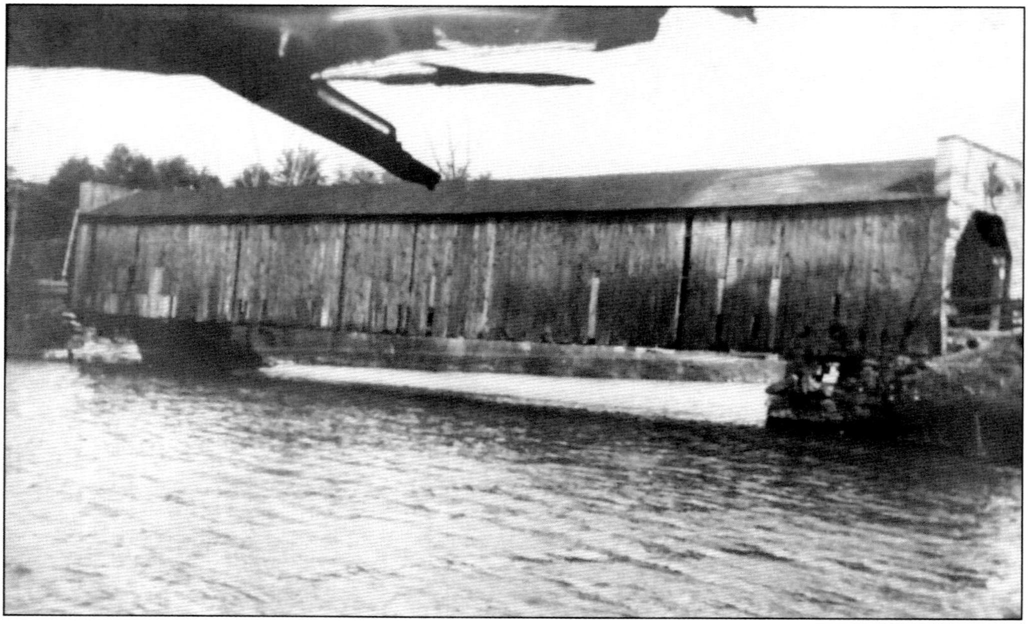

Horton's Bridge, pre-1914. From this view looking east, the covered bridge over the Little River on Granville Road was built in 1835 at a cost of $2,150. In 1882 it was found to be in "a bad condition" and "would have gone into the river in a few weeks if not attended to." The bridge was reinforced with a heavy frame at each end and with the new retaining walls, became "as strong as when first made."

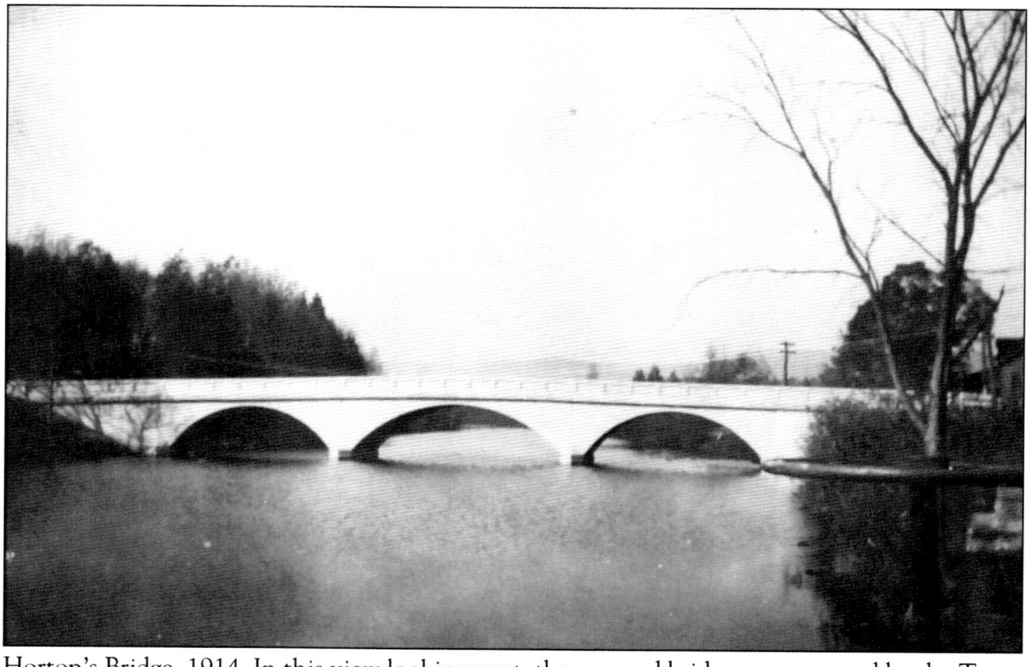

Horton's Bridge, 1914. In this view looking west, the covered bridge was removed by the Town of Westfield on June 2, 1914. Simpson Brothers of Boston was awarded the contract to build the new bridge.

Horton's Bridge, seen pre-1914 in this view looking north. On April 7, 1914, this old, covered wooden lattice truss bridge was ordered closed to travel. The town voted to replace this bridge with a reinforced concrete bridge.

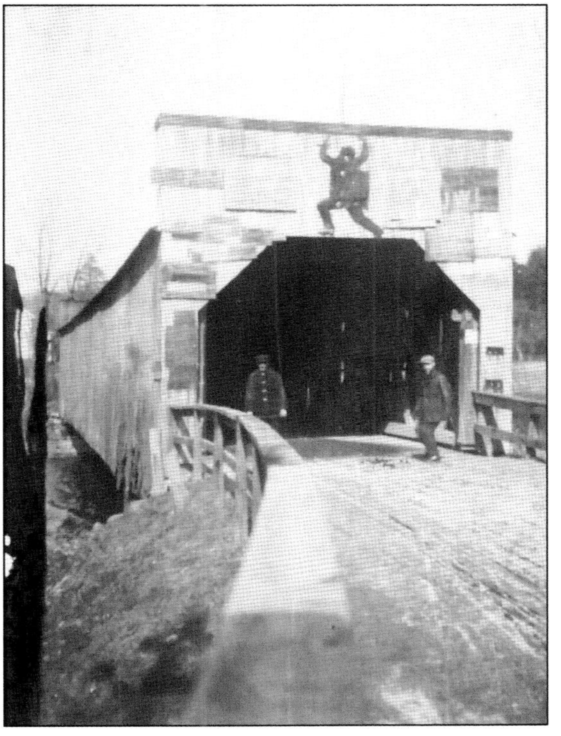

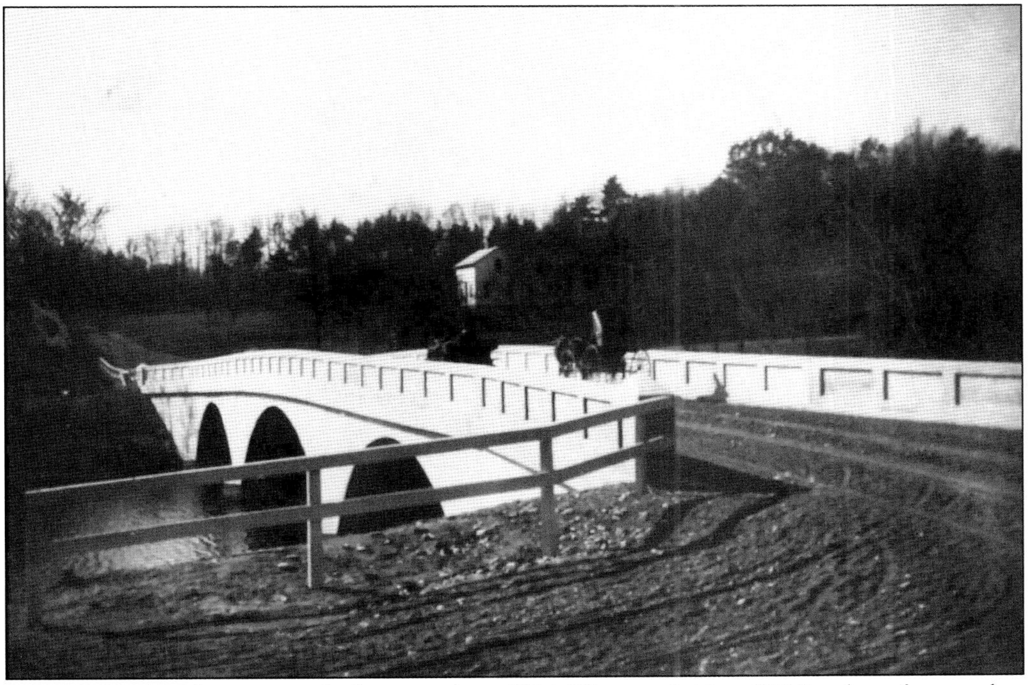

Horton's Bridge, from a view looking south in 1914. The new bridge, 218 feet long from end to end of the wing walls, was completed on October 17, 1914. The bridge has one 50-foot and two 40-foot arch spans. The 24-foot clear roadway was opened for travel on September 16, 1914.

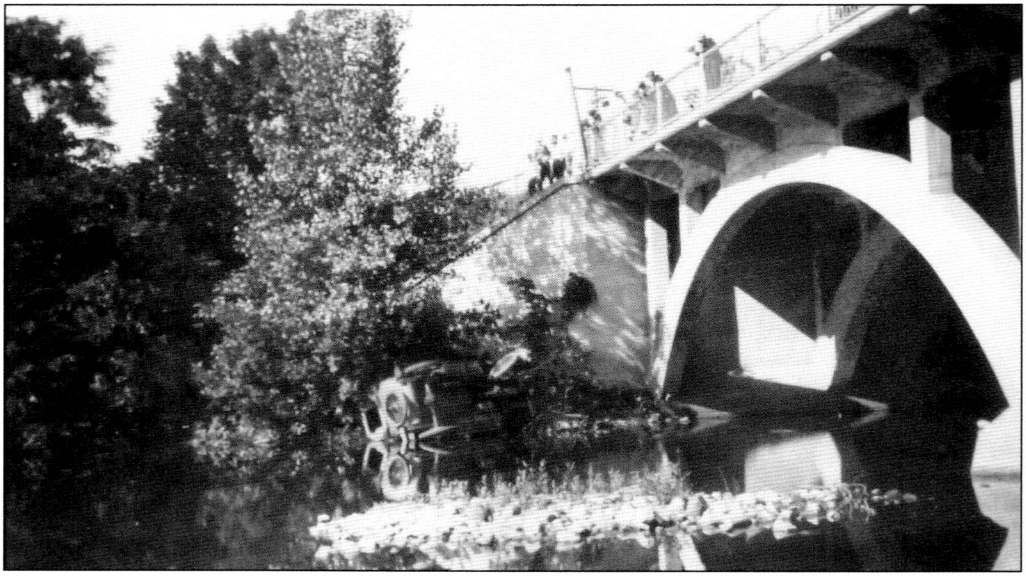

Accident at Cowles Bridge, June 1925. Stanley Szuba of the Tannery Road area in Westfield lost control of his car when his left front tire blew out. The car went off the road, turned a complete somersault and plunged 30 feet into the Little River. Szuba clung to the steering wheel during the accident and walked away with only a few cuts and bruises.

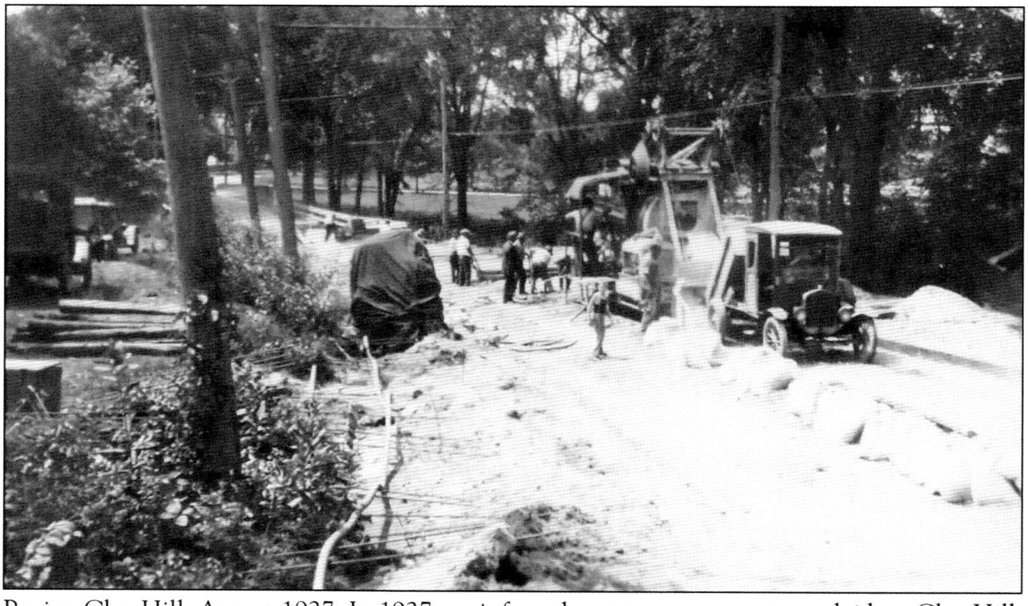

Paving Clay Hill, August 1927. In 1927 a reinforced concrete pavement was laid on Clay Hill, from north of Powder Mill Brook to just beyond the railroad bridge. This same area is being rebuilt today.

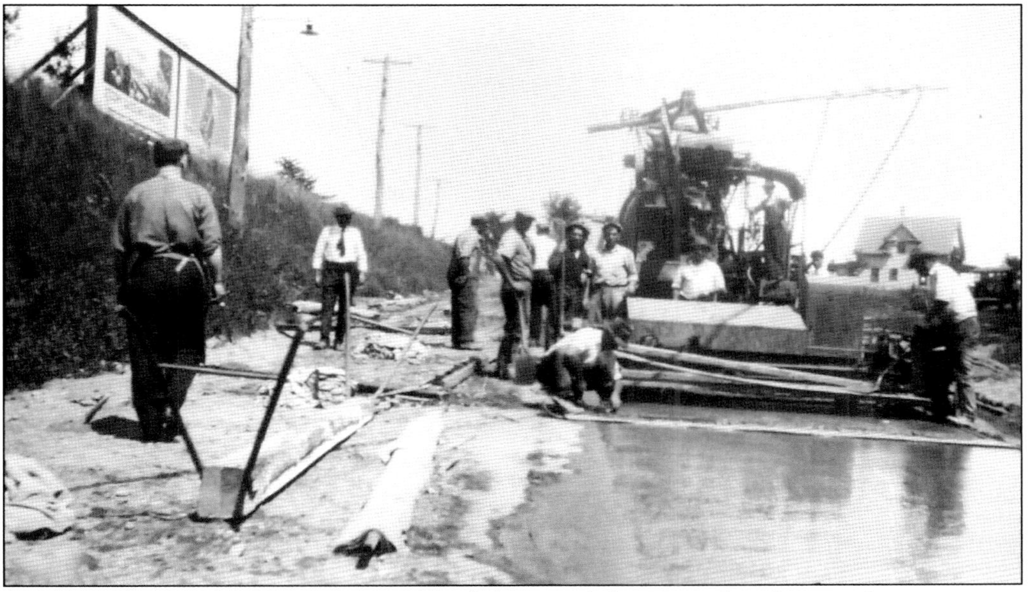

Paving Clay Hill, 1927. In 1920 a special decree of the Hampden County Commissioners ordered construction on College Highway. Paving Clay Hill was the final project of this order.

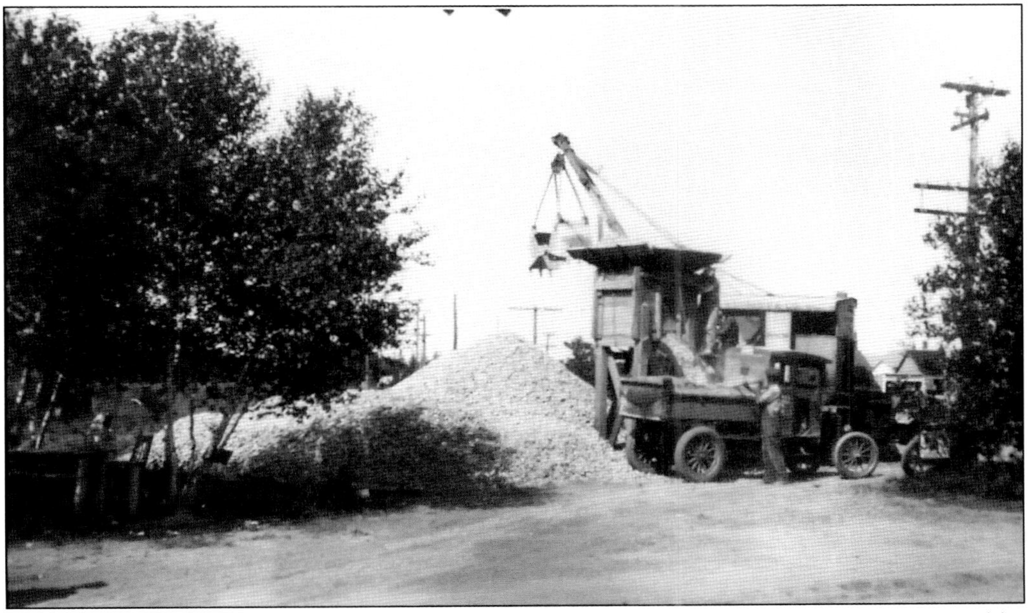

Paving Clay Hill, 1927. According to the *Annual Report* of the superintendent of public works, O.E. Parks, "The concrete section is twenty feet in width and eight inches in thickness. Combination shoulders and gutters, average width of about six feet of asphalt penetration macadam was laid the entire length of both sides of the road." The work was completed by Daniel O'Connell Sons, Inc., of Holyoke.

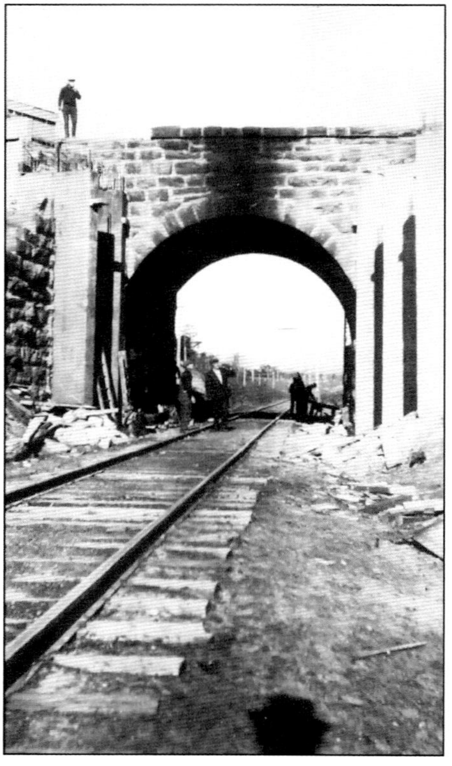

Clay Hill Bridge, 1927. "The narrow bridge on a bad curve at the top of Clay Hill was a dangerous spot," according to the *Westfield Valley Herald*. In 1926 the county commissioners ordered the City of Westfield to make alterations "at the crossing of the Northampton Road over the tracks of the Holyoke and Westfield Railroad."

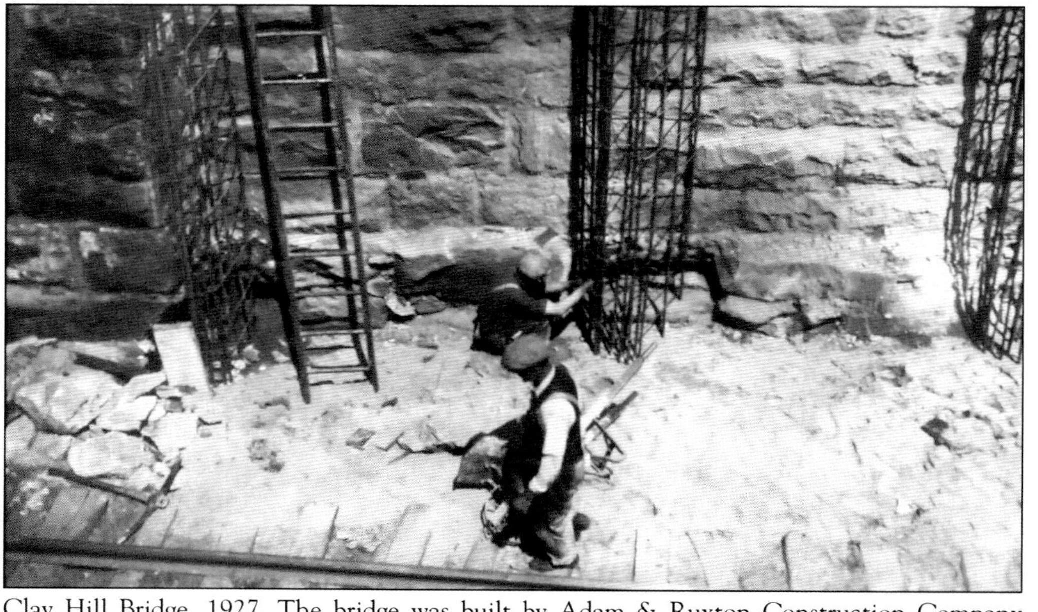

Clay Hill Bridge, 1927. The bridge was built by Adam & Ruxton Construction Company of Springfield. Daniel O'Connell Sons, Inc. completed the road surfacing. Future roadwork became the responsibility of the City, and future bridge repairs were the responsibility of the railroad. The cost of this project was shared by the New York, New Haven & Hartford Railroad ($4,487.43), Hampden County ($4,487.43), and the City of Westfield ($9,815.84).

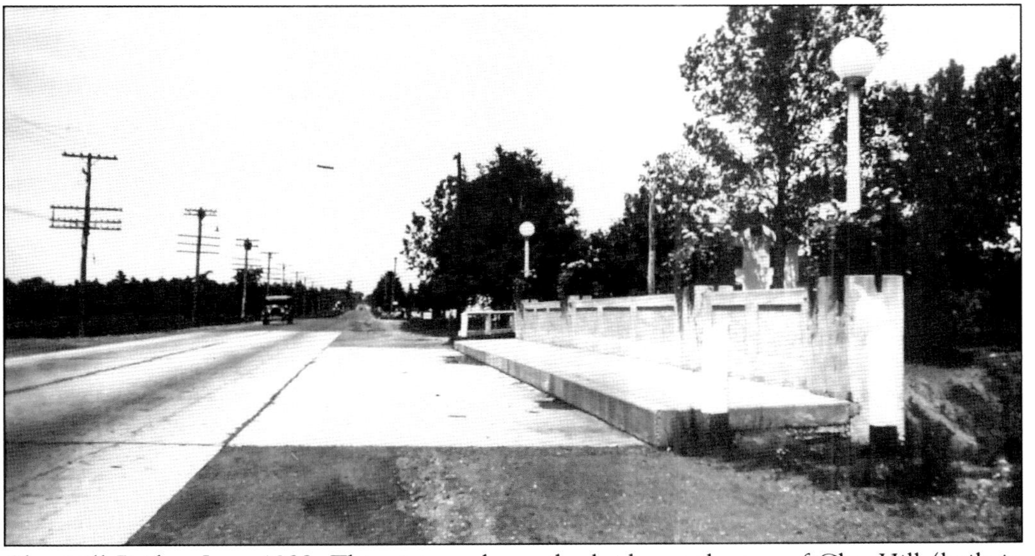

Clay Hill Bridge, June 1933. This picture shows the bridge at the top of Clay Hill (built in 1927) as it looked in 1933. This view was taken looking north towards the current turnpike entrance. The Clay Hill Bridge is being rebuilt today.

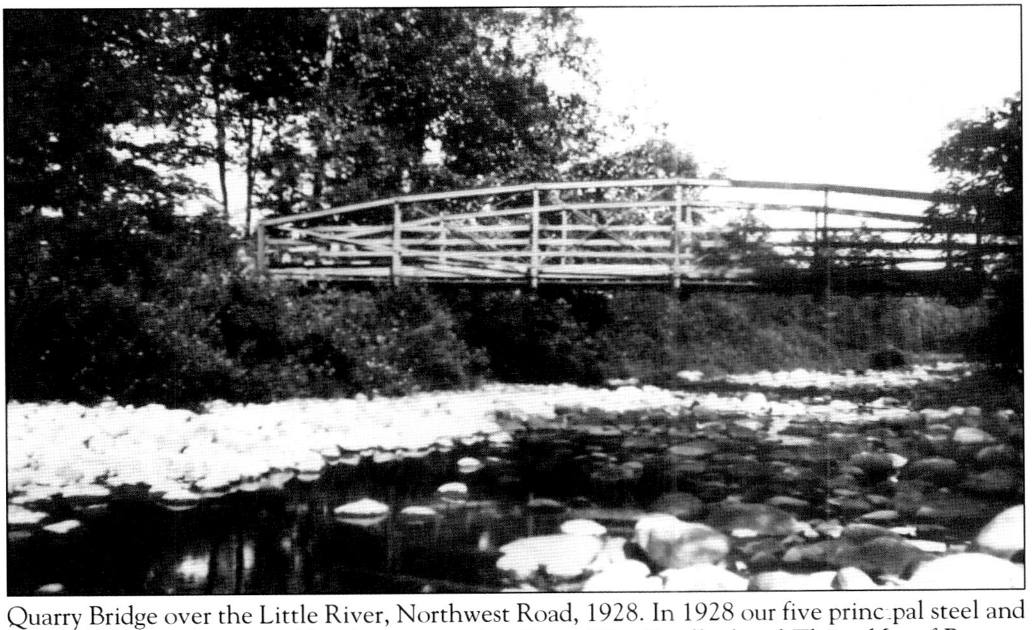

Quarry Bridge over the Little River, Northwest Road, 1928. In 1928 our five principal steel and iron bridges were inspected by the engineering firm of Fay Spofford and Thorndike of Boston, Massachusetts. The Quarry Bridge, built in 1887, was found "not suitable for loads in excess of six tons and was so posted." This historic lenticular bridge was closed in 1995.

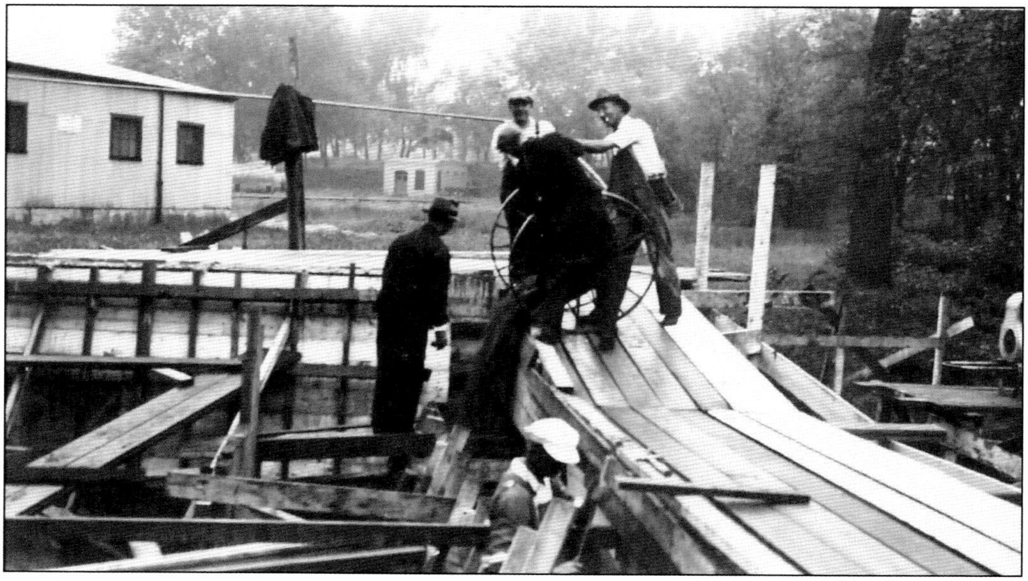

North Elm Street Bridge over Powder Mill Brook, September 1933. When building this reinforced concrete slab bridge, "portions of the stone masonry in the abutments of the old bridge were utilized in the new construction."

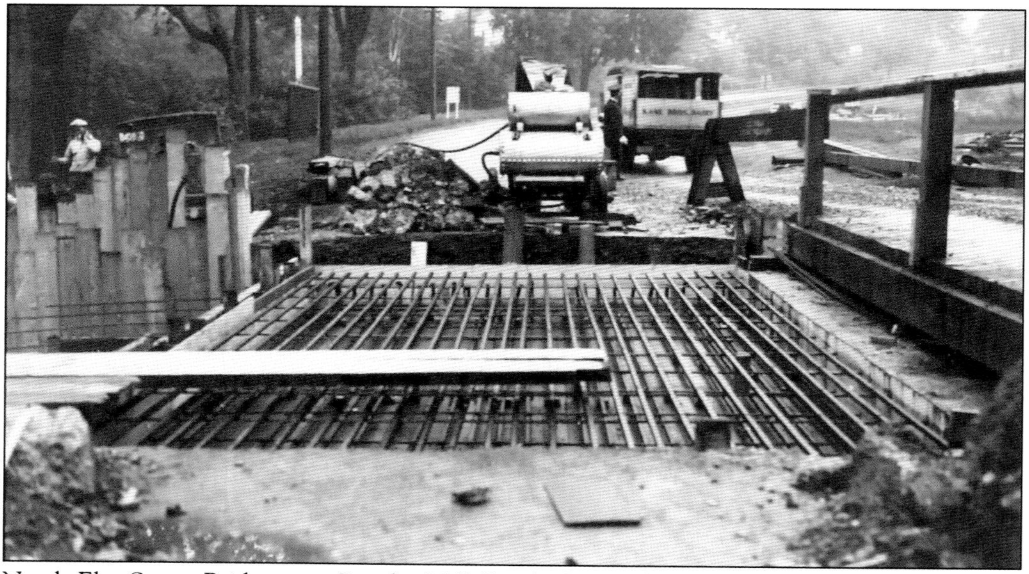

North Elm Street Bridge over Powder Mill Brook, September 1933. The cost of constructing this 20-foot bridge was shared between the State of Massachusetts ($4,000), Hampden County ($2,000), and the City of Westfield ($3,146.64). This bridge is also being rebuilt today.

Union Street Bridge, June 1933. Soldier's Relief workers are shown pouring a concrete abutment on the bridge over Sandy Mill Brook, converting the wooden decked bridge to concrete. The cost to the City of Westfield was $2,231.64.

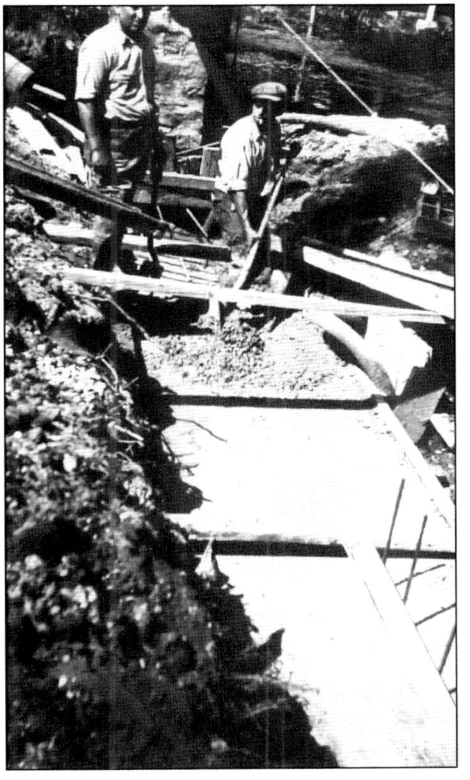

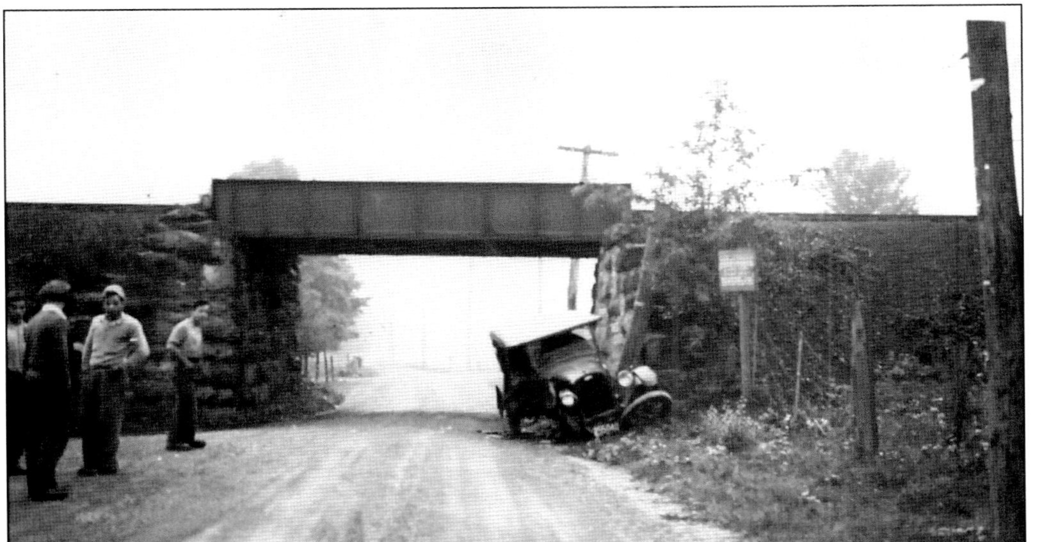

Accident at East Mountain Road, September 20, 1933. This Model T went off the road on East Mountain Road near Holyoke Road. The men looking on are probably Soldier's Relief workers who had been working on a culvert on East Mountain Road at that time.

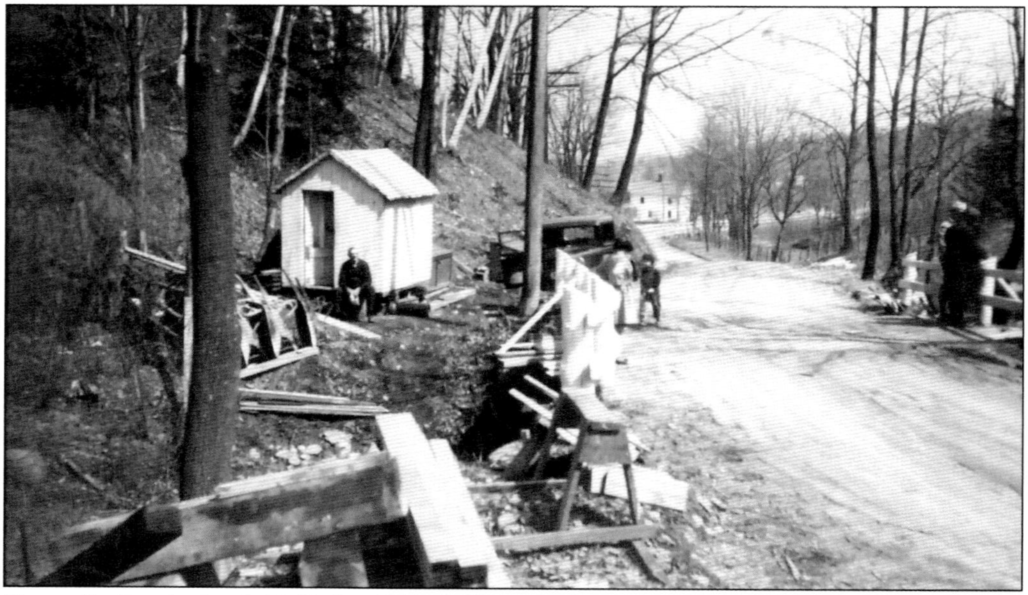

Granville Road, April 1933. In 1933 Soldier's Relief workers built a new concrete bridge on Granville Road "west of Mundale Filters." The former service men who worked on the bridges and highways typically worked three days a week. This 6-foot bridge cost the City of Westfield $1,651.21.

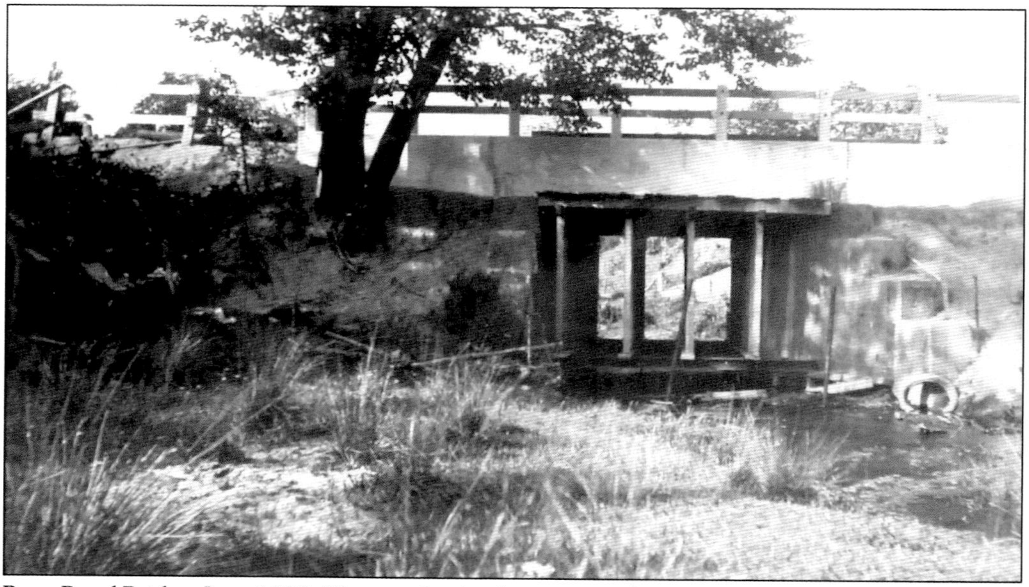

Root Road Bridge, June 1933. The wooden bridge over Timber Swamp Brook was rebuilt in 1933 by Soldier's Relief workers. Following a five percent wage cut for city employees in 1932, the recipients of Soldier's Relief received a ten percent cut in 1933, reducing their wages from 50¢ per hour to 45¢ per hour. This 10-foot concrete bridge was constructed at a cost of $909.25.

Eight

The Younger Set

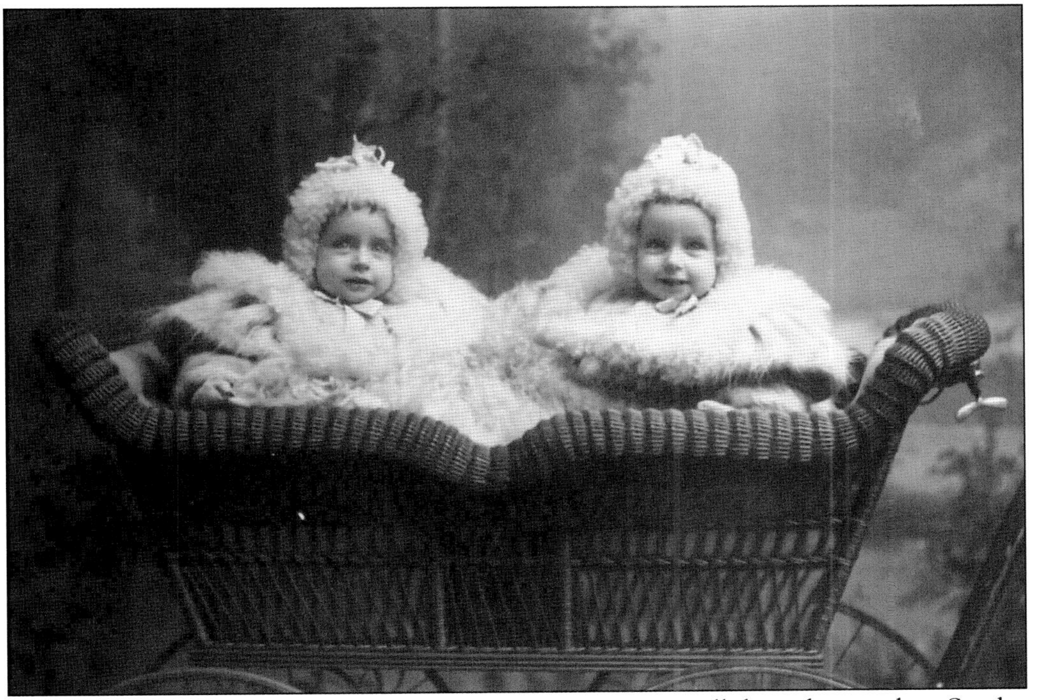

Out for a stroll in 1895. These babies, Irene and Margaret, are all dressed up in their Sunday best as they sit in their wicker carriage.

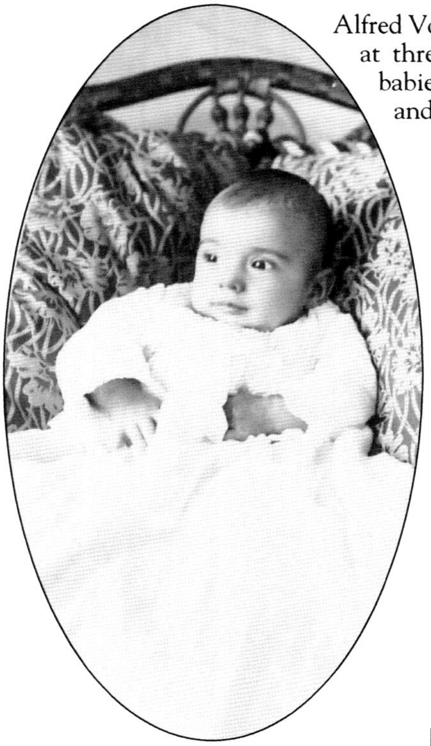

Alfred Vondell. This beautiful, wide-eyed baby is Alfred Vondell at three months old. During this era it was customary for babies of both sexes to wear long dresses trimmed with lace and fine embroidery.

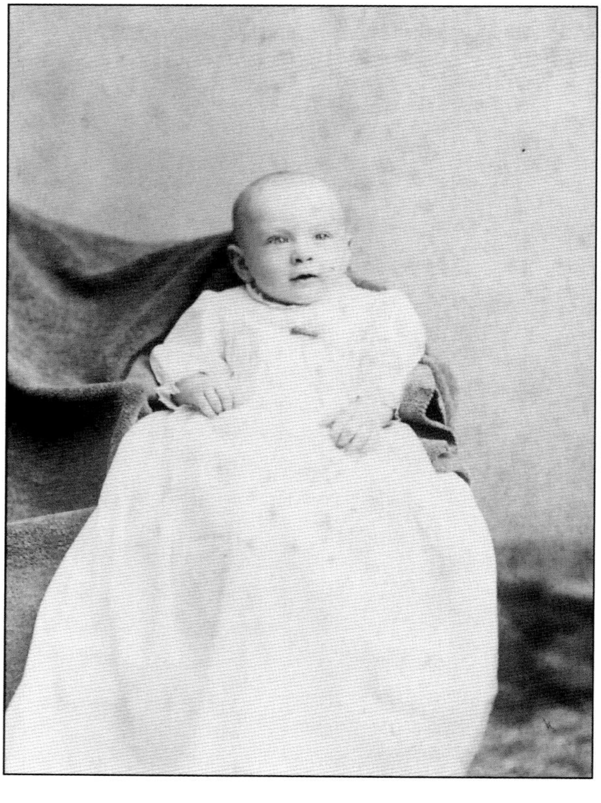

Merrill F. Hosmer, late 1890s. He later became a physician.

Thelma Louise Vondell. At age ten-and-a-half months, Thelma is all dressed up for the photographer.

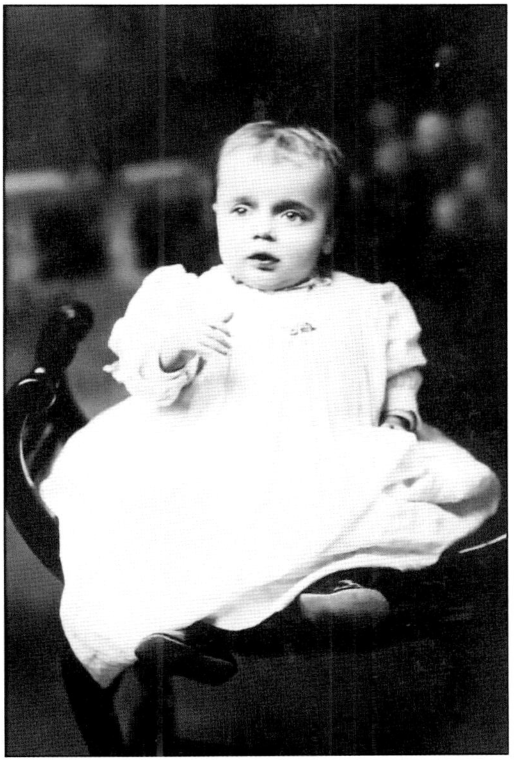

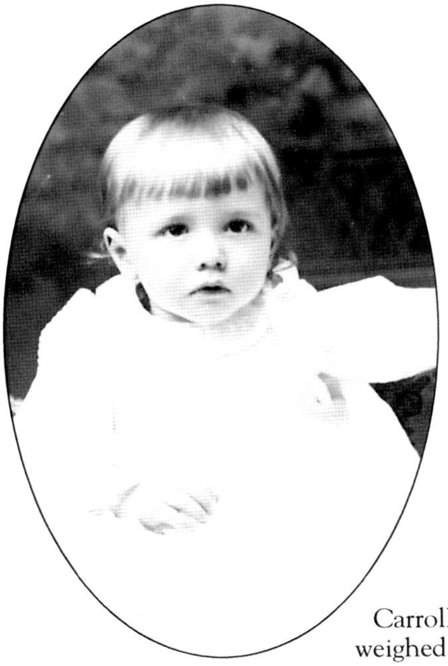

Carroll Barnes Allen. At age twenty-one months, Carroll weighed 24 pounds.

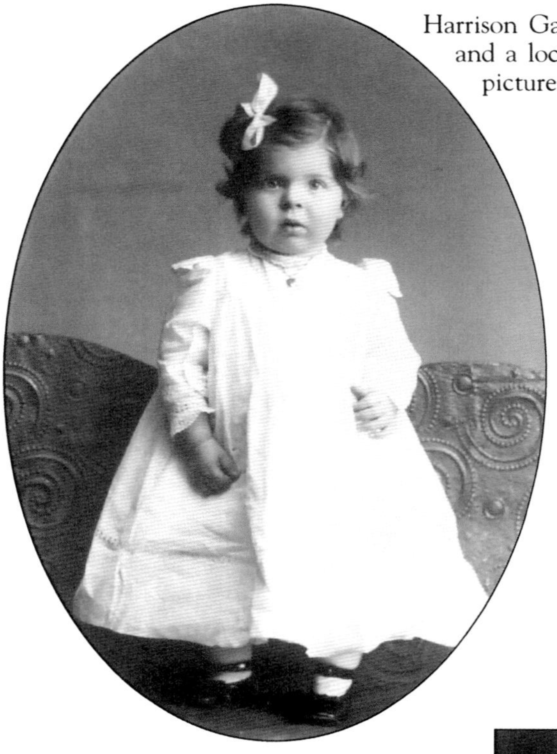

Harrison Gates White. Shown wearing a hair ribbon and a locket, Harrison was one year old when this picture was taken on February 10, 1903.

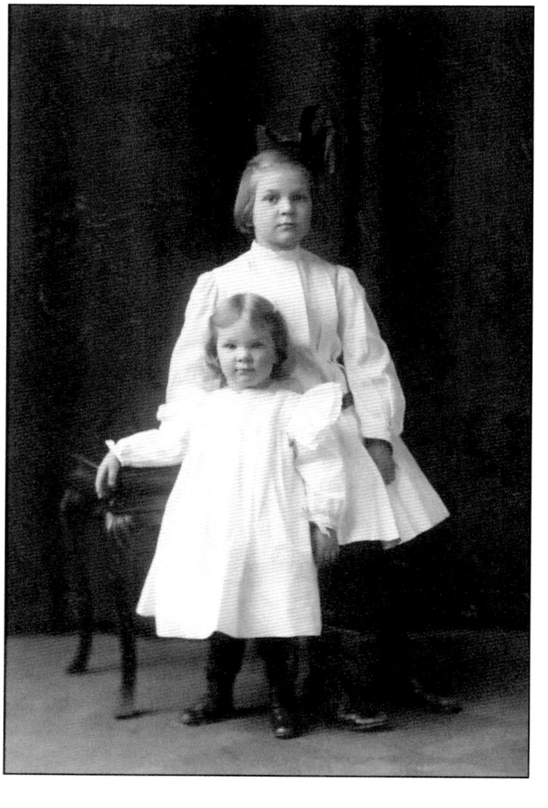

Howard sisters. All dressed in white, Elizabeth E. Howard (age six) poses with her sister, Madeline F. Howard (age two years and six months).

Ward Rees (from a tintype). Born in 1864, Ward is shown here wearing a cerise dress without the leggings. Little boys in those days wore dresses until they went to school. He later became a druggist and a city assessor. He lived at 11 Shepard Street. (See also page 27.)

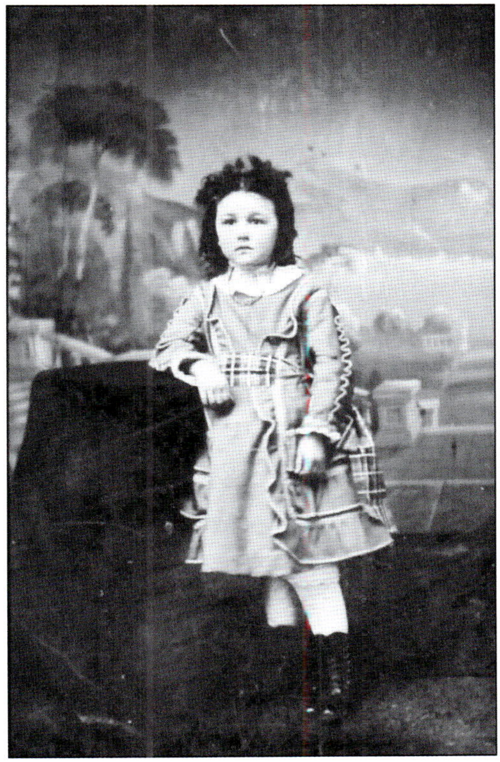

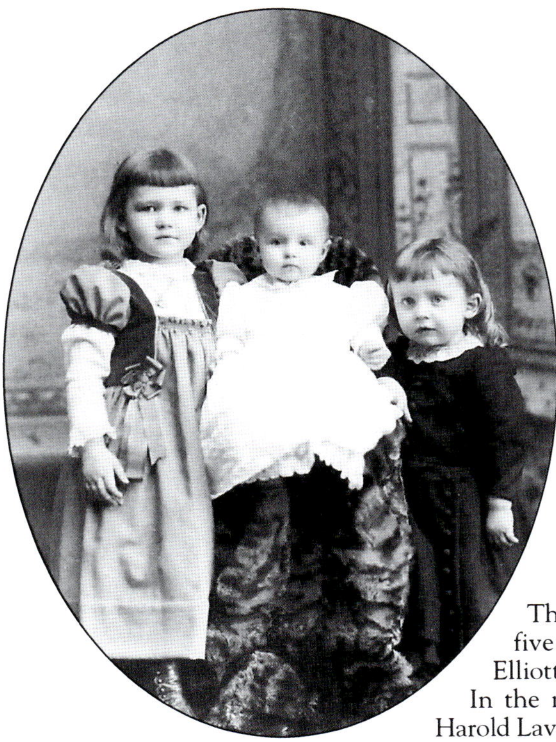

Three Allen children. Ethel Grace (nearly five years old) stands on the left with Raymond Elliott Allen (nearly three years old) on the right. In the middle between his sister and brother sits Harold Lavelle Allen, age eight months.

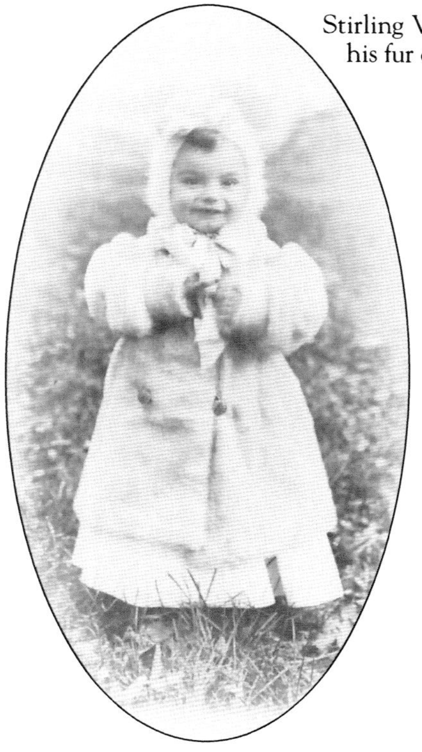

Stirling Vondell, age two. Stirling smiles proudly as he shows off his fur coat and hat.

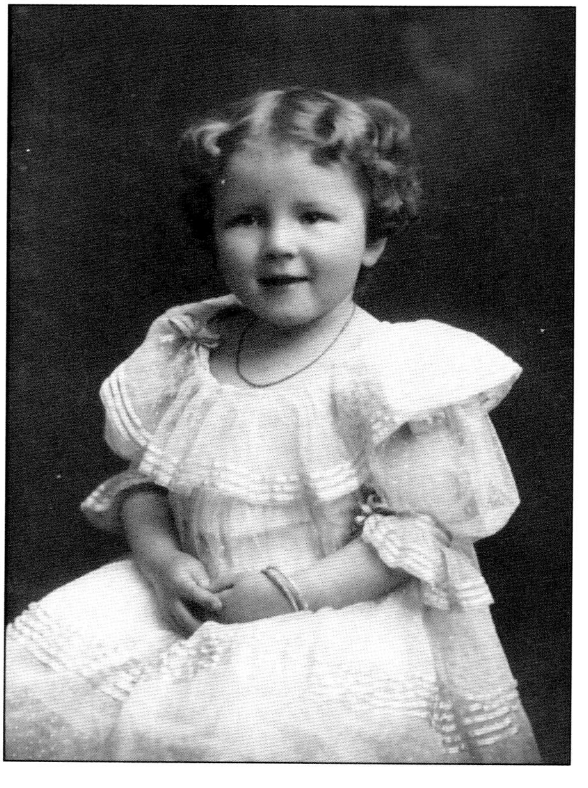

Katherine J. Dean. At age three, Katherine is sitting pretty in a beautiful dress of dotted swiss with ribbon trim.

Johnnie Mahoney. Corkscrew curls like Johnnie's were a fashionable hairstyle for children in the early 1900s.

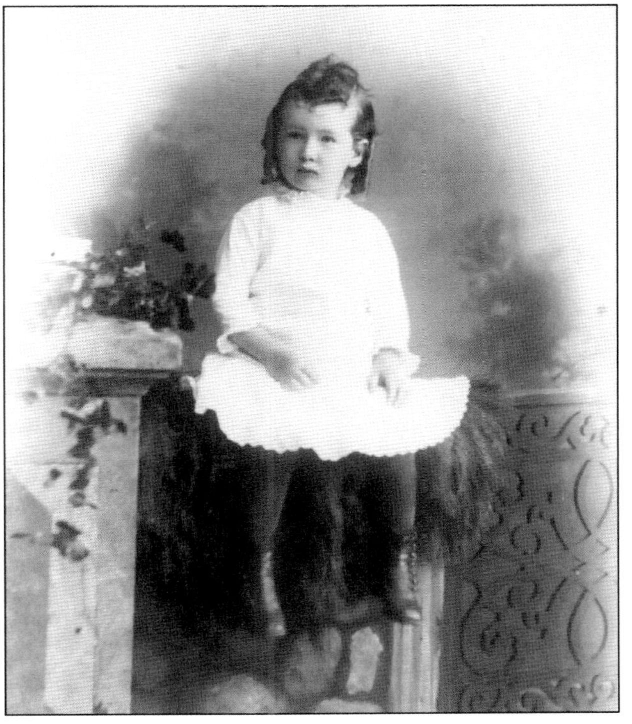

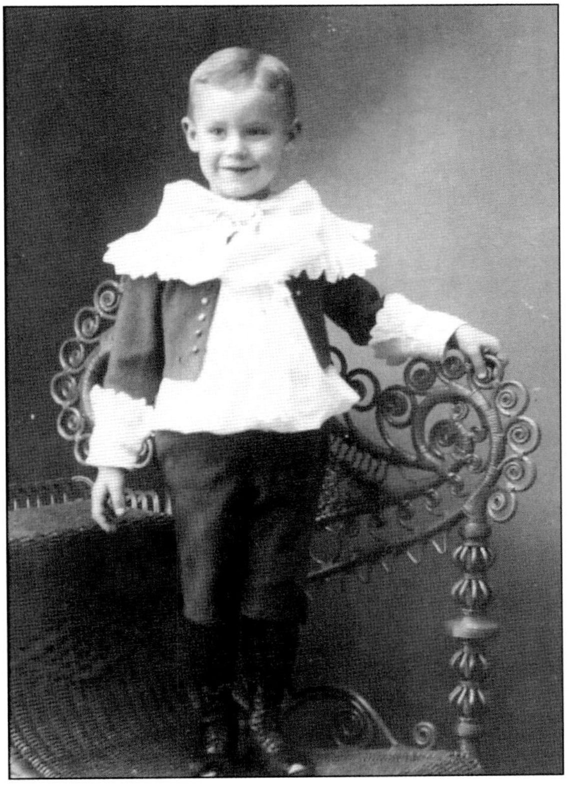

In the Lord Fauntleroy style. Boys' clothing in the 1890s was influenced by illustrations in Frances Hodgson Burnett's novel *Little Lord Fauntleroy*. This style is illustrated here in the fancy collar and cuffs and the knee-length breeches worn by this handsome young boy.

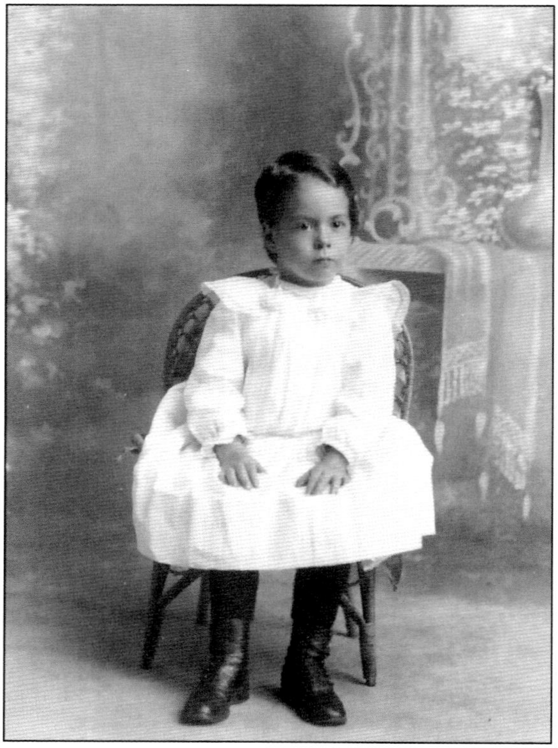

Gertrude Sackett. This cute little girl grew up in Westfield. In 1909 she lived at the Alquat Hotel and was working as a clerk at M.C. Ryan's.

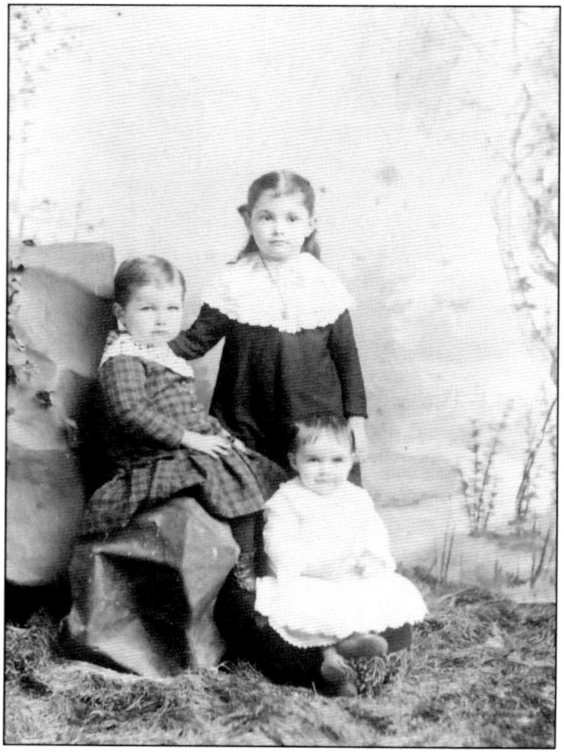

Cone sisters with their brother. Cora Viola Cone (six years and six months old) stands behind her brother, Leon Clinton Cone (three years and one month old) and younger sister, Millie Parks Cone (one year and two months old).

Mary and Lorenzo Lambson, ages six and four years old. This lovely portrait was done by F.J. Tooke Studio at 32 Elm Street. Their specialty was portraits, and many Westfield families will remember having had their pictures taken there.

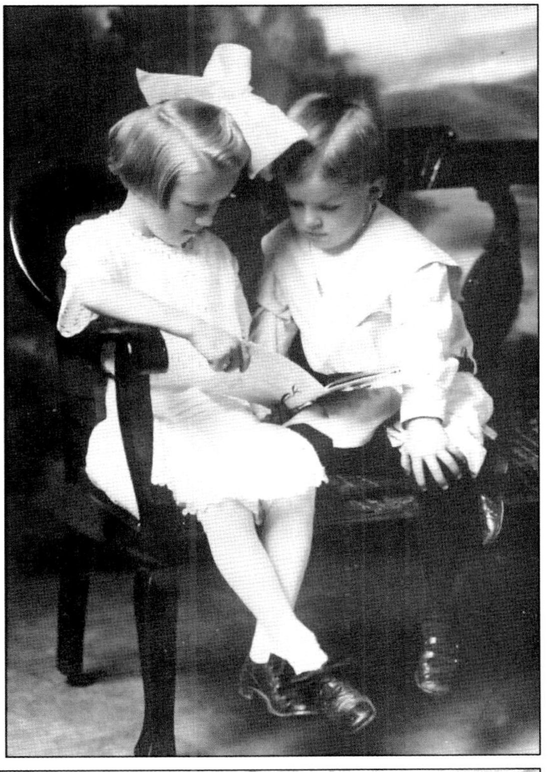

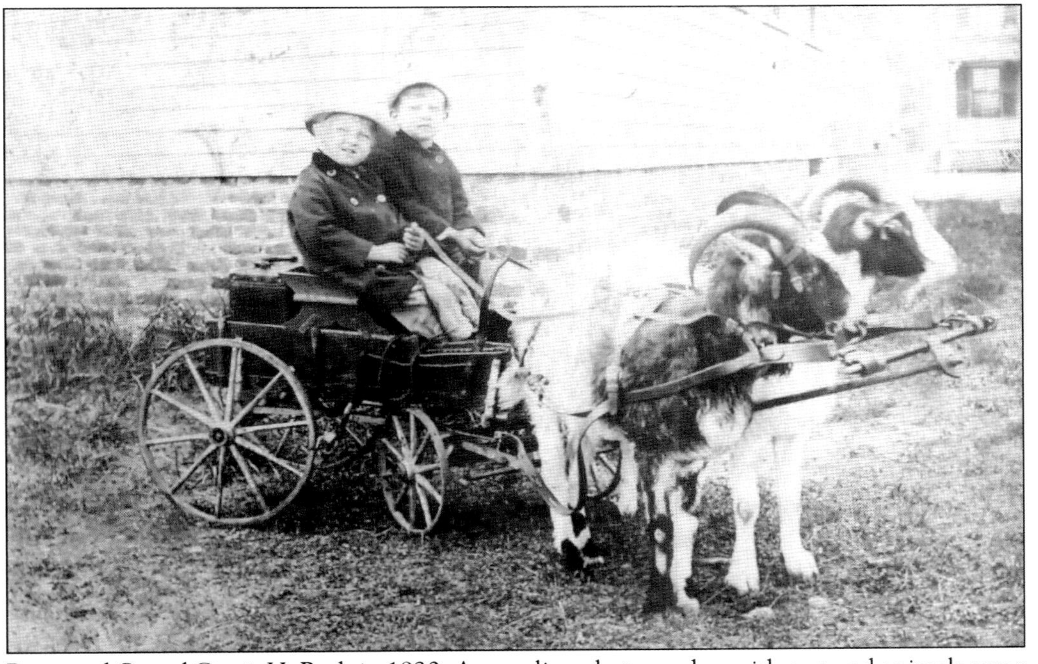

Raymond C. and Curtis H. Bush in 1920. A traveling photographer with cart and animals came to the Bush home at 25 Harrison Avenue and took this picture of the two boys. Raymond was six years old at the time.

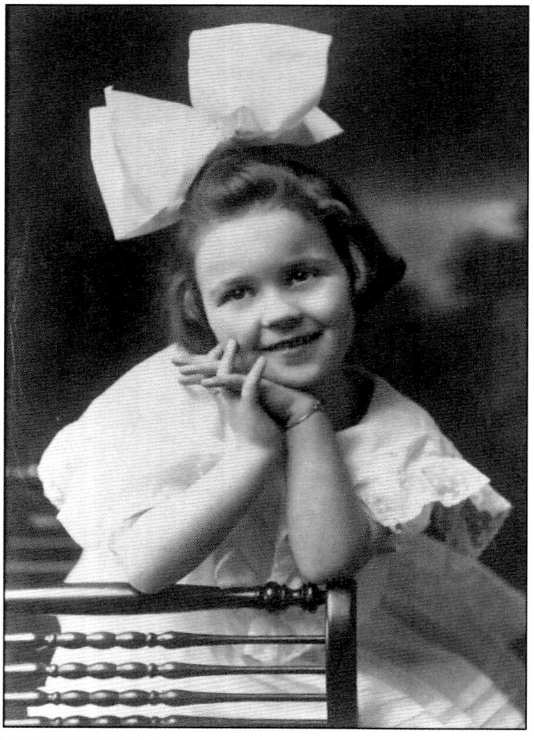

Marjorie Ellis in 1915. Wearing a large hair bow was a popular style for little girls in the early 1900s, so Marjorie certainly was in style!

The Patterson children, 1910. These children are holding toys that are still popular today. Paul has a kite, Margaret a doll, and Norman seems to have a yo-yo hidden in his hands (notice the string around his middle finger).

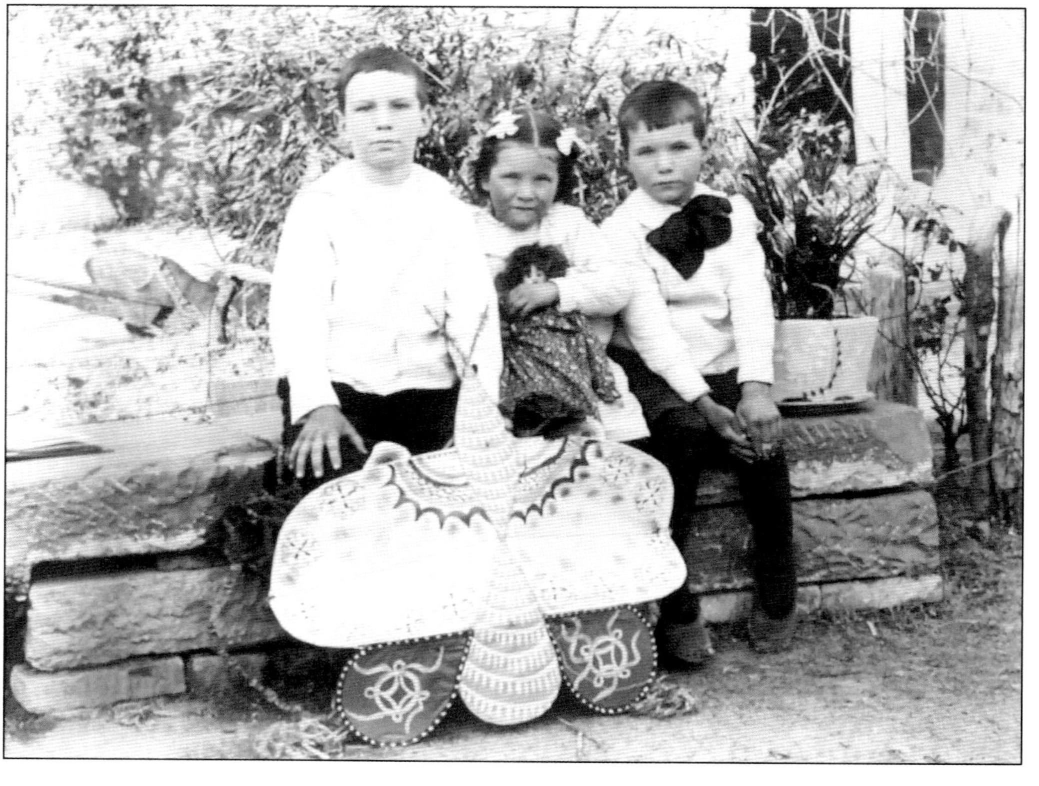

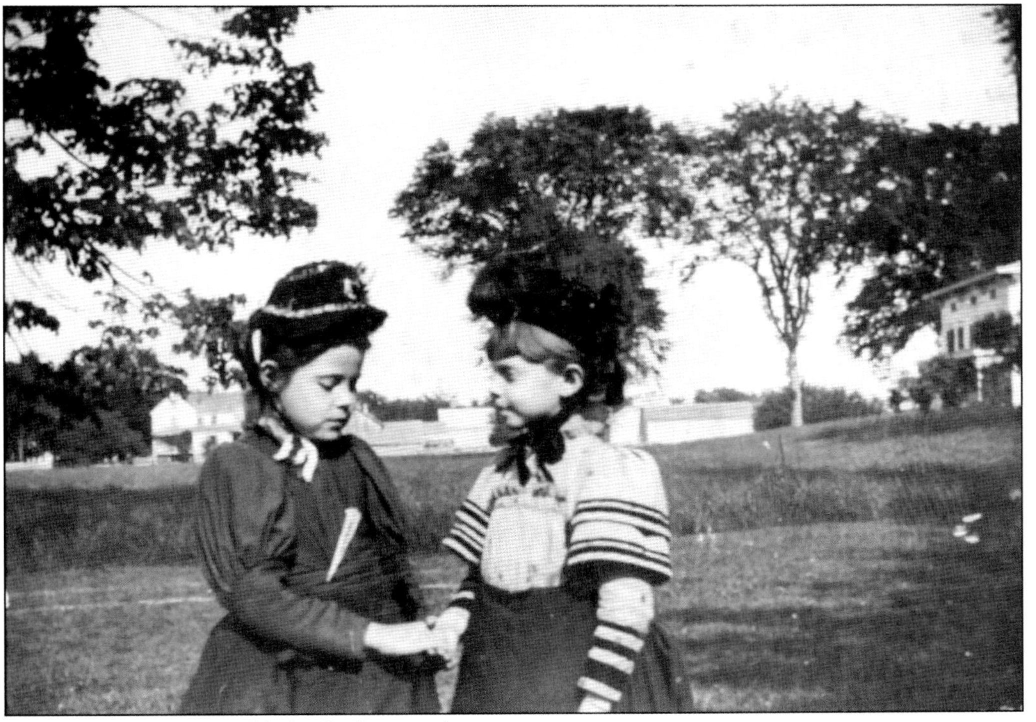

Dressing up. Here are Gladys Perkins and Eloise Fowler playing on the grounds of the Laflin's home sometime prior to 1896. The house on the right with the narrow piazza is located at 30 West Silver Street.

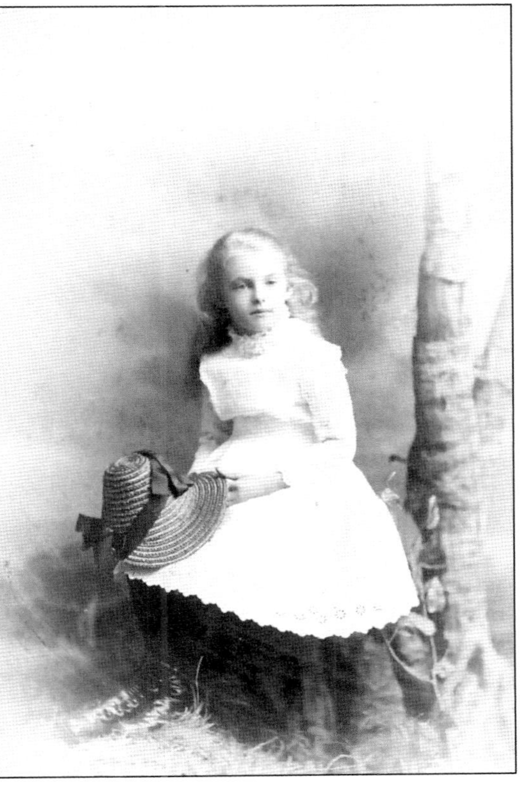

Ethel Sackett. This little girl looks quite elegant in her beautiful lace dress as she holds a large straw hat.

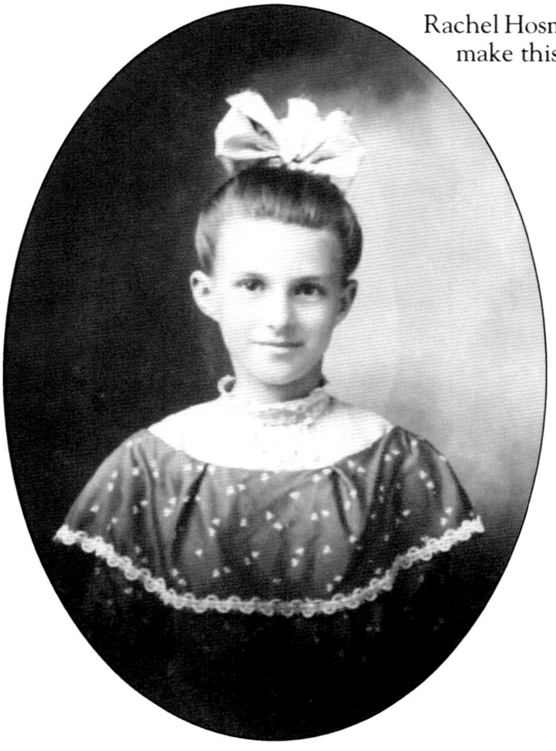

Rachel Hosmer. A cape collar and sophisticated hairstyle make this young lady look quite grown up.

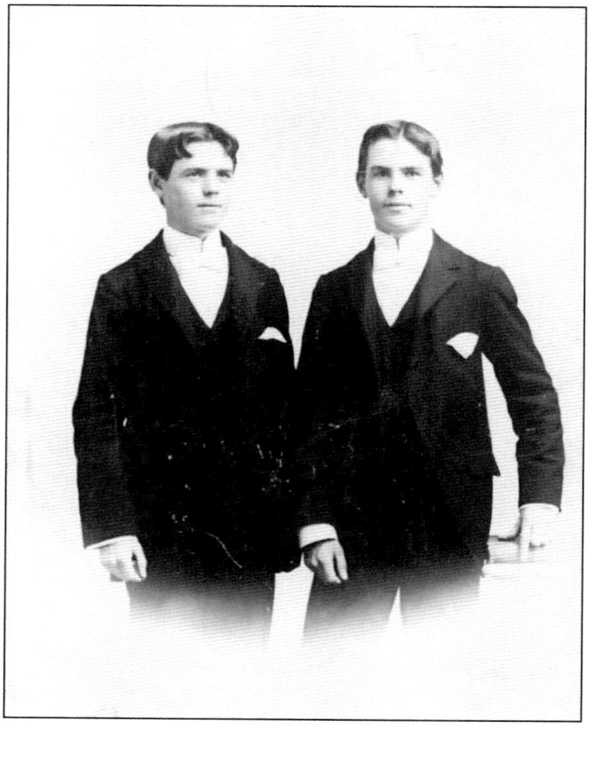

The Stiles brothers. These fine looking boys grew up to be well known in Westfield. Charles D. Stiles (on the left) became an accountant and lived on Ridgeview Terrace in 1920. Chester H. Stiles (on the right) became superintendent of schools.

Nine

Schools and Sports

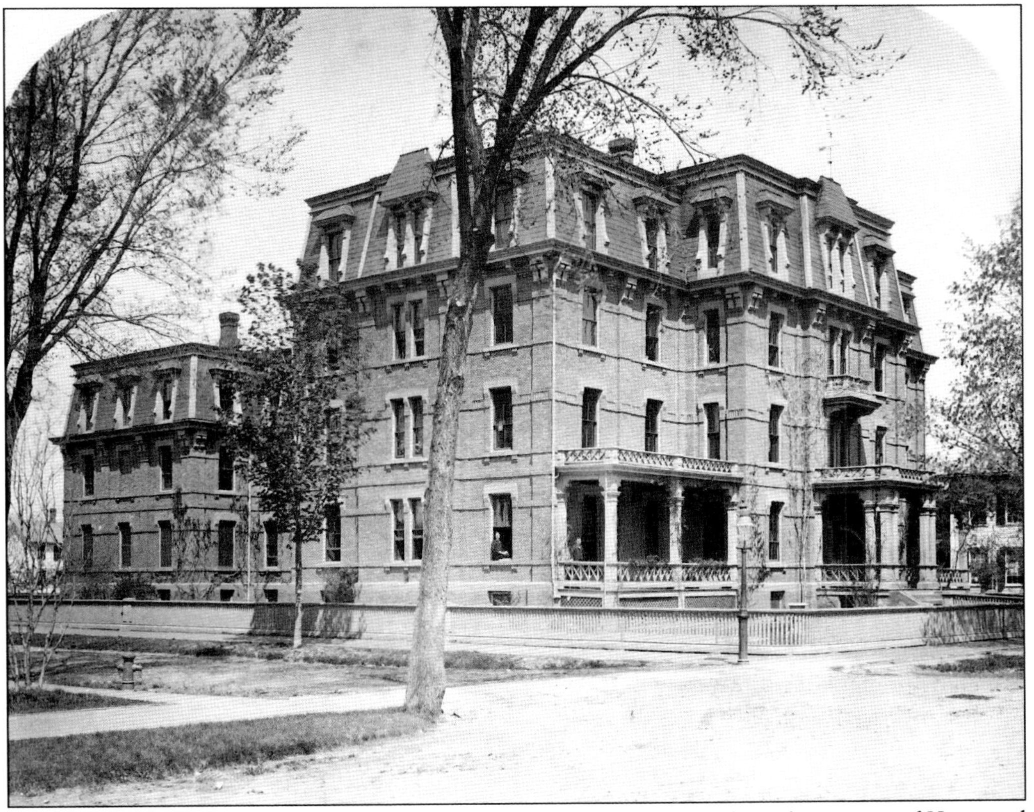

State Normal School Boarding House, 1874. This building, located on the corner of King and Washington Streets, was erected in 1874. It was a dormitory for the State Normal School and was known as Normal Hall. It provided quarters for 175 residents at $3.75 a week and was used for three decades. Later, it became the Alquat, the Washington Hotel, and the Pilgrim Hotel. The building was destroyed by fire on January 8, 1971.

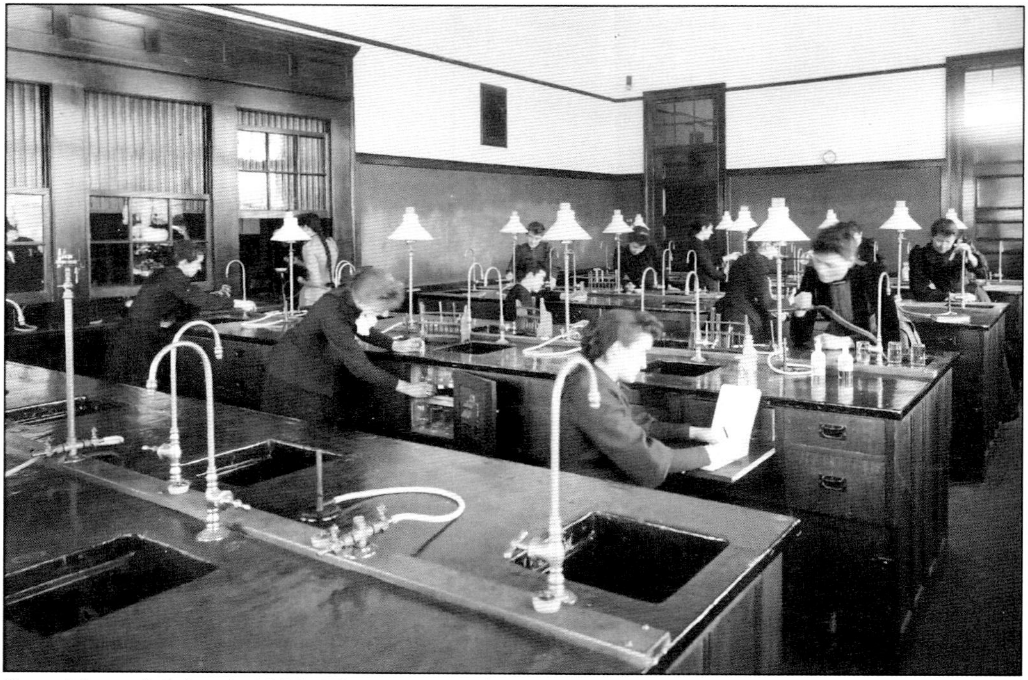

State Normal School, 1895. This nineteenth-century chemistry lab was located on the third floor of the Normal School. The building is now city hall.

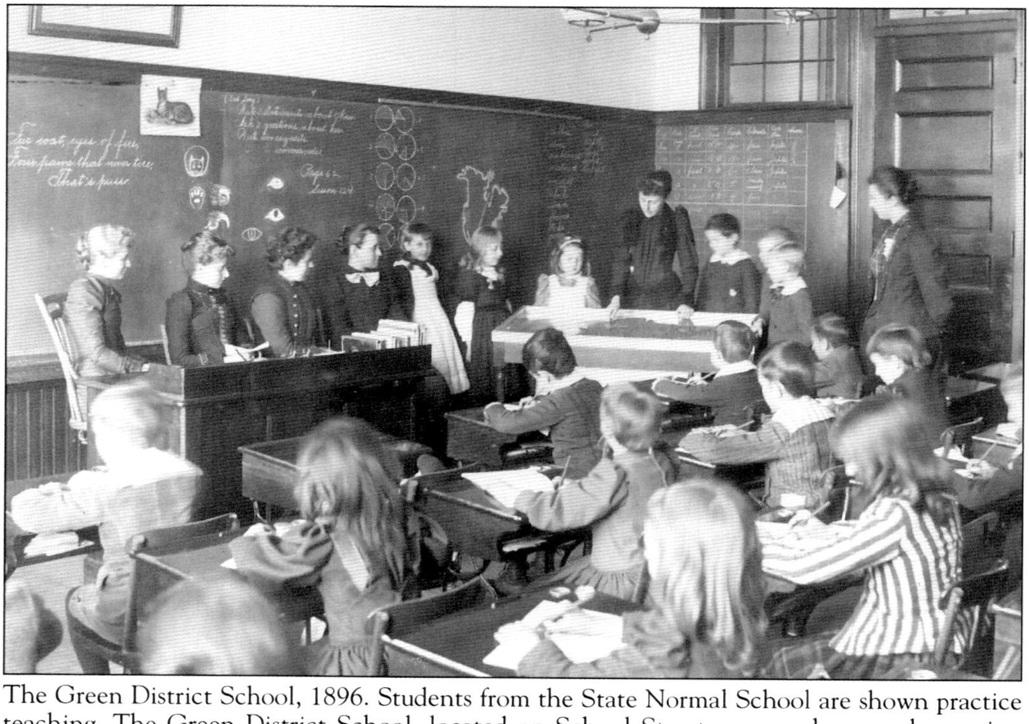

The Green District School, 1896. Students from the State Normal School are shown practice teaching. The Green District School, located on School Street, was used as an observation school by the Normal School until the state opened its own training school in 1900.

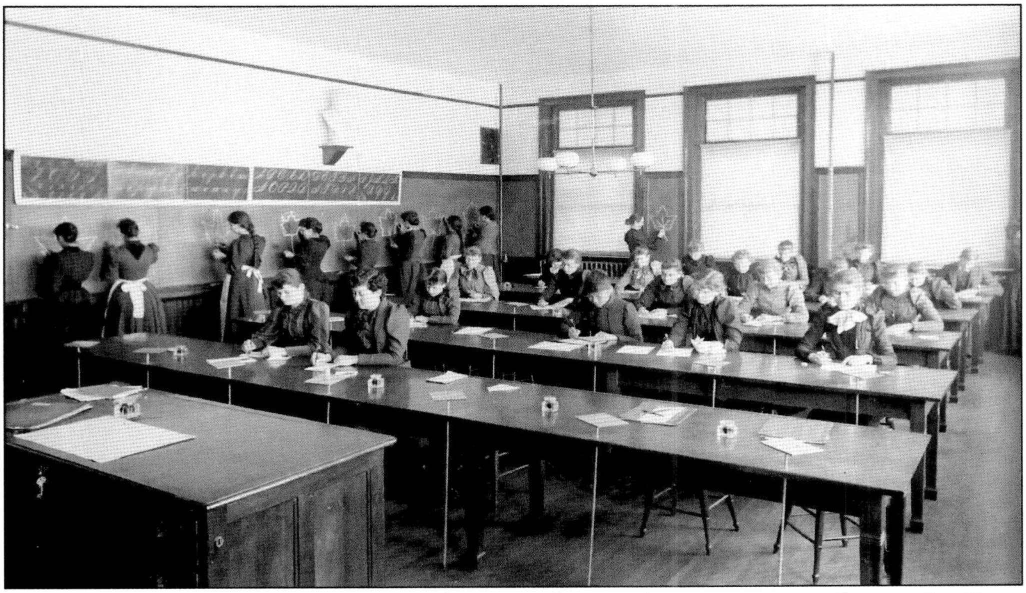

State Normal School, 1897. These students are drawing leaves in an art class at the State Normal School.

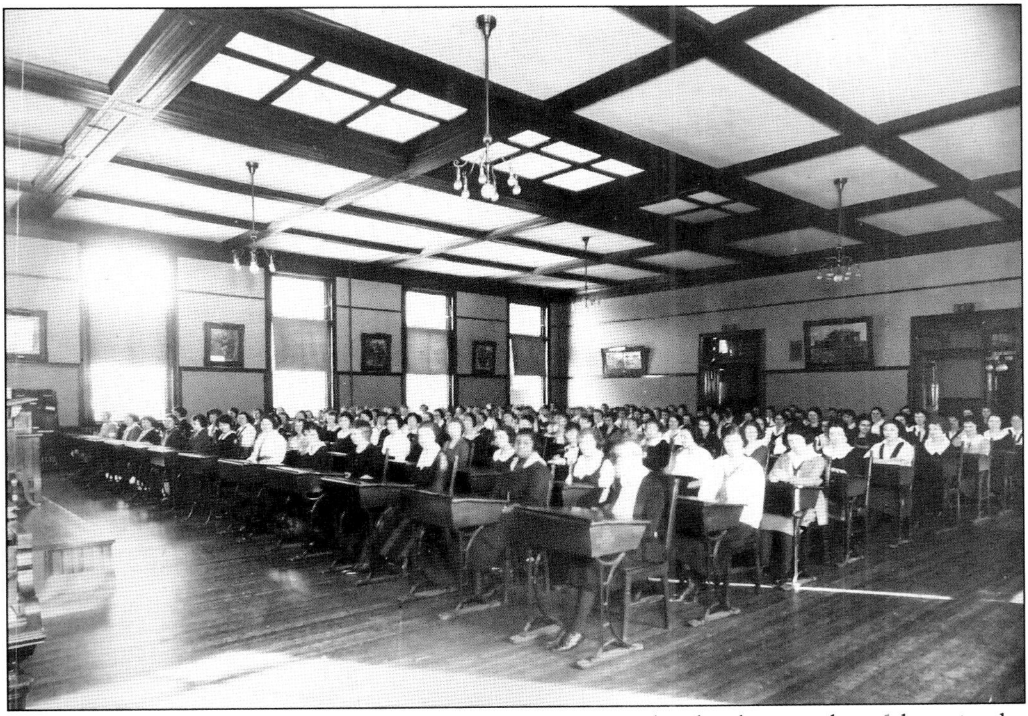

State Normal School, 1915. Students of the State Normal School are gathered here in the Assembly Hall.

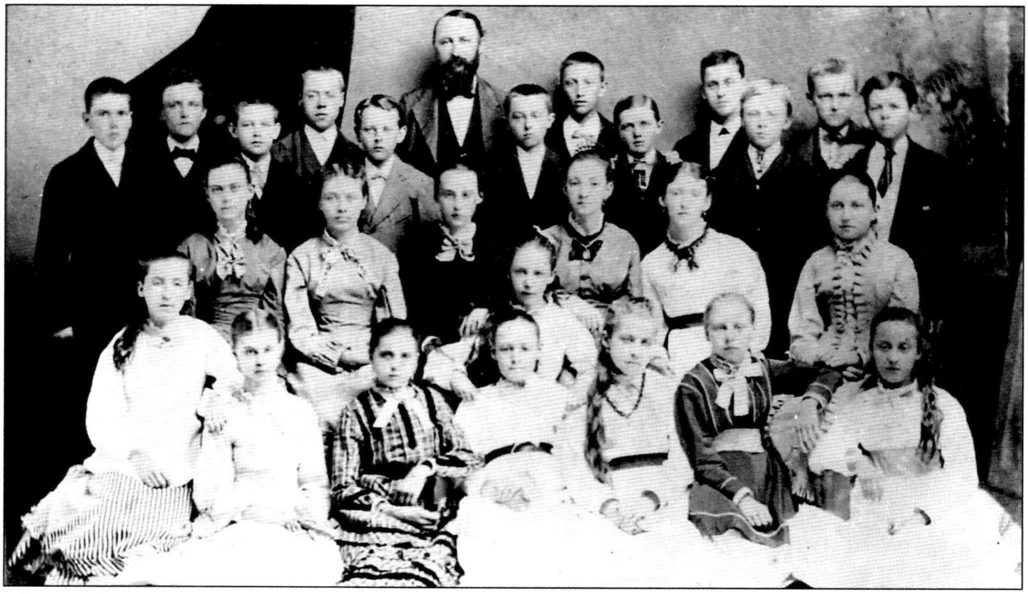

The graduating class of the Grammar School of the School of Observation, 1876. From left to right are: (front row) Anna Hasler, Carrie Mosely, ? Moore, Nellie Eaton, Minnie Weiser, Kitty Green, and May Lewis; (second row) ? Wheeler, ? Bascom, Bella Waterman, Ada Fowler, Jessie Solomon, Kate Mallory, and Lizzie Owen; (top row) R.D. Reed, Bill Bowers, Bert Dibble, Frank Green, Harry Gowdy, Luther Case, Albert Record, Arthur Mosely, "Chet" Abbe, G. Whitaker, George Collins, and George Cushing. Standing with the class is Principal John H. Halderman.

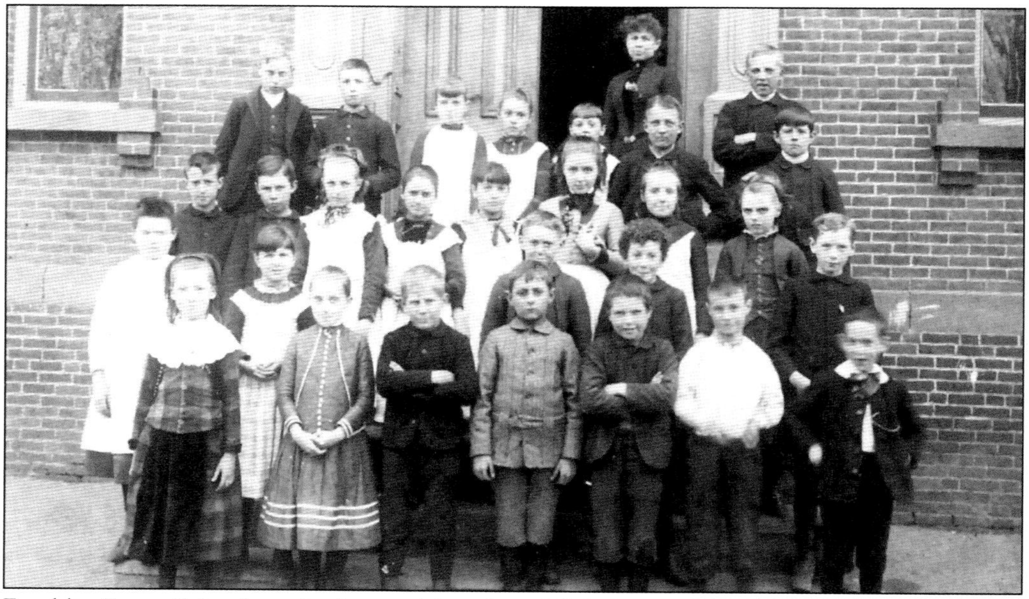

Franklin Street School, grades four and five, June 1889. Some of the above are: Harry Spencer, Ralph Douglas, May Dibble, Hattie Dyson, ? Cowles, Fred Williams, Charles Williams, Walter Parentian, Willie Lay, Clara Avery, Hattie Howard, Bessie Osborne, Gracie Upton, Florence Holcomb, Gracie Case, George Nichols, Francis Jones, Cassie Martin, Mamie Noble, Rosie Carroll, Bessie Cooley, Willie Jones, Ralph Loomis, ? Martin, Julie Jones, and Henry Brooks.

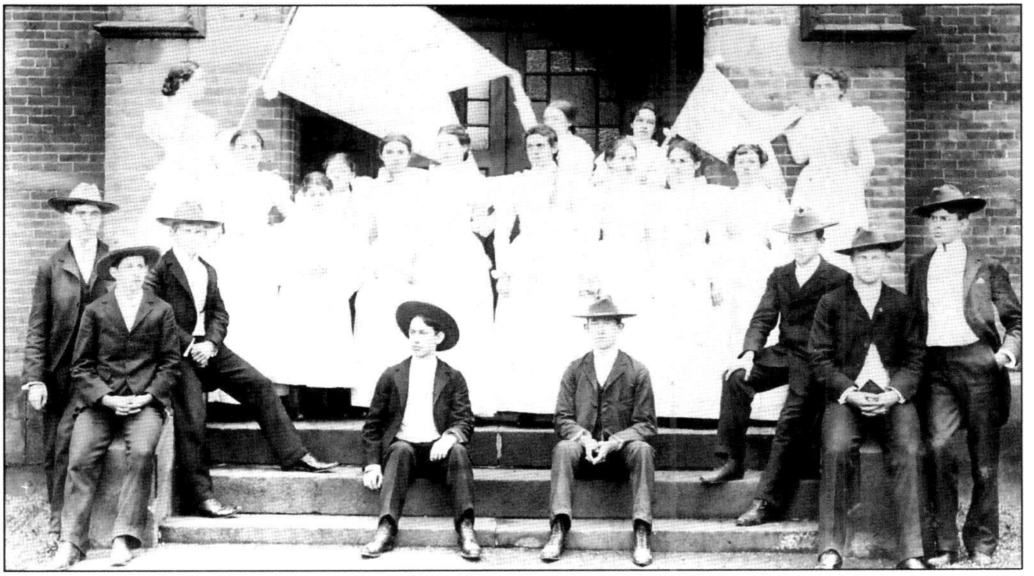

Westfield High School Class of 1897. The graduates (not in order) are: Helen Dwight Brooks, Mabel Austin Farnham, Addie Beatrice Fiske, Helen Christine Pease, Marie Louise Strong, Henriette Zelda Dyson, Harry Williams Gladwin, Edith Huntington Reed, Blanche Estella Pease, Clarissa Belle Searle, Mabelle Anna Stewart, Frances Elsie Caffrey, Edward Gillett Crotty, Archibald John Douglass, Henry William Lloyd, Marion Campbell Noble, William George Parenteau, Austin William Phelon, Edward James Sammons, Lillie Adeline Shepard, and Myrtie Maud Whiting.

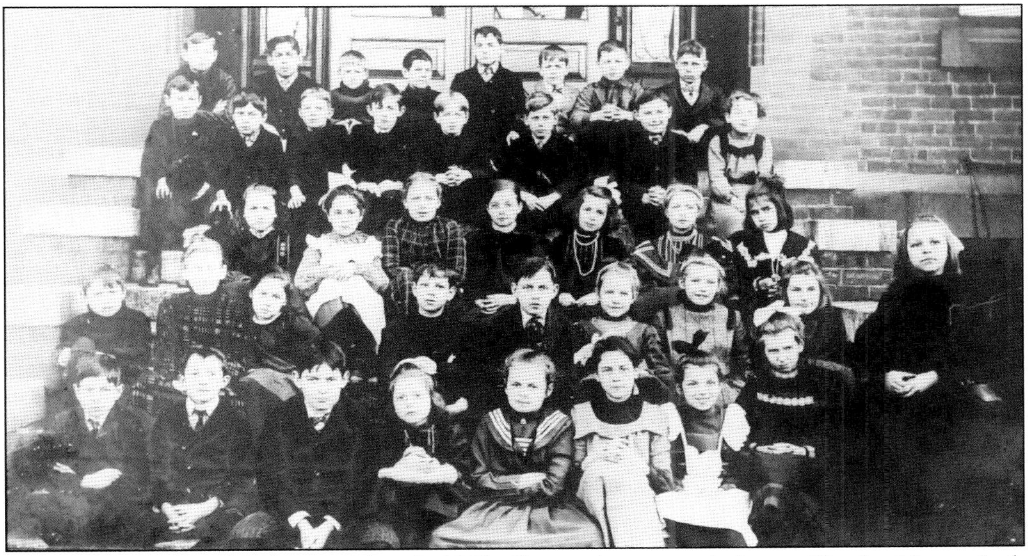

Normal Training School, December 7, 1903. Shown (not in order) are: Charles Harvy, Jack Varney, Percy Audly, Joseph Simson, Harold Bridger, Arthur Price, Peter Deveno, Roy King, Charles Plumb, Joseph Litono, Adnah Snow, Fran ?, Frederick Taylor, Raymond Noble, Fred ?, Ruth Emerson, Emily Berga, Ethel Douglas, Florence Bennett, Emily Brown, Edith ?, Edith Cadle, Mildred Putman, William ?, Renak Danel, David Atwater, Chinton Harvy, Florence ?, Mar ?, Inese Kelly, Florence Powers, Edith Reed, Dorothy ?, William ?, and Sidney Barton.

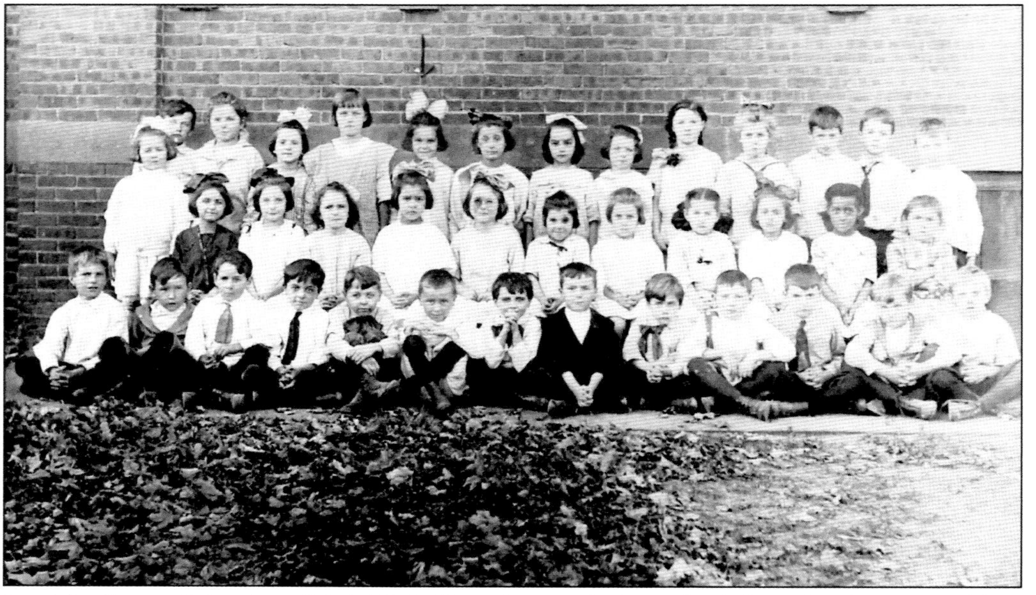

Franklin Street School, *c.* 1912–1913. Seated seventh from the left in the first row is Tom Ferriter. From left to right are: (second row) Elinor Burke, two unidentified, Mildred Barnes, two unidentified, Helen Ryan, unidentified, Stella Brown, three unidentified; (top row) Stephen Lucas, Anna ?, Anna Carroll, Jennie ?, Doris Dowling, Cecelia ?, Mary O'Hare, Mariann Harran, Charlotte Myers, unidentified, David ?, and two unidentified.

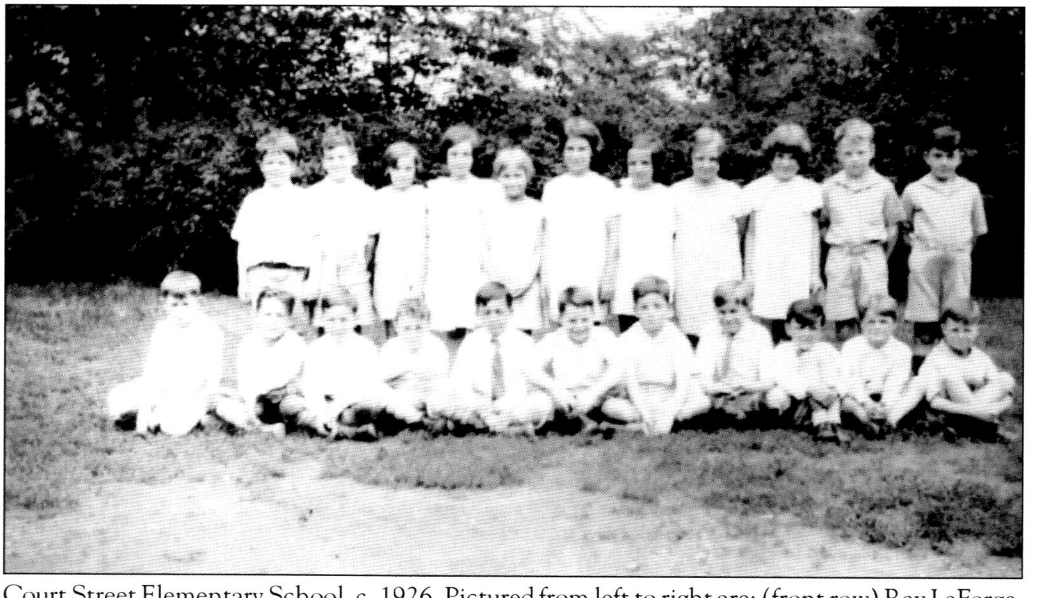

Court Street Elementary School, *c.* 1926. Pictured from left to right are: (front row) Ray LaForge, Bob Modena, David Nicoll, Richard Mahoney, Pat Dowd, Richard Pendleton, Tom Cooley, George Barden, Don Ludwig, unidentified, and Jack English; (back row) Roger Webster, Art Marcoullier, Gertrude Bean, Katherine Carney, Shirley Bein, Ellen Gillett, Priscilla Gillett, Martha Richardson, Shirley Hull, Jack Bell, and Tom Powers.

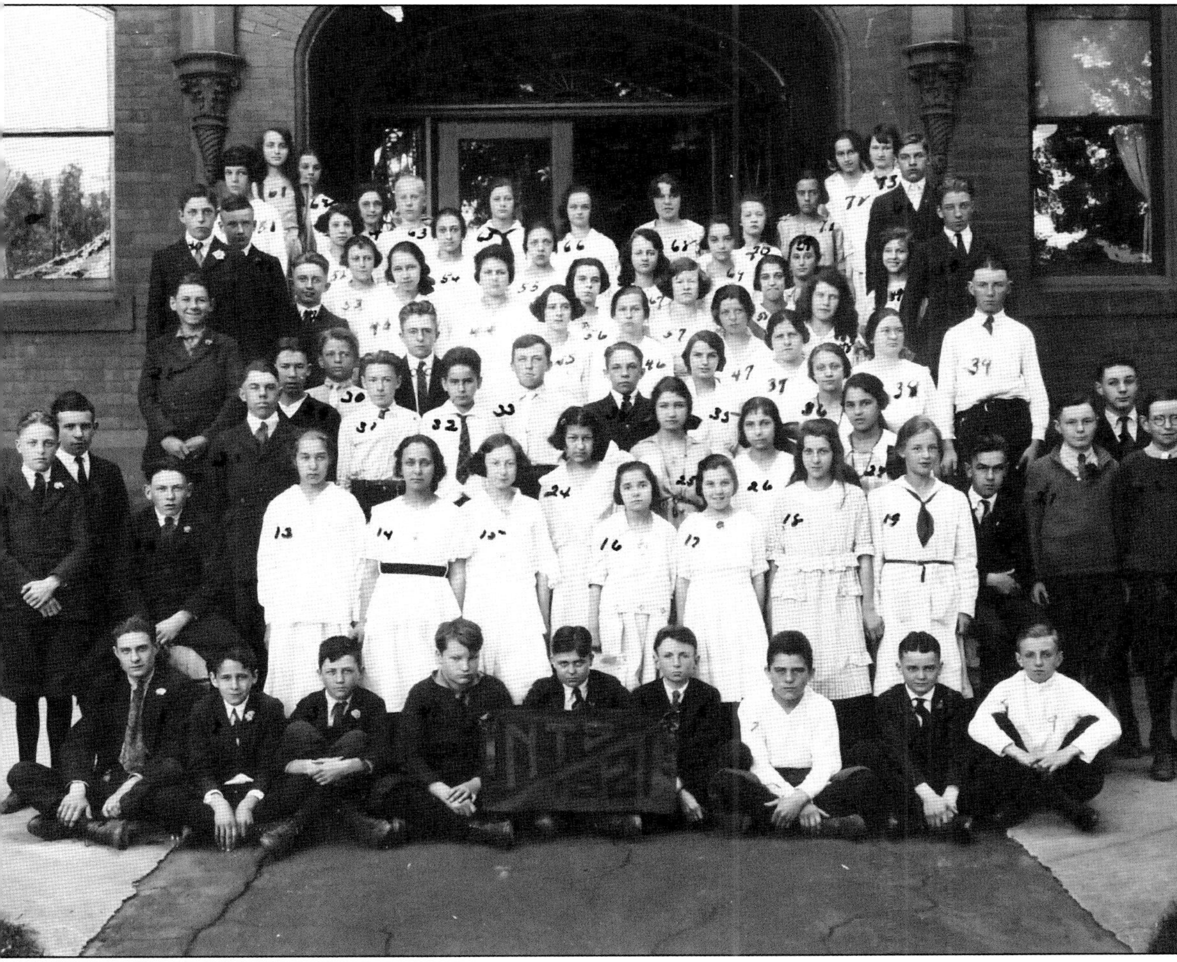

Normal Training School's eighth grade class, 1921. From left to right are: (front row) Harold Fowler (1), Herbert Burlingame (2), James Connor (3), Donald Bates (4), Ted Janes (5), Kiddo Maloney (6), Dick Fink (7), Tom Ferriter (8), and Victor Dintzner (9); (second row) Russel Barber (10), William Plummer (11), Billy Armstrong (12), Mary Mochak (13), Sadie Milstein (14), Rose King (15), Rose Kupec (16), Helen Ryan (17), Pauline Sizer (18), Guila Hawley (19), Robert Pomery (20), George Mallory (21), unknown (no number), and Walter Chandler (22); (third row) Ralph Blodgett (23), Cecelia Rosoff (24), Evelyn Stetson (25), Rose Gagne (26), and Louise Wemette (27); (fourth row) George Onofry (28), Reign Rix (29), Don Hammond (30), Albert Smith (31), Harry Fiske (00), John Waters (32), Steve Lucas (33), Merle Lent (34), Maisie Dubrava (35), Doris Nesbit (36), Mary Armstrong (37), Margaret Mahoney (38), and Howard Burke (39); (fifth row) Albert Gagne (40), David Harrington (41), Louis Britton (42), Edith O'Connor (43), Esther Mulvehill (44), Anna Carroll (45), Stella Brown (46), Marion Harran (47), Theresa Shea (48), Isadora Warren (49), and Charles Cary (50); (sixth row) Doris Dowling (51),Floris Degere (52), Esther Carr (53), Silvia Kimball (54), Mary Wadsworth (55), Doris Kenney (56), Marjorie Roberts (57), Edith Labrovits (58), Marjorie Williams (59), and Lee Wyman (60); (top row) Hannah Goodman (61), Catherine Adams (62), Sadie Chapman (63), Mildred Barnes (64), Rose Gehring (65), Charlotte Rice (66), Helen Kernan (67), ? Bissell (68), Mary O'Hare (69), Elinore Burke (70), Mildred Ostrander (71), Josephine Remp (72), and Anna Evans (73).

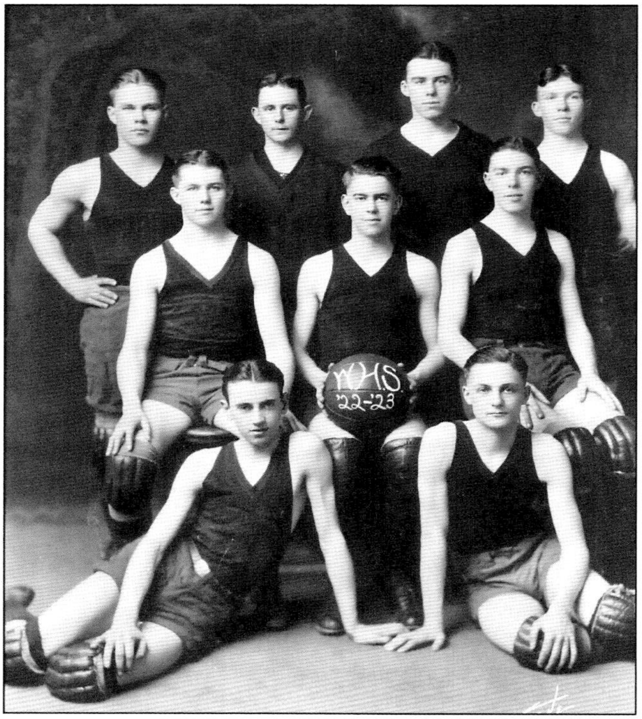

Westfield High School basketball team of 1922/23. From left to right are: (front row) Patrick Egan and Joseph Jachym; (middle row) Allyn Stillman, Irving Keefe, and Lawrence Gibbons; (back row) Harold Harvey, William Bullens, Thomas Little, and John Mahoney.

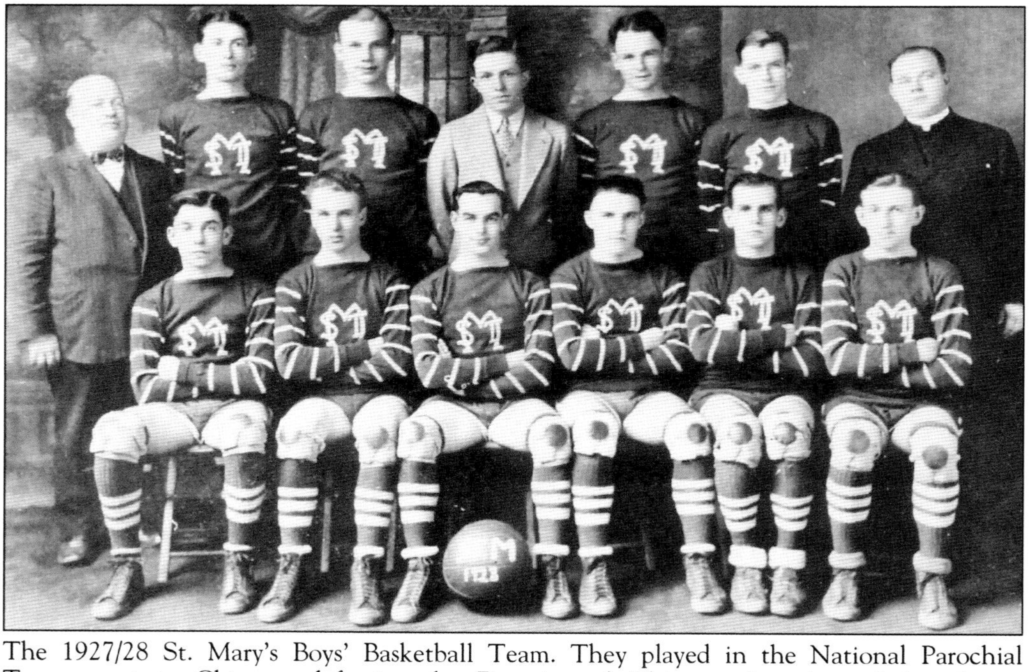

The 1927/28 St. Mary's Boys' Basketball Team. They played in the National Parochial Tournament in Chicago, defeating the Detroit and Chicago champions, before losing to St. Patrick's of Pueblo, Colorado, in the last minute. They are, from left to right: (front row) Schoenrock, Cashman, Moran, Slattery, Coach, and Siska; (back row) Coach "Happy" Houlihan, Devine, Grubert, manager Hickson, O'Rourke, Halloren, and Rev. Donoghue.

St. Mary's High School girls' basketball team, 1924/25. Members of the team, from left to right, are: (bottom row) Helen Leary and Theresa D'Allessio; (middle row) Mary Mosely, Anna Henchey, Mary Baker, and Marguerite Browne; (top row) Mary Reardon.

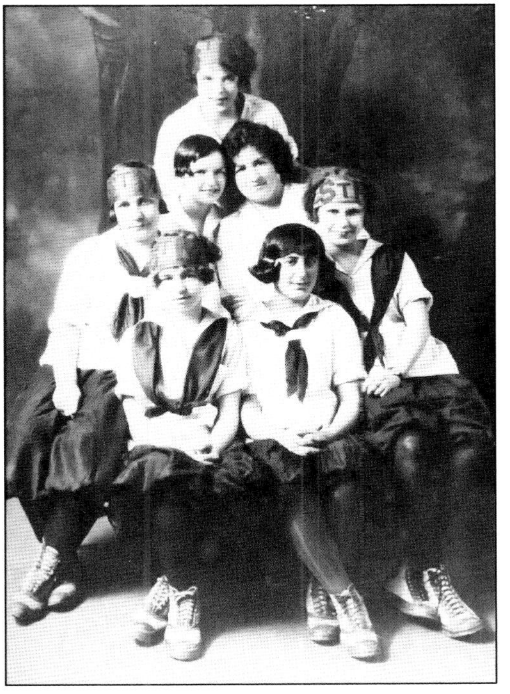

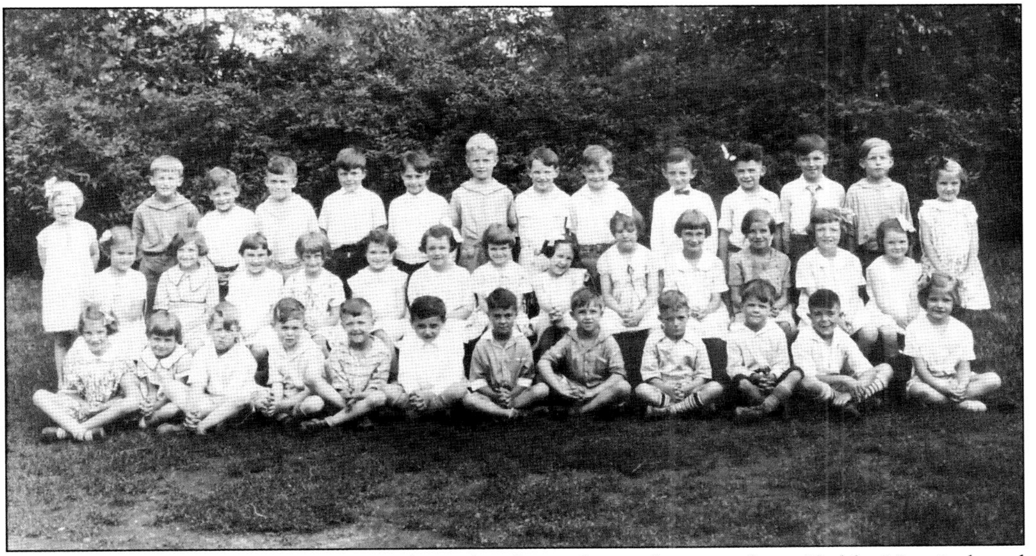

Court Street School group, 1930. This school was located across from Noble Hospital and was called "Old Mother Hubbard School." Pictured from left to right are: (front row) Jane Smith, Eleanor Bien, Erskine Bush, unknown, Dick Cantell, John O'Conner, Don Tryon, Bob Marshall, Fred Gracie, John Webster, unknown, and Priscilla Gates; (middle row) Mary Kingsbury, Gert Bean, Frances Haynes, Muriel Loud, Frances Roraback, Dorothy Goodkind, Marion Woodworth, Virginia Ludwig, Mary McCallough, unknown, Peggy O'Neil, Norma Whittemore, and Peggy McMahan; (back row) Marcia Kane, Bill Robinson, Don Robinson, Bud Malone, Bob Benaway, Ted Bridgeman, Fred O'Donnell, Bill Wallace, John Dowd, Dick Chandler, Dick Ring, Charles Sawyer, and Patty Bell.

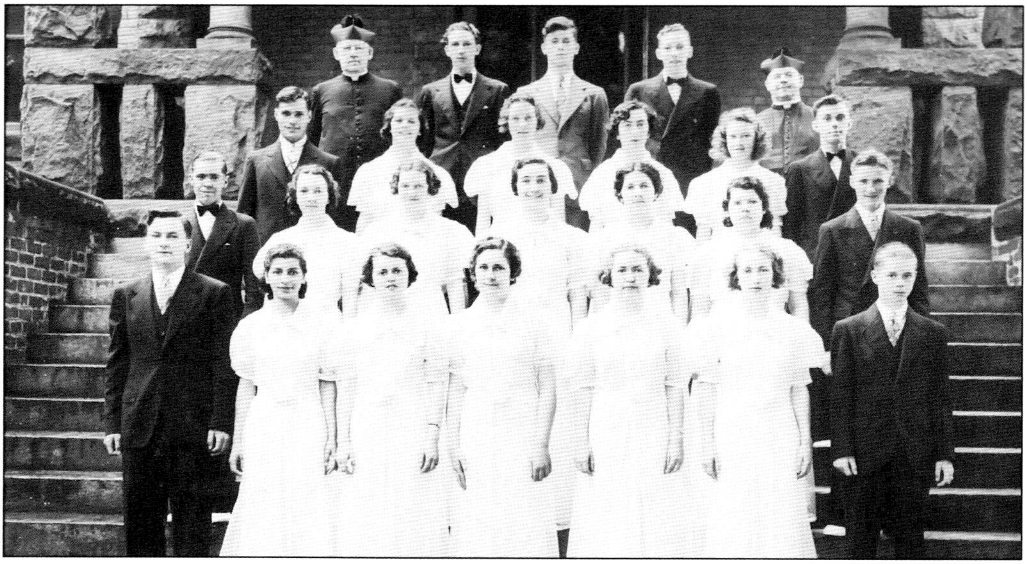

The 1937Graduating Class of St. Mary's High School. From left to right are: (front row) Thomas Devine, Gertrude Lenza, Rita Dineen, Agnes Lucey, Catherine Crean, Margaret Armstrong, and Robert English; (second row) Gordon Wells, Mary Teahan, Margaret Conniff, Mary Albano, Mary Petrucelli, Dora McLenna, and James Troy; (third row) Leon Rondeau, Agnes O'Connor, Margaret Courtney, Edna Clare, Frances Barry, and Roland Boutin; (fourth row) Rev. James Curran, Herbert Stevenson, Edwin McGrath, John Griffin, and Rev. Florence Donoghue.

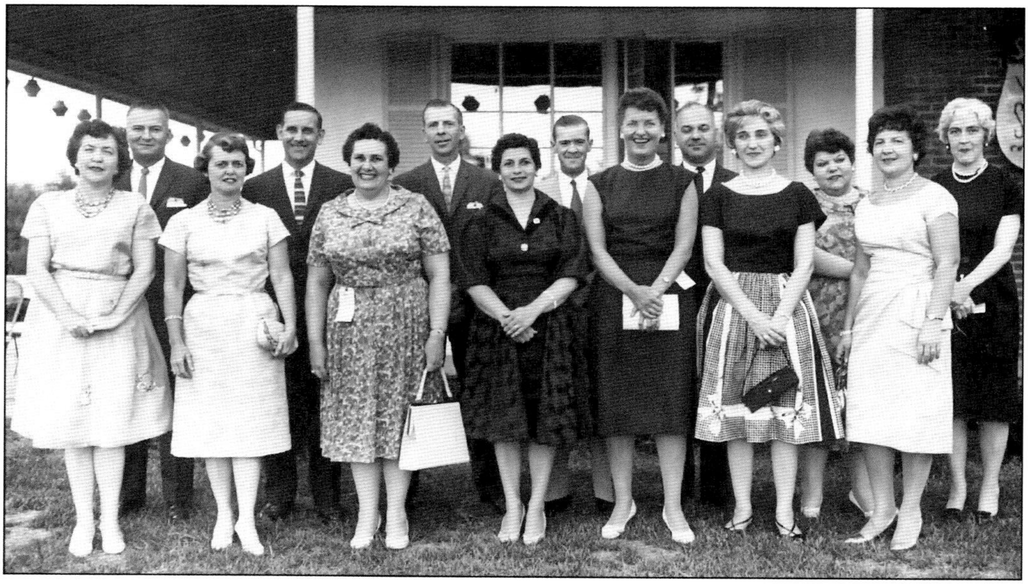

St. Mary's High School Class of 1937, Twenty-fifth Reunion, held at Shaker Farms. From left to right are: (front row) Catherine Crean Anderson, Rita Dineen Dupont, Agnes Lucey Pais, Gertrude Lenza Harrington, Margaret Courtney Heaton, Mary Albano, Dora McLenna, Mary Petrucelli Allen, and Edna Clare Lorenzatti; (back row) Thomas Devine, James Cavanaugh, Peter Nadeau, Gordon Wells, and John Kocsis.

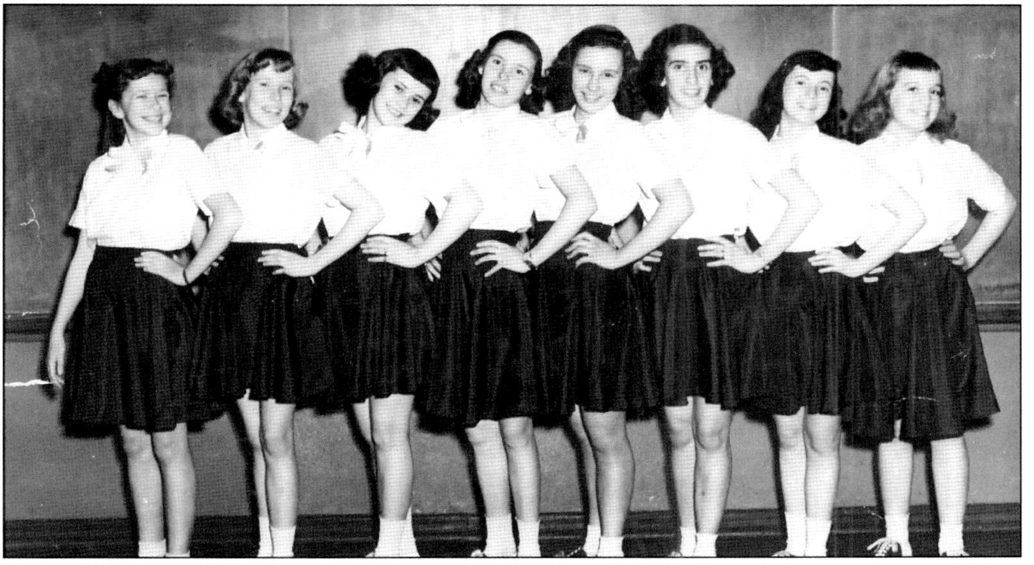

Normal Training School seventh grade cheerleaders of 1947. From left to right are: Helen Holmes, Peggy Barnes, Jane Thibault, Mary Barnes, Dorothy Burke, Beverly Danforth, Carol Scanlon, and ? Devine.

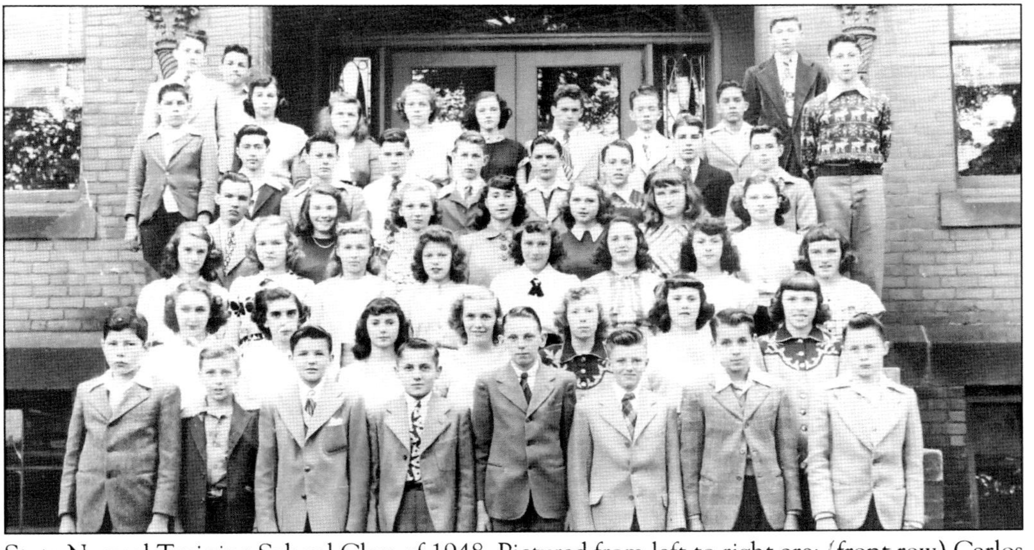

State Normal Training School Class of 1948. Pictured from left to right are: (front row) Carlos Iglesias, Robert Freeman, Arthur Mzanski, Robert Ring, Robert Elder, Gerald Boylan, Robert Mahar, and Robert Hibert; (second row) Katherine Wermuth, Bev Danforth, Carole Scanlon, Jeannette Goodniss, Margaret Barnes, Jane Thibault, and Mary Barnes; (third row) Carole Baudin, Dorothy Tebo, Gail Marcoulier, Joyce Palecki, Dorothy Burke, Cynthia Emard, Bernice Turcotte, and Joanne Ryan; (fourth row) Robert Agan, Claire Condron, Phyllis Monczka, Abelina Rodriguez, Phyllis Wright, Roberta Justin, and Dolly Kelso; (fifth row) Joseph Ferreria, Ronald Carrier, Robert Cooper, Irving Barnes, Edward Kelso, Richard Hills, Richard Fink, John Shepherd, and John Murphy; (back row) Thomas Hannon, Paul Wellspeak, Linda Stodden, Marianne Murphy, Polly Knox, Marlene Fouche, Richard Brazee, Gerald Rose, Roger Hills, James Naughton, and Daniel Mastrionni.

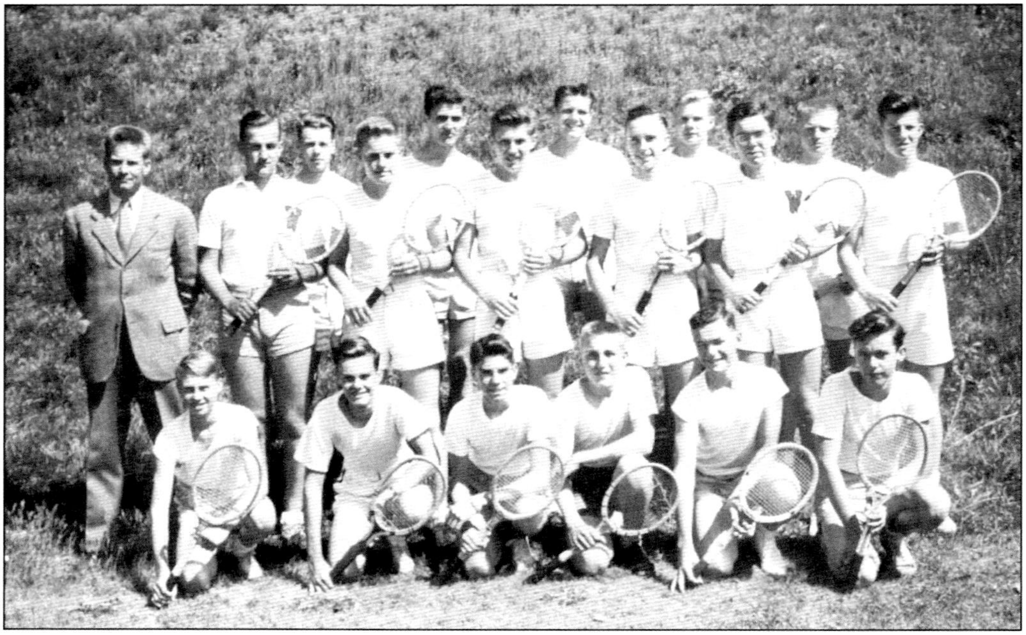

Westfield High School tennis team, 1950. Members of the team, from left to right, are: (front row) Harland Thayer, Fred Leopold, John Little, Joe Patrick, Eddie Stockbridge, and George Freeman; (back row) Coach Homer Gammons, Don MacLean, Robert Wind, Bob Brinkman, Robert Therrien, Jack Moltenbrey, Jack Robinson, Victor Marcotte, Ralph Eustis, Louis Crawford, Bob Ertel, and George Haskins.

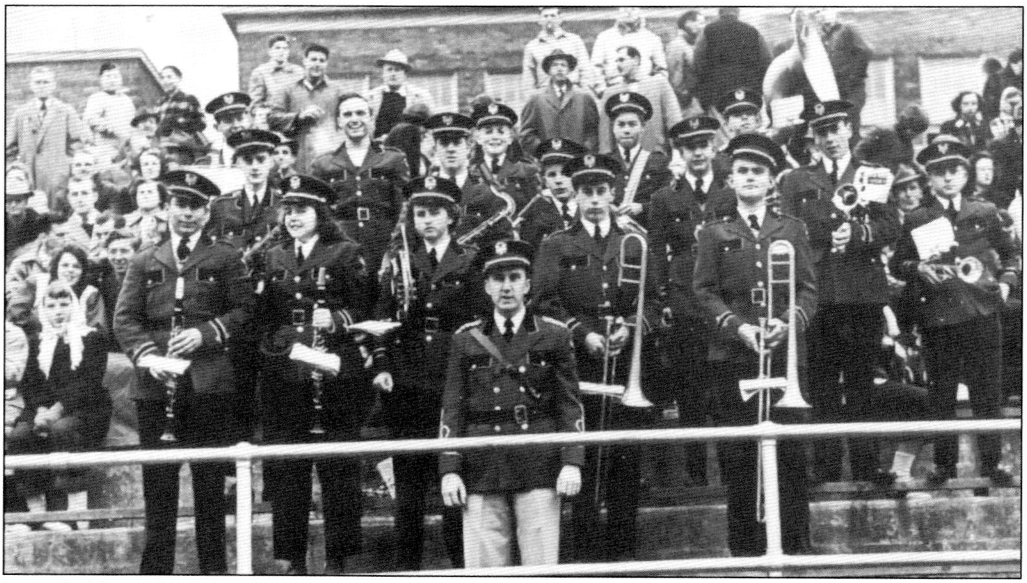

Westfield High School Band, 1950. In the center is Douglas Ward, director. Shown from left to right are: (first row) Alfred Wood, Marilyn Kellogg, Ruth Hannum, Richard English, and Conrad Boyer; (second row) Richard Davich, George Haskins, Robert Schultz, Theofolis Balabanis, Clyde Jones, and Robert Ring; (third row) Marcel Schmidt, Jack Wright, Herbert Wood, Leonard Kellogg, and William Weber.

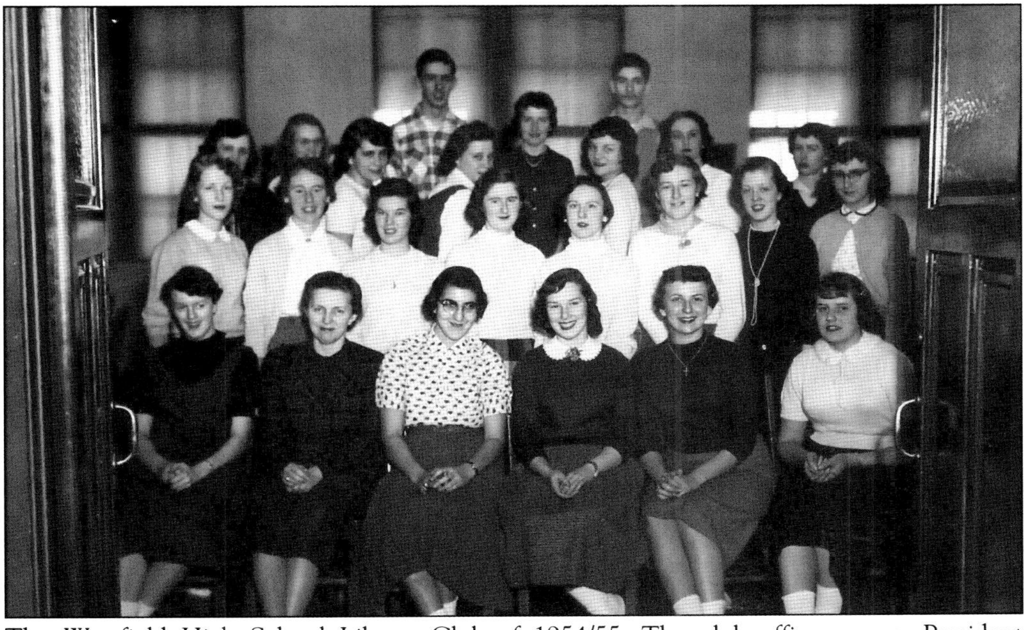

The Westfield High School Library Club of 1954/55. The club officers were: President Elizabeth Boccasile, Vice President Nancy Dickinson, and Secretary Judith Reinert. Other members, some of them pictured above, were Roger Allen, Pauline Amlaw, Jane Arterton, Carolyn Avery, Elizabeth Banks, Bette Collier, Catherine Deedy, William Hahn, Carol Heiden, Phyllis Hicks, Jane Holcomb, Nancy Kenyon, Jeanne Kindy, Marie Laudato, Sandra Lee, Pamela Lemire, Joan McDonald, Theda Markham, Nancy Mayhew, Frances Merver, Mary Montovani, Helen Nagorka, Janet Olinski, Janice Peebles, Ronald Rainville, Pat Renaud, Gladys Strong, Sharon Stubbe, Helen Sweeney, Doris Thouin, Louise Welliver, and Roberta Yefko.

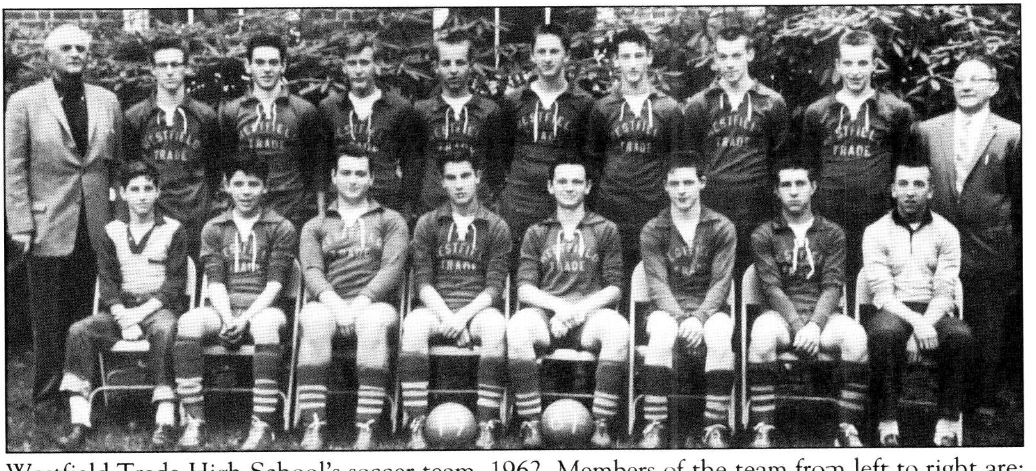

Westfield Trade High School's soccer team, 1962. Members of the team from left to right are: (seated) Ralph Tirrell (manager), Arthur Lafreniere, Raymond Salois, Edward Avery, Robert Tenero, Francis Neylon, Robert Tercyak, and John Bashonski (manager); (standing) Coach Joseph J. Jachym, David Mikuski, Michael O'Connor, Raymond Frappier, Bruce Nielsen, Thomas Galczynski, Richard Limoges, Thomas Jachym, Francis Janisieski, and Mr. Edward W. Cerveny (activities manager).

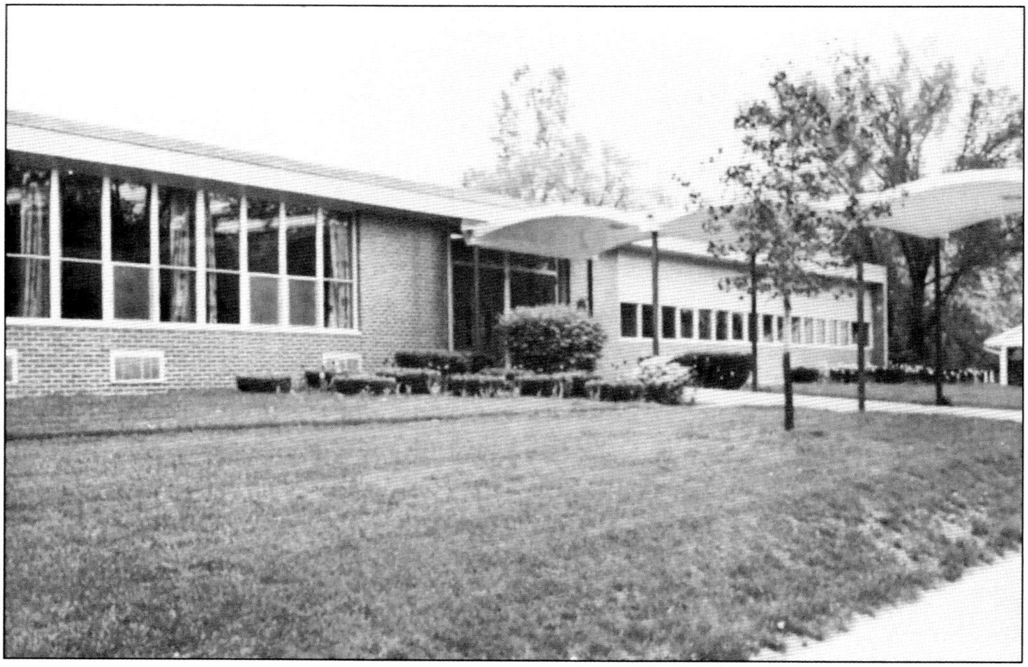

Westfield Trade High School, 1970. This school building on Smith Avenue opened in 1963, and it has recently been expanded and connects to the former Westfield High School building pictured below. The name has been changed to the Westfield Vocational-Technical High School.

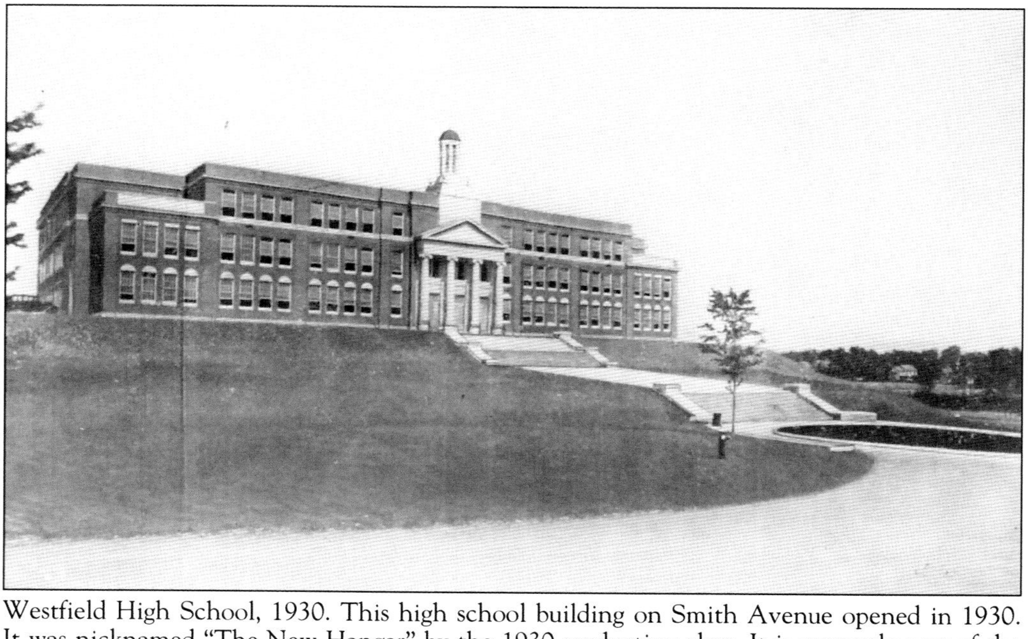

Westfield High School, 1930. This high school building on Smith Avenue opened in 1930. It was nicknamed "The New Hangar" by the 1930 graduating class. It is presently part of the Westfield Vocational-Technical High School.